# AMERICAN VOUDOU

## JOURNEY INTO A
## HIDDEN WORLD

# AMERICAN VOUDOU

## JOURNEY INTO A HIDDEN WORLD

## ROD DAVIS

University of North Texas Press
Denton, Texas

The paper in this book meets the minimum requirements of the American
National Standard for Permanence of Paper for Printed Library Materials,
Z39.48.1984.

Permissions
University of North Texas Press
PO Box 311336
Denton TX 76203-1336
940-565-2142

Library of Congress Cataloging-in-Publication Data

Davis, Rod, 1946–
    American voudou : journey into a hidden world / by Rod Davis.
        p.   cm.
    Includes bibliographical references and index.
    ISBN 1-57441-049-0 (alk. paper)
    1. Voodooism—United States. 2. Hoodoo (Cult)   I. Title.
BL2490.D37                              1998
299'.675'0973—dc21                      98-21264
                                        CIP

Design by Accent Design and Communications
Photographs by Rod Davis

For Jennifer and Moriah, and the future

# CONTENTS

# PREFACE

FOR MOST OF my life all I knew about voudou[1] was what I saw in the movies: dancing zombies, chicken heads, and pins in dolls. It had something to do with the Caribbean or New Orleans. It was black. Sometimes you'd hear about it in the blues. I didn't go so far as to equate voudou with satanism, though many others did. To me, "voodoo" was mostly a weird name. It wasn't even real and certainly was nothing to take seriously.

How I subsequently came to be standing before an Elegba altar in a South Carolina forest tasting the blood of three roosters sacrificed to my spirit is therefore a tale not just about voudou, but about its effect on one who ventured into what in many ways is one of America's least-traveled frontiers.

For nearly five years before undertaking the odyssey described in this book, I had flirted with the vo-du, the spirits of West Africa (from which voudou, in all its Anglicized variations, derives), but never engaged them fully. A journalistic assignment in New Orleans in 1985 had given me my first real exposure, other than the common bits of voudouesque vocabulary— "mojo" (a charm); "hoodoo" (an alteration of voudou common in the South), etc.—I'd picked up while living in Baton Rouge in the late sixties, a graduate student at LSU. That was about it until a stormy romance fifteen years later with a young woman from a traditional Catholic family from the well-heeled section of New Orleans around Tulane called Uptown.

A lifelong rebel, Pam was drawn to voudou for the same reason a lot of people in the Big Easy were, because it was outside the mainstream and likely to stay that way. Voudou was to the young, artistic bohemia of New Orleans as common a cultural crossroads as a bookshelf full of Anne Rice's vampires or John Kennedy Toole's neurotics. Many, like Pam, had picked up voudou charms at back-street shops, or smiled knowingly at mention of the word in conversation, possibly had experienced readings or been to Marie Laveau's grave; but few actually knew anything about the religion itself. Or probably cared. What was of interest to the disaffected of the city was neither the spirituality nor the theology, but the marginality. Voudou was not white and it was not of the ruling class, and if you wanted to try to distance yourself from all that suffocation and decay and slow, steady corruption, you would attach to the new perspective of your black-clad, white-lipsticked, alienated freedom anything that could identify you as not being of Them. And so without knowing it, the white exiles of New Orleans, the ones who try to make the bridge between the white and black souls of the city, and all too often fall off that bridge, partook of the political content of the African religion. They validated that content by seeking its alliance, slight and oblique though it was.

For Pam, there were also strong artistic motivations. We once bought a pheasant bone earring from a traveling hoodoo merchant so she could use it in a painting, the first of many she would use to explore vivid voudou techniques, at once expressionist and formal. Yet she knew very little more about the religion than did her peers, or at that time did I, and for good reason:

voudou had been driven so far underground you couldn't find much about it even if you wanted to expend the energy. Only the most esoteric of African Studies scholars had written about it seriously. In the popular culture virtually nothing was available, and what was, was wrong. Most books purporting to be about American voudou were either luridly racist, such as Robert Tallant's *Voodoo in New Orleans,* a ubiquitous and unfortunate presence in French Quarter bookstores, or poorly researched compendia of alleged hexes and rites.

In the absence of the printed word, I turned to real life. Occasional trips to New Orleans and to South Carolina, and another assignment, this time for the late, great magazine, *Southern*, enabled me to make the acquaintance of numerous present-day believers whose oral accounts and daily practices ushered me into a richness of experience I couldn't have gained from a library full of material. As my circle of contacts and friends grew, so did my knowledge of the theology of voudou, the history of its importation in the holocaust of slavery, its well-proven revolutionary content and consequent near-extermination, and the rise of the negative image which now flourishes. The more I learned, the more I realized how little I really knew—how little, in fact, anyone outside the voudou world really knew, especially in the United States. If at the start of my engagement with the religion I was asking, "What is voudou?" it became increasingly obvious there was a more encompassing question: *What happened to it?*

If ever the nation harbored a cover-up, it did with voudou. So effective was the suppression that virtually nothing of the authentic African form, with the notable exception of Caribbean-shaped santeria, remains on North American soil. Successive generations of African Americans have left a widespread network of root doctors, hoodoos, healers and prophets, particularly in the South, but not even they can tell you the names of the great voudou deities, of the rituals and prayers for celebration and sacrifice, or of Ifa, the ancient and complex art of divination that lies at the core of voudou philosophy.

Had Catholicism or Judaism disappeared on transport to the New World, we now would be overrun with studies, laments and investigations. How could such a thing happen? Why? And surely one of these studies would observe that in Boston or New York or Chicago, something of the vanished theologies remained in the lives of people even today—a kosher deli, a corner store selling pictures of the saints. And that would raise other questions. Did those religions really disappear? Did they go underground? Does anyone remember them? Are they practiced in secret?

Ironically, voudou also might be said to be all around us. Anyone who has listened to jazz (said to be from an African word for ejaculant) has perceived the legacy of voudou in the arts, and anyone who visits any of thousands of black churches can observe not just the obvious African influences, but the vestiges of voudou as well. It's like a parallel universe. Here and there the membrane tears open. At such ruptures do we sense the true zing of African-American culture. It's that zing, I think, which lends even the word "voudou" its special cachet of eeriness. Voudou doesn't give people the shivers because it celebrates the dead—what religion doesn't? The shivers come from a deeper chill, a very bad memory: once upon a time, in America, an entire pantheon of gods was murdered. But the deicide was not final. The souls survived.

—═—

In the 1980s, voudou enjoyed a minor resurrection, especially among artists and intellectuals, black and white. David Byrne's film, *True Stories,* featured a voudou seer in a reasonably sane context, and books such as Luisah Teish's *Jambalaya:*

*The Natural Woman's Book of Personal Charms and Practical Rituals* sought to establish voudou in the context both of women's issues and the spiritual searching of the mostly white New Age movement. Ethno-botanist Wade Davis's *The Serpent and the Rainbow*, a science-adventure account of *zombi* pharmacology, was a landmark: the first serious nonacademic study of voudou as an extensive, complex system of social organization since Maya Deren's 1953 *Divine Horsemen*, or the great scholar Melville J. Herskovits's on-site examinations of Haiti and Africa in the 1920s and 1930s. And art historian Robert Farris Thompson's influential *Flash of the Spirit* broke new ground in linking African-American artistic themes to the religion of West Africa —in other words, to voudou.

A second wave of interest in voudou, though mostly incidental, emerged in the nineties, in scholarly and ideological works examining African culture and the diaspora of slavery. These were essentially directed at the Caribbean, not the United States per se. Some, such as Paul Gilroy's *The Black Atlantic: Modernity and Double Consciousness*, or Leslie Desmangles's *The Faces of the Gods: Vodou and Roman Catholicism in Haiti,* carried forward the case made by, among others, Sidney W. Mintz and Richard Price in *The Birth of African American Culture* in 1973, that the New World could be better viewed—because of the special horrors of the slave trade—as the forced incubator of a new culture rather than as a place where African values and culture could be said to have been distinctly or discretely transplanted. These views emphasize a very heterogeneous, pan-Carribbean interconnection combining many different African sources into something neither "purely" African nor American. Gilroy calls it an "inescapable hybridity." In another time, the mutated culture would have been known as *creole*—or *criollo*—born in the New World. Other authors, such as George Brandon in *Santeria from Africa to the New World: The Dead Sell Memories,* and Joseph M. Murphy, in *Working the Spirit: Ceremonies of the African Diaspora*, have focused efforts less on consciousness and identity theory and more on expanded observation of voudou practices, primarily its Caribbean relative, santeria. The generally acknowledged best of the new wave is Suzanne Blier's remarkable 1996 *African Vodun: Art, Psychology and Power,* which explores, mostly in an African setting, spiritual and artistic connections in African culture.

Yet, except for Zora Neale Hurston's pioneering travels in the South in the twenties and thirties, no one had made a systematic effort to chronicle the real-life practice and extent of voudou *in the U.S.* And then it came to me: that's what I had to do. I had to find what was out there now. Only then would I begin to understand anything at all, and only then would I have anything of value to report. I outlined a path: an arbitrary crisscross route from New Orleans across the slave belt states of Mississippi, Alabama and Georgia, dipping down to Miami, where the voudou of Cuba and the Caribbean is endemic, and up to New York, too, where priests and practioners increase in number each year. But mostly the Bible Belt, because that's where it lives.

After writing the manuscript, though, a strange, and perhaps instructive interlude occurred. My former publisher was bought by a multinational conglomerate and the book became a kind of *zombi* itself—orphaned, as they say in the business when a book loses its original patron. All along, voudou priests and priestesses had warned me rather strongly about "obstacles" in getting to print a book which didn't take a stereotypical view of voudou, or follow the predictable academic catechisms. The book would come out when it was time, I was told. I didn't believe it.

I should have. Several years of seemingly endless and often dispiriting rejections and renegotiations became a lingering exegesis of the priestly cautions. The voudou renaissance is, as I had predicted, here to stay—you can even find "voodoo" websites now on almost any internet search engine—but the prejudices about the religion are as potent as ever, even in the carrels and corner offices of the publishing cartels.

Nor has voudou's renaissance done much to quell the long-standing contentions over the efforts by African Americans to reclaim voudou worship on their own terms, rather than through heavily modified, mediatory forms such as Cuban santeria. This book's own small efforts in witnessing the revival have drawn startling vituperation, and at least two strong objections to its alleged "Afrocentrism." Responding in detail would involve a book-length discussion of its own; to avoid that I will accept the "Afrocentrist" label, insofar as it means I side with the attempts of African Americans in the United States to lay unfettered claim to their own heritage on their own terms.

This implies neither a superiority nor purity of African heritage over any other. I also fully acknowledge the danger of any people claiming cultural hegemony. I live in the South; how could I not know that? Yet, in the context of the legacy of slavery, I hardly see the search for voudou authenticity—basically a deeply spiritual quest for African roots—to represent cultural totalitarianism in any form. I do see a value in putting voudou on a par with any religious belief system from Europe. Or Cuba, in the case of the quarrel with santeria. Not that my opinion matters. The issue of what is "African" and what is a "new" culture forged on this side of the bloody Atlantic is not up to me to decide, nor to academic specialists. It is for African Americans themselves, acting in response to their own sense of the sacred.

—===—

Approximately a year before I started this project, while ignorance and curiosity were careening inside my head, I had the opportunity to call on Wade Davis (no relation) at his home in Vancouver. His introduction to voudou in Haiti had been similar to mine in America: he had never known much about it, nor had reason to. He, too, subsequently had proceeded through a paucity of background information only to come afire through direct experience, the excitement of which came from the simple discovery of suppressed evidence. We agreed that little was known of American versions of voudou, which are more assimilated into Christianity than are Haitian models, and to my great satisfaction we also agreed on our initial reactions as Westerners.

"Have your encounters with voudou had any effect on your own religious beliefs?" I asked Wade as we sat drinking coffee in his basement study. The walls around were lined with maps, African and Haitian artifacts, well-stocked bookshelves and a basket of clothes for the baby his anthropologist wife, Gail, was carrying.

"I'm still looking for my gods," he answered. "I'm tragically secular. Those of us who don't know our gods and we first see something as raw and immediate and visceral as spirit possession—as you have, too—we have two responses. Fear, which finds its outlet in cynicism and disbelief. Or awe. My answer was always awe."

My answer is the same.

Rod Davis

---

[1] For an explanation of the various spellings of voudou, see page 9.

# ACKNOWLEDGMENTS

Thanks first to members of the African-American community throughout the South for sharing with a stranger the most sacred parts of their lives. I also thank all those mentioned in this book; each of you gave generous amounts of time and provided a fresh clue in the search for the legacy of voudou in America. I would especially thank the Reverend Lorita Honeycutt Mitchell Gamble, her son Gary Williams, and members of their extended family and her congregation for their continuing support in New Orleans. Thanks also to New Orleans dancer and priestess, Ava Kay Jones.

Much of the detail of the practice of the religion today would not have been possible without the wise counsel of the Oba, priests and people of the village of Oyotunji, South Carolina, who shall always remain close in spirit. I was also helped along the voudou trail by Sarah Albritton in Ruston, Louisiana, and Julia Mae Haskins in Demopolis, Alabama, and in Miami by Chief A. S. Ajamu and Lydia Cabrera. I further thank my friend Pamela Becker, for her early assistance and participation in the project, and also to friends Kathy and Donna Knox, and Sarah Whistler for help and ideas along the way, and to Howard Sandum for invaluable advice and support. I appreciate the assistance of the libraries and staffs of Tulane University and the University of Texas for help in research and to American Airlines for assistance in transportation, and to the Whittle Corporation for a helpful assignment in New Orleans. Finally, my appreciation to colleagues Jim Morgan and Linton Weeks, whose idea for a cover story on voudou in the late *Southern* magazine opened the door to this book, and to my editors Charlotte Wright and Fran Vick at the University of North Texas Press, for their faith in my vision and commitment to this witness.

# PART ONE

# THE
# STREET

# 1

# MIDNIGHT RITUAL

AT 1:00 A.M. the open air market along the Mississippi River edge of the French Quarter was still brightly lit, although the handful of people threading through the vegetable stands, bins of T-shirts, tables of tourist memorabilia and hanging clusters of garlic were mostly either vendors or drunks. My companions were neither. One was a Christian minister and voudou convert and the other was a middle-aged, middle-class woman whose week of initiation into the ancient West African religion was ending that night with her presentation to the marketplace, for prosperity, and to the Catholic Church, for the beneficence of God. They were both black, and I white, but all three of us had traveled a long road. It would be longer still, and before it was over I would taste the blood of sacrifice, feel the strange sluggish plasticity of another consciousness in my body. For my two friends, the way ahead was now one of discovered destiny and alliance with the powers of the universe, for they had accepted unto their lives the exiled African pantheon of spirits. In the ancient kingdom of the Yoruba people, an area roughly equivalent to what is now Nigeria, they are known as the orisha; in neighboring Benin (formerly the slaving kingdom of Dahomey) as the "vo-du," a word from the language of the Fon people.

Even in the wee hours of the Quarter we stood out. More natural to the habitat were the angst-ridden Tulane or University of New Orleans students outside the clubs on Decatur, sporting hang-dog forelocks or peroxide bobs, doing coke and Jagermeister shots, or the two men in black motorcycle vests, S&M chains and crotch-hugging leather shorts—remains of a culture that had collapsed of its own appetite, much as had the city around us. When the moon came up over New Orleans, decay and psychosis were as sweltering as the air, and, like the air, you had to breathe them. If Las Vegas is about corruption, and LA about power, and Miami about violence, New Orleans is about death; or, more specifically, one's attitude about death—that is, religion. It is a place to go off the deep end and find company. That was where I was, among the holy.

Both Gary and Lorraine were dressed in white. They'd driven up to the market, among the big trucks bringing in the next morning's produce, in Gary's blue Datsun, and gotten out like flashes of incandescence against the night sky. Gary was still in the colors of purity because, although initiated, he had not quite completed his year of apprenticeship. Lorraine was wrapped in white gown, lace, hat and heels because her year had just begun. Both had come to voudou, as had—until very recently—any U.S. black seeking the authentic African experience, through the Cuban form known as santeria. Worshipers of santeria refer to initiates as "yaguos," a Cuban adaptation of iyawo, a word from the Yoruba, West of Africa, which means both a mother and a child of the spirits. Thus Gary and Lorraine were both yaguos, although Gary was on the eve of becoming a full-fledged priest. Lorraine would be called "yaguo" by her friends in the voudou community for many months to come.

After a week of dancing, singing, sacrifices, readings and prayer from the priests who had been delivering her into the mysteries of santeria, the yaguo Lorraine was so high she could have floated, but the trip had to be strictly on foot. The idea was to "make the corners" of the market, which meant walking the oblong perimeter and pausing at each of the corners so that Gary could throw the four coconut divining shell fragments, known as obi, and ask the spirits of the market, such as Oya, goddess of the wind and the cemeteries, and Elegba, the divine trickster and lord of the crossroads, for good fortune and promise of success. I could sense white people staring all around us, and it made me feel bristly, but Gary and Lorraine let it roll off, as if the rest of the world didn't exist. A short but powerfully built man, Gary lent his arm to Lorraine as she teetered on her heels atop the concrete and asphalt. In her free hand she carried a horsetail whisk, an emblem of Obatala, the god of wisdom and organization.

At the first corner, they stopped. It had been raining, and Gary had to find a place without puddles. When he did, he took a bottle of Florida water, a sacred, lightly scented religious toilet water also used by many Catholics, from a paper sack and poured it on the glistening asphalt. He also threw out a few pieces of candy in cellophane wrappers, as offerings. Invoking the spirit of Elegba—to whom one must pray in order to reach any of the other African deities—Gary tossed the obi on the street. They fell two black, two white, which means two fell showing the white meat and the other two the dark husk: the configuration ejife, which means yes—a good omen for Lorraine.

But it wasn't the final cast. The prophecies which come from the obi, as in all the divination systems in Yoruba-based voudou, are binary—only yes and no questions can be answered, which requires a series of interrogatives; for example, "Will you have success?" If the answer is "yes," you may ask if the success is to come in business (yes/no), and if "yes," you may try to narrow to the type. A "no" answer requires that you expand or change the scope of the inquiry.

Before asking the next question, Gary bit a small segment from each piece of coconut—substituted in the New World for the kola nuts used in Africa—and spewed the mixture onto the ground, then threw the obi again, and poured water over the pieces. This time it was three black, one white. The next throw was two and two, and then three black, one white again. Gary said that the yaguo got affirmative answers to her requests, but that the final three/one configuration (etawa; a qualified yes) indicated that "her dead ancestors are talking. She's got to put something up (on her altar) when she gets home."

We advanced to the next corner. This was the first time Gary had escorted an initiate to the market and he was intent on observing all the protocol, just as had been observed for him in New York, where he had received his initiation as a child of Elegba. Gary's mother, the Reverend Lorita Honeycutt Mitchell, had seen to it that four of her six children were delivered into the power of the spirits since one of her twin boys, Andrew, had been saved from cancer through the intervention of the spirit in the form of St. Lazarus, who is paired in the world of voudou to the African deity Babalu Aye, the deity of catastrophic illnesses such as smallpox.

It was at the Reverend Mitchell's East New Orleans house—a modest shingle bungalow with a cow's tongue hanging from a hook on the front porch and a dead goat buried in the back yard—that the weeklong initiation of the yaguo Lorraine had been taking place, and where I had spent several days leading up to this night.

Gary, twenty-three, was Mitchell's eldest son, gifted in both prophecies and preaching, and what he was doing at the market was more than escorting a yaguo; he was taking the first steps toward bringing voudou back to the control of his family, the control of African Americans. In doing so he was joining what in the past few years has become a movement of spiritual reclamation pinioned in the South, where it started, but stretching across the country and presaging the most unexpected and intriguing religious renaissance in the United States in this century. It will certainly change the shape of American culture well into the next century, as population increases among the developing nations in which voudou variations may, by some estimates, involve up to fifty million adherents (Gert Chesi, *Voodoo*, 1979). Which is all the more remarkable when we remember that for half a millenium, as voudou spread to the New World via slave ships, virtually no effort was spared in the attempt to exterminate its presence, power and influence.

—==—

From about 1440 to about 1880, contract vessels delivered to Caribbean and Atlantic ports millions of hijacked Africans. The precise numbers have been raised and lowered over the years; 15 million enslaved humans delivered to the New World has generally been the accepted figure, though the total was revised down to 9.5 million (with an error range up to about 12 million) by Philip D. Curtin in *The Atlantic Slave Trade* in 1969. The most recent book on the subject, *The Slave Trade*, by historian Hugh Thomas, puts the total at 11.3 million delivered to the New World, with almost 2 million perishing in the infamous Middle Passage. Most of the survivors, about 4 million, went to Brazil, says Thomas, with 2.5 million sent to Cuba and about 4.1 million spread throughout the rest of the West Indies. Published estimates of slaves brought to North America before Congress outlawed the trade in 1808 have run from 400,000 to 600,000; Thomas puts the figure at 500,000, though that doesn't include the numbers from illegal slave trading, which he estimates at only about 5,000. The numbers, of course, are but approximations of the totality of the evil: "The attempt by many meticulous historians to decide figures to the last digit in a number is a vain one," Thomas concludes. "I am not even sure that is necessary."

The slaves, far from being a homogenous lot, represented numerous nations, cities, regions, languages, and so on, but almost all came from the western coast of Africa. As human beings, not chattel, they brought their cultures with them, including their ancestral religions—which were promptly outlawed. Various edicts, including the order of Pope Alexander II in 1493 and the infamous Code Noir of Louis XIV in 1685, precluded all but Christian worship, which often began with forced baptism aboard slave ships. Denied their own rituals, the slaves developed a method of dual worship—a combining process usually known as syncretization. Linking their deities (arrayed in a pantheon more than accidentally similar to Roman and Greek systems) to Catholic saints, slaves could pretend to pray to St. Barbara, for example, while really delivering their wishes to the vo-du thunder god, Songo (Anglicized as Shango; or Chango in Spanish), whose symbolic African colors of red and white and favored weapon, the double-headed axe, exactly matched the trappings of the Catholic ringer.

Having syncretized, voudou mutated—or evolved, depending on one's point of view—into a form with an unmistakable African core but mixed, in different regions, with a wide variety of other beliefs and faiths. From Brazil to New Orleans, transplanted voudou borrowed freely from native Indian cultures, European witchcraft, and other non-voudou African slave religions, for example the Kongo-based palo mayombe. And it co-opted precisely as much Catholicism as locally necessary to prevent the African content from being crushed by Europeans who at first merely scorned it, then, after voudou-inspired revolts beginning in 1791 led to the overthrow of the French on Santo Domingo and the founding of the Free Republic of Haiti in 1804, feared it as the single element that could precipitate their greatest fear: widespread, multi-centered, unstoppable slave revolts.

Today, as a generic term, voudou can be used to refer to almost any of the New World theologies emanating from the Yoruba religion and kingdoms. I have not intended its use here in a restrictive or purist sense. In different areas, voudou has different rituals and doctrines, running a sectarian range roughly comparable to that from Judaism through Protestantism to Catholicism. In Haiti, the religion metamorphosed into vodun or vaudoux; in Cuba, santeria; in Brazil, candomble; in Trinidad, Shango Baptist; in Mexico, curanderismo; in Jamaica, obeah. In the American South, it became voodoo and, in the most extreme caricature, hoodoo, the petty hexing (pins in dolls, love potions, etc.) which most people, black and white, confuse with the real thing. For the last several decades, another designation, orisha voudou, has been popularized by a group of African Americans seeking to de-syncretize voudou from Christianity and thus distinguish it from Cuban and Puerto Rican dominated santeria.

Throughout this book, I have avoided the orthographic form, "voodoo." The word in that spelling has come to signify centuries of racist falsities and perversions, not the least from Hollywood. Vodun, voudoun, vaudou, vaudoux, and vo-du are but some of numerous variations that seem less freighted with pejoration, but my preference is "voudou," the Creole-based spelling common in eighteenth- and nineteenth-century Louisiana. New Orleans newspapers styled it "voudou," as in "Voudou Nonsense," from a fairly typical headline in *The Daily Picayune*, June 26, 1871, recounting a St. John's Eve celebration; or "The Birth of Voudouism in Louisiana," June 26, 1874 [see Appendix I for more complete accounts of media treatment of voudou]. The writer George Washington Cable also used the spelling in novels such as the *The Grandissimes*. My choice of this spelling is admittedly arbitrary, but I think it necessary to break the lin-

# TOUR THE WORLD FAMOUS

## *NEW ORLEANS HISTORIC* VOODOO MUSEUM

### TOURS

Featuring The Great
Marie Laveau

## SINCE 1972

THE ALTAR ROOM

724 Dumaine
New Orleans, La.

70116

**(504) 523-7685**

READINGS
RITUALS
CRAFTS
SUPPLIES
LECTURES
TOURS
GRIS-GRIS
DOLLS

Open 7 days a week
10:00a.m.-10:00p.m. or later

C.M. Gandolfo
Curator

*plus*

ADVENTURE LOUISIANA TOURS

FIND OUT WHAT'S COOK'N

Offers
the most
intriguing and exciting tours,
guaranteed NOT to be a
run-of-the-mill experience.

## SWAMP TOUR PLUS

### VOODOO WALKING TOUR
### VOODOO TOUR VIA VEHICLE
### VOODOO RITUAL SWAMP TOUR

RITUAL TOUR

ADVENTURE LOUISIANA TOURS features
customized tours

*Major Credit Cards Accepted*

Brochure advertising Voodoo Museum, French Quarter.

guistic thought-lock emanating from the "voodoo" word picture. In addition, its etymology is distinctly American, befitting the scope of this book.

Some American practitioners, especially in santeria, avoid the problem by referring to "orisha worship." But others, myself included, think it is important to retain use of the word voudou itself. As an influential priest once told me, "The word will not go away. I wouldn't want it to go away. Keep in mind it has been maligned in the Western mind and Hollywood has given it a very ugly image and so nobody wants to be called vo-du, in the same way people didn't want to be called nigger . . . (but) it's perfectly legitimate and I think that you should use it and the more current that it becomes in the American mind, then people will understand it better and it will become vindicated of all the ignorance and viciousness that Hollywood has imposed upon it."

Only in Africa did vo-du (orisha) worship retain its lineage, without the intervention of Christian slave masters, to the ancient court of the Egyptians and their reverence not for the single patriarch deity developed under Judaic tribes as Jahweh, but for the entire cluster of existence, from the stars and the moon to the fecundity of the earth mother herself. What a story, what a grand chronicle could be constructed of the migration of these great mythical powers to the glories of the New World, already ablaze with the Aztecs, the Inca, the Anasazi, the Cherokee, the Navajo, Hopi, Sioux, Apache, Iroquois! But it didn't happen that way. Not for any of the indigenous religions, and especially, unsparingly, not for the "dark continent" import.

The religious history of America—I would say the social history, too—became that of the Bible, and to a lesser extent, of the Torah. In the case of the Native American religions the substitution was simple. Genocide. A religion without a living people to practice it is just another footnote in a history textbook. African theology was a different matter—the slave population grew, instead of dwindled. Eliminating the slave religion, and replacing it with Christianity, required centuries of repressive laws, executions, maimings and brainwashing. But it worked. Which is why we were performing one of the most devout rituals of the voudou culture at the French Market under cover of night, instead of among throngs of well-wishers on a weekend afternoon, or on Sunday morning TV.

—===—

At the third corner, Gary ran into difficulty with the obi. He had to throw several times, because the numbers weren't coming up right. You try not to leave with a bad sign. The worst would be four black husks, meaning oyekun, or danger—stop—the strongest warning possible. I know because I got one of those several months later in Atlanta and only by sacrifice to Elegba and Ogun, the god of metal, did I avoid a potentially dangerous accident in a pounding thunderstorm. But Lorraine wasn't getting an oyekun. She was drawing the one/three combination, okana, which is basically a strong warning to seek further consultation. So you ask again until you isolate the negative elements, and then through further yes/no dialogue with the ancestors, whose voices are revealed via the obi, you establish the proper course.

As Gary did this, he prayed to Elegba in the Yoruba language and in Spanish chants he had learned from Cuban santeros. Though now facing a separatist revolt from the African-American orisha voudou revivalists, the Cubans, whose ancestors' brutal sugar plantations absorbed huge quantities of slaves, are generally credited with preserving the rituals of orisha voudou through the long centuries of bondage. It was Cubans who re-introduced the traditional, as opposed to ersatz, practice of the religion to the U.S. black community in the late 1950s in

New York, where it remained relatively cloistered until the late 1970s or early 1980s.

I looked around as Gary and Lorraine studied the obi. The truckers were checking us out, and so were the club crowd and some of the vendors. You could tell we were doing something plenty weird, and that it involved a white man and two black people in some kind of odd costumery, and we weren't drunk, and it wasn't a party, and it had a method. That was probably the part that sent off the vibes—we had a purpose. That's always been the thing about voudou.

After we finished at the last corner, it was time to walk through the market itself, to present the yaguo publicly. As we walked up the sidewalk between the stalls, Gary remembered he was supposed to pick up some vegetables for home. About a dozen people were involved in the initiation, and it is customary for the host, in this case Gary's mother, to feed them.

We passed a vegetable stand and Gary looked at a display of plump, ripe tomatoes.

"How much are these?" Gary asked.

The vendor, a short, fat man I had overheard people calling Fredo, looked at Gary and the yaguo. "We're not open."

Gary examined the tomatoes. "Oh, I thought you were."

"Well, we're not."

An electrified split-second came and went. You could barely see it in the tight smile on Gary's face. "You looked open," he said again, then shrugged and escorted the yaguo away.

Earlier, while waiting for Gary and the yaguo to arrive at the market, I had seen business done at that stand. I walked over to Fredo. "You're open," I said. "You've been open all night."

Fredo's eyes narrowed as he checked me out. "We're closed."

"What do you mean you're closed?"

"I mean, we're closed."

"That's bullshit."

"Why don't you get on out of here?"

"Why don't you go fuck yourself?"

He said something equally snappy. I made a couple of quick calculations and figured this was a bad place to pick a fight. Gary and the yaguo had moved down the walkway. I joined them, Fredo's epithets still buzzing. I wanted to smash his face, but mostly I was angry with myself. I had lost my temper and nearly provoked a fight.

"Forget it," said Gary. "They're just ignorant people. They don't know anything about us."

Lorraine, who in heels towered nearly a head above Gary and me, was bound by silence. I was deeply sorry to have nearly created an incident on one of the most important evenings of her new life, and I apologized to both of them. "I just have a temper sometimes," I said.

Gary's eyes darted my way from under his white leather cap. "Yeah," he said. "I do, too."

We turned up outside the market and went back to the car. It was time to go to a Catholic church to complete the presentation. I suggested a chapel on the other side of the Quarter—Our Lady of Guadalupe, named for the Virgin of Guadalupe, the Aztec/Catholic patron saint of Mexico. Some tourist literature refers to Our Lady of Guadalupe as the Old Mortuary Church, because of its use during the yellow fever plague of the 1830s. It's also nicknamed "the voudou church," and in it you can sense the closeness of the two religions; at least one link is a statue of St. Expedite, "the voudou saint," who supposedly makes things happen faster. Church lore has St. Expedite, who looks like a Roman foot soldier with a halo, coming from medieval Italy, but the version around New Orleans is that he was adopted by slaves unloading crates stamped with the word "expedite." I lobbied a little for my choice, but Gary decided on St. Louis Cathedral, the big structure anchoring Jackson Square, which was much closer.

Our Lady of Guadalupe Church, on Ramparts Street in New Orleans, adjacent to the French Quarter. Also known as the Mortuary Church and sometimes the Voodoo Church.

We got in the Datsun and parked as close as we could on Decatur—it was difficult for Lorraine to walk far in those shoes.

We made our way slowly up one side of the square, which by day is filled with tourists, one-man bands, clowns, every kind of street hustle imaginable, but post-midnight is deserted except for the kinds of people you assume you don't want to run into at that hour. Just at the top of the square, before we turned toward the church, we saw a couple embracing, with considerable energy. Gary and I looked at each other and laughed, and then the female half of the pair, a tank-top blonde, looked at us, and she laughed, too. "Hope y'all are having fun," she called out. "We are."

At the steps of St. Louis Cathedral, Gary threw the obi again, and poured holy water, and spoke to Elegba, and to Olorun (known in santeria as Olofi), the creator of all things, much as the Christian God, before whose temple we were gathered. I watched the obi cast, and there was a difficulty again. "Would you mind turning your back?" Gary asked. "The coconuts aren't throwing right." I did, and I guess it worked out. We left.

Lorraine was then to go back to Reverend Mitchell's house to receive the baroque, ornate porcelain pots, or superas, used to contain the essences of the various spirits who had been summoned for her during the initiation week. Then the yaguo would return to her own house. There, before she could enter, Gary would repeat the four corners ceremony and spread covers over the mirrors. For the next year, Lorraine/yaguo would follow a rigid pattern of living in accordance with the itá, or life reading, that was the fulcrum of initiation.

Among other restrictions during her initiation year, there would be no movies, no dancing, no parties. She couldn't go out at night unless she had to work, and she must always wear white, except at work. She was very happy about all of it. As they drove away into the night and I stood along the Square and waved, it looked as if we'd gotten together for a late night drink and now we were all going back home. It wasn't anything like that at all.

# 2

# LOOKING
# FOR LORITA

IT HAD TAKEN me a few days once I got to New Orleans to track down the Reverend Mitchell and thus be a witness to the ceremonies for Lorraine that had culminated at the French Quarter. I almost hadn't found her at all. Hard times had come since I'd last seen her, two years earlier. Her old phone had been disconnected and her new number was unlisted. Nothing, either, when I drove over to her tiny ministry, the St. Lazarus Spiritual Church of Christ, a converted $125-a-month shotgun shack among the row houses and junk yards of Metropolitan Street northeast of the Quarter. I could tell by the trash and tall weeds that she wasn't there. Lorita Mitchell would never let her church fall into disrepair.

A crucifix stood amid the detritus like a sentry, but the vestibule door was locked tight. No notes, no signs, no forwarding information. Nobody around to ask. I tried to see inside the boarded windows but couldn't. Two years ago, inside that room, I'd been to an astounding service, my first encounter with the Spiritual Church, a mix of Catholicism and charismatic Protestantism—and voudou, I would argue. The Spiritual Churches are considered to have been founded in 1925 in Chicago, though some say that New Orleans was the starting point circa 1920. Certainly today, the denomination, which consists of numerous associations around the country, is most prevalent in the South. In the course of a four-hour ceremony, I had watched Reverend Mitchell swirl in her white robes while preaching Jesus and dancing her flock into possessive trances to drum-led call and response hymns. I had seen her prophesy destinies and beseech the healing powers of Christ using a bead-wrapped palo mayombe staff.

A woman like that didn't disappear. She was still in town, still preaching the Gospel, and still practicing voudou. I would find her when it was time, and in truth that's how I wanted it. A thing you learn about voudou is that you don't rely on plans and timetables. If the search were a drawing, it would resemble the Dahomean snake-god Dambada-Wedo, which encircles the earth and creation, tail in mouth, without beginning or end, and history moves through it like a rat. To see the movement of voudou is to know what the snake knows, go where the snake goes.

I ran down several useless telephone numbers and even traced Reverend Mitchell's old eastside apartment, where I'd seen, as opposed to participated in, my first sacrifice ritual. I drove back toward downtown and picked up Esplanade to Broad Street, in the general direction of the State Fairgrounds, to the F&F Botanica, where Lorita learned her trade giving readings in an adjacent shed, kicking back to the Cuban owner Felix a healthy cut of her income, about $25 per consultation, not counting fees for sacrifices. She and Felix had been heading for a falling out, and I figured they'd had one. He said he didn't know where she was.

I decided to look for leads through other botanicas—shops which sell religious supplies, herbs and iconography, and cater to both voudou and Christian (mostly Catholic) customers. Although they vary in degree of legitimacy—and honesty—most are true touchstones to voudou in a community offering spiritual advising and similar divination services. They aren't as plentiful in New Orleans as in say, Miami or the Bronx, where Cuban and Puerto Rican communities are filled with botanicas and the santeros (practitioners of santeria) who patronize them, but I spotted a shop on Elysian Fields, a long boulevard east of the Quarter. The Solano Botanica looked like a 200-year-old grocery store on a Mississippi backroad.

The interior was dusty and dark, as was Solano himself—a small, sour-faced man smoking a stubby cigar and wearing a Dallas Cowboys T-shirt. Fleshy circles under his eyes made him appear vaguely malevolent, and he tried to spook me, saying if I wanted to study voudou I would have to become "involved." I wasn't sure if he meant become initiated or merely buy something, such as an expensive plastic-wrapped supera on one of the shelves. It was the opening gambit in a head game some occultists like to run.

I told him I was just looking for Reverend Mitchell. I described her. I figured if he knew anything about voudou or santeria he would know about Lorita. He said he didn't.

I had turned to go when someone knocked on the door. Solano opened it, admitting an older, heavyset black woman in a blue flower print dress. She seemed perturbed, and I lingered to see why. Ignoring me, she told Solano she was having trouble collecting money owed her and wanted some herbs. Solano rebuked her for not coming around earlier. She said she had, and they were quibbling about it when I broke in, introduced myself to the woman, and tried my questions on her.

She reacted immediately. Yes, she'd heard of Lorita Mitchell, especially when I used the surname Honeycutt, the name of one of Lorita's four ex-husbands who himself had been a minister. "Honeycutt, she's around," the woman said. "I don't know where, but I think she's at Reverend Francis's church over in the Ninth Ward."

Antioch Spiritual Church in New Orleans, near the Ninth Ward neighborhood where Lorita Honeycutt Mitchell grew up.

I found the Antioch Spiritual Church of Christ where the woman said it was, and cajoled the Reverend Oscar Francis, also known as Bishop Francis, into giving me Lorita Mitchell's new phone number. I called the next morning. The heavy New Orleans drawl, thick with husky directness, was unmistakable. "Yeah, dahlin', why don't you come on over tomorrow about six," she said. "We're having another initiation. I'm sorry I can't talk to you anymore 'cause I'm up to my elbows in blood." She laughed and I could hear a din of voices in the background. "But you know about that, don't you?"

It turned out I'd been pretty close all along. Lorita's new house wasn't far from her old apartment, though she'd obviously moved up a little: these blocks boasted paved streets, three-bedroom brick ranch styles. Her next-door neighbor was a deputy sheriff.

I parked in the driveway and walked through the yard gate as dozens of white and brownish feathers swirled past me in the wind. At the front porch a blackened cow tongue, "for people with big mouths," hung from a big hook in the ceiling. Lorita's youngest daughter Juanika greeted me, leading me inside and down a short hallway. Offerings of corn, bread, yams and cooked sacrificial meat filled small wooden bowls on the floor. A bunch of okra had been tacked up just inside the door. So had a dead pigeon, hanging upside down.

Juanika guided me into the living room. Four young women from Lorita's church sat primly on the two large sofas. One was holding Lorita's infant granddaughter, Antoinée. They were all watching a movie starring James Caan on TV, called *Hide in Plain Sight*. Gary was there; so were three Cubans I'd never seen.

I was introduced and escorted into the kitchen. Wonderful aromas of garlic, spices, onions and sizzling grease enveloped three women laboring amid steaming pots of spaghetti sauce, pasta, vegetables and piles of freshly cut goat and fowl. One of the women was her: the Reverend Lorita Honeycutt Mitchell, forty-six, minister of the Lazarus Spiritual Church, priestess of Oshun, initiate of palo mayombe, and matriarch of her clan. She stood barefoot in purple sweatsuit before a frying pan, sautéing chicken feet and chitlins. Her skin was very dark, flawlessly smooth, her eyes doe-like, luxuriant, powerful. She smiled at me with toothpaste-commercial intensity. "Glad you could make it," she said, continuing to stir.

I was quickly introduced to the other people in the house: Lorita's daughters-in-law, some members of her Spiritual Church who had come to help out but were not voudou, and the three Cubans: Rogelio, Alfredo and Doris. They were all from New

Jersey and had flown down, at Lorraine's expense, to preside over the initiation. They were needed because Lorita, although a priestess, did not yet have the authority to perform the full ceremony. Voudou, like most religions, is hierarchical. An initiation requires several levels of the priesthood beyond that to which Lorita had ascended.

Rogelio was to be the padrino, or godfather, of the initiate, and thus would preside over the ceremony. He was also Lorita's personal padrino, and, like her, was a priest of the patron deity Oshun, the goddess of beauty. Alfredo was an oriaté, a specifically Cuban ranking of priest with special powers of divination important to the ceremony. Doris, a priestess of Obatala, was primarily there to assist with logistics. Rogelio took my elbow and escorted me to the back porch, which had been converted to the main initiation room and also housed the various altars to Lorita's personal spiritual guardians. The gesture was not so much to be friendly as it was to demonstrate that, although we were in Lorita's house, Rogelio considered himself to be in charge.

Lorraine, in a loose white cotton smock, sat in a corner of the porch on what was called her "throne," actually a small wooden post covered in silver wrapping paper. Around her a special canopy had been arranged with draperies of yellow, red, blue, silver and white cloth. Superas and offering bowls lined the walls. Some contained entrails; one propped up the head of a pig. Maybe a goat.

In the center of the floor, a wooden chopping block and knife lay next to a tub filled with the remnants of sacrificial fauna. The yaguo looked serene but tired. They all looked tired, for that matter. There'd been very little time for sleep since the initiation started, and most of last night they had been up making sacrifices to the spirits in order to achieve ocha, the ultimate goal of the santeria quest. Ocha means power.

Each altar featured the statues, herbs, flowers, colors and offerings pecular to its god. Lorita's Oshun shrine, for example, was maintained in a wicker cabinet filled with superas, a fan, a small black doll, and mirrors.

I ducked Rogelio, grabbed a beer and went into the living room. Lorita was taking a break from the cooking, and came in to sit next to me on the couch. We had a lot to catch up on. Someone brought her a Coke, and while the Cubans and the church members and the relatives and friends went about their business, Lorita told me the story of how, only a year earlier, she'd met Rogelio in New Jersey. A strange, contradictory, angry tale, it was really her way of telling me she was fed up with her guests and couldn't wait to be rid of them. I'd only been there an hour and understood completely.

Someone interrupted us to tell Lorita that the yaguo had to "go." Miffed, Lorita excused herself to escort the initiate, as was her duty. But Lorraine must've done something wrong, and I could hear Lorita scolding her. "She's just a rich lady with long fingernails," Lorita muttered as they passed through toward the bathroom. "She's not used to being told what to do. But the Lord is good for bringing you down to the level of everyone else."

Rogelio swirled in from another room, primped up in a long, semi-translucent yellow shirt, untucked, in the Caribbean style. He joked about borrowing one of Lorita's furs, because an unseasonable cool front had blown down from Canada. Lorita's body tensed. The Cubans had been eating her food, using her phone for long-distance calls, sleeping in her bedroom, and now, it seemed, were also wearing her clothes. "He treat me like a slave," she whispered.

Yet he was her padrino. And more. He had, in the last year, initiated four of her children: Gary, Juanika, and the twins Andrew and Anthony. It was terrible to feel she was being used by the man to whom she had entrusted so much.

In a few months she would break with him forever. By then she would have enough initiates in New Orleans, all black Americans, not to need the Cubans anymore. Consciously, and with the cunning of the streets, Lorita was making her own dynasty. It was funny—Lorita never liked the word voudou, feeling it had long ago been propagandized as the stuff of evil and sorcery.

"Santeria" was okay, because the Cubans had convinced her santeria was something else. But santeria is voudou as surely as Catholicism is Christianity, and in her own way, forging untutored but determined into the nearly vanished world of the orisha in America, Lorita Mitchell was as true a daughter of the African powers, the vo-du, as had ever landed on these shores.

—=—

Next time I saw her, near the end of initiation week, she had poured herself into a form-hugging denim sheath and was in full Oshun—sensual, stunning, a volcano of vanity, all hallmarks of the goddess whose mythological links include Venus, Isis and Aphrodite. It was the night before I would go to the Quarter with Gary and Lorraine—and time for what in santeria is called the medio, a feast. The hard work of preparing the sacrifices for the spirits, of the nights of praying, and the haggard demeanor of those who had participated, was replaced by a party—beer, wine, singing and dancing.

The yaguo sat under her canopy on straw mats, greeting but not speaking to those who came to pay their respects. She wore a plain white dress, and, on her head, for Shango, a silver crown with red parrot feathers. Her face bore white markings feigning mutton chop sideburns and a mustache, to symbolize the old man aspect of her patron deity, Obatala. Her neck was strung with the vari-colored beads of Shango, Elegba, Obatala, Ochosi and Ogun.

Another white dress hung on the wall to her right. More formal in its detail and frills, it would be worn by the yaguo only twice—that night for dinner and again in her grave. It had been hand-sewn by members of Lorita's church—for a fee. An initiation ceremony, in santeria, can cost $5000 or more, maybe double that in some instances, and Lorita had in mind putting as much of the money into the hands of her own people as possible. Even the fees for the carpetbagging priests, ranging from $700 to $1500, would mostly be spent in town.

Lorita greeted her yaguo in the royal manner, throwing herself forward full-length before the throne, arms stretched above her head, beseeching her spirits to join in the homage. The yaguo reciprocated to show respect. The Cubans followed suit, as did the other visitors, except a couple of church women to whom all this still seemed bizarre, even sacrilegious.

Alfredo, on congas, and Louis, on shakeree—a large, hollowed gourd around which has been draped a loose netting of beads—had taken up spots to one side of the porch and began "looking for the voice in their drums." They found it, and within minutes the fifteen or so guests in the hot, crowded room were singing and whirling to the beat. Lorita and Gary spun across the middle of the floor. Rogelio, now in white trousers and red shoes, head covered with white lace, was a technicolor cyclone. Alfredo paused sometimes to pass around a bottle of rum, or to mop sweat from his face. I stepped outside for some air, nearly tripping over a crate of guinea fowl.

A few small children darted in and out. I swatted away mosquitoes, which, like the flies, were drawn in by the livestock and I guess by the sweaty humans, too. The back yard needed mowing, but was not unkempt. In it lay a hula hoop, an old truck axle and a sagging clothes line. Over in the far corner, I could see a worn circular patch in which Lorita several months ago had set up candles and glass jars and buried a goat. She told me she had needed a special cleansing ceremony to remove a vicious curse from herself. She believed it had been placed on her by friends of her first padrino, a Cuban priest named Ricky Cortez, with whom she had quarreled violently and had sought to replace with Rogelio.

The serenading of the yaguo continued. Dollar bills and other presents piled up on the mat in front of the throne. It was like being at a crowded weekend party in a small off-campus apartment. I squeezed back in near the doorway next to a woman from Lorita's church holding Antoinée. The woman swayed and smiled, and the baby closed her eyes to sleep. After a while everyone got tired, and the drummers stopped, and it seemed that the spirits had left the room. Nothing formal ended the dancing; we just filtered out to eat.

Someone handed me a plate of goat ribs, sausage, guinea fowl, red beans and rice. Someone else took seven plates of food into the throne room to set before the yaguo, for her spirits. I asked the Cuban santera, Doris, if you could be a vegetarian santero, if there might not be any vegetarian saints or orishas who preferred meatless offerings. She laughed.

I ate all my beans and rice and, hoping not to offend anyone, scraped everything else into the trash bin. I filled up on cake and talked to James, a big, quiet man who ran a private security business which employed Lorita's son Andrew. Like many people in New Orleans, James wasn't voudou, but that didn't mean he didn't put stock in it. He had come to Lorita after a former girlfriend hexed him by killing a cat. His business went bad, he said, until Lorita cleaned him with chickens, passing them over his body to draw the spell from him, and then killed them to keep the spell from spreading. Now James was okay and had begun going to Lorita's church and did some repair work for her.

Everyone I would meet had a story like that, proto-Biblical— fall from grace after contamination with evil, wandering through the wilderness of despair, then salvation at the hands of a true prophet of Jesus. It was no accident that, in black American culture, the prophet of Jesus was, often as not, also a party to a world of spirits and spells emanating straight from a half-forgotten African past.

It got late and I was tired. I said goodbye to Lorita and set up a time to meet Gary and the yaguo Saturday night for our impending trip to the French market. I went out into the night. The cool front had opened up the clouds, and as I drove back downtown, the stars came out. They were brilliant—glittering outposts in the heavens.

# 3

## THE GODS AND THEIR WAYS

ONE SULTRY MORNING a couple of weeks after the initiation at Lorita's home, I drove down to the lower end of the Quarter to meet Ava Kay Jones at the Old U.S. Mint, a refurbished brick office building now used as a museum, library and public meeting place. I had met Ava about the time I met Lorita, when Ava was working as lead dancer for her Voodoo Macumba Dance Troupe. Since then, she had not only taken further steps towards becoming an orisha voudou priestess—steps that would lead me in a circle back to her many months down the road—but had also opened a botanica, Jambalaya. Until it closed, another victim of the New Orleans economy, it was the only voudou establishment in the Quarter with any claim to authenticity. Lorita's Lazarus Spiritual Church Supply, and the other authentic ones, were all elsewhere in the city.

A small, voluptuous, articulate purveyor of both her faith and her talent, Ava became the center of attention whenever she walked through the Quarter in her white dress, big earrings and white kerchief, as striking a picture of a m'ambo, a Haitian priestess, as even the long-time residents were likely to encounter. Some people didn't know what to make of her—she didn't fit known stereotypes. Others treated her almost like a celebrity. More than once, whether we were snacking on coffee and croissants or splitting po'boys at an oyster bar, I watched black wait staff scrutinize her minutely, as though something inside, half-forgotten, were registering. Ava sensed it, too. It was one of the reasons she had made her choice, to give up a career as an attorney to devote her life to the orisha.

She and her troupe, a half-dozen dancers and musicians, turned devotion to the gods into a delicious tornado of snakes and drums, scarves and machetes, athleticism and grace. One night I walked down to Congo Square, where drum-playing and dancing had once been outlawed, to see Voodoo Macumba's open air performance for delegates from a book publisher's convention. The guests had arrived in horse-drawn carriages and taken their places under a striped lawn tent, with no idea what was about to hit them. When it was over, the images of the virile,

Ava Kay Jones, center, dancing with python in public performance of her Voodoo Macumba Dance Troupe, at Congo Square, New Orleans.

muscled male dancers, Ava writhing with her pet python, the strange black kettles, the drumming, the heat—had reduced the evening to a kind of awkward quiet. Polite applause, very little talking as the delegates went back to the cloppity-clop of the carriages, the normalcy of their hotels.

She saw that as evidence of her usefulness, too. Voudou was not something that settled in easily. Even defensiveness meant someone was paying attention, and there was much to which she wanted to attend. In her appearances and performances, the flamboyance of her very demeanor, she tried to set the record straight in her own way. Having made a "name" in town as a voudou savant, she was sometimes interviewed in local media, and occasionally invited to lecture on her beliefs. That was what I was doing at the Old Mint. The State of Louisiana had hired her to explain voudou to a new crop of state tour guide volunteers whose jobs would be to escort groups through the French Quarter. I wanted to hear it.

I was early, and ducked over to Ursulines Avenue to a coffee house to read the paper and pass the time, musing about when I had first met Ava in this very place. She had been with a musician friend who called himself "Sidiki," who told me the word jazz was from an African word "jass," meaning jism. Ava didn't fluster at direct talk about sex. Lorita never did, either. It had nothing to do with black or white; it was all about ideas of sexuality. In voudou, sex was not a sin. It was part of life.

I finished my coffee and walked back to the Mint. I was spending a great deal of my time with these two women—priestesses, daughters of gods, people I could never have imagined on my own. I was not fully aware of the complexities at the time, but later, I would look back in wonder at the paths each had taken to her African spirit, how the oracle of fate, known in voudou as Ifa, had aligned each in precisely the right way, had imagined them completely.

Lorita as Oshun and Ava as Oya, ancient and eternal rivals—more appropriate earthly manifestations could not have been chosen. In their distant world, an amalgram of history and mythology, Oya and Oshun shared one trait—both were river goddesses, powerful symbolism in all religions; on all other matters they quarreled, starting with men. Shango was Oya's husband and Oshun's lover. Their personalities, too, were oil to water. Fiery, temperamental, outrageous Oshun and serious, controlling, earthy Oya, the former the embodiment of beauty, the latter of the strange, compelling world of death, of fundamental knowledge, of eternal change.

Here below, the distinctions between the two orisha in their human guises took the form of sociology. The backgrounds of Lorita, a ghetto-reared survivor of the mean streets, and Ava, a middle-class infiltrator in the white worlds of dance, law and university degrees, had kept the two voudou priestesses, among the first authentic initiates in the New Orleans voudou renaissance that began in the 1980s, in completely different social worlds. Except for the link of Ricky Cortez, the enigmatic santero who had separately introduced each of them to santeria voudou, neither would have been aware of the other's existence. Yet even after entering the religion, and thus hearing of each other through the grapevine of botanicas, clients and practitioners, the two women remained mutually aloof. Lorita sizzled with jealousy at the mention of Ava Kay, and Ava felt that she would be unwelcome if she called on Lorita. Exactly as Oshun and Oya would have behaved.

Thinking of Ava or Lorita in their god-like states became a fascinating kind of game for me, a way of converting the vagueness of the spirits into flesh and blood. In the voudou world, not unlike the realms of the ancient pagan religions, avatars of thousands of human spirits are coalesced into what Jung might call archetypal personalities—hundreds, perhaps thousands of deities. Their cosmos was filled with combat, intrigue, treachery, heroism, lust, tragedy—sagas much like those of the gods of the Vikings, the Romans, the Greeks, the American Indians, the Hindus.

Sometime in the mists of memory, the vo-du were converted from living matter—usually through violent death caused by hubris—into immortal prototypes which pretty much cover the range of human character. A dozen or so have become the most prevalent in the New World. Besides Elegba, or Esu (Eleggua in santeria), Ifa, Oshun, Oya, Obatala, Shango and Babalu Aye, there are Ogun, the god of metal and war; Ochosi, the hunter, especially popular in Brazil; Osanyin, the herbalist; Yemonja, the goddess of the sea and fertility and queen of the witches; Olokun, also an ocean deity, generally considered male, and considered by some to be the patron of the African races, as Ogun is for Europeans; and Dambada Wedo (Damballah-Hwedo in Haiti), the serpent ruler, entwining the earth and the past.

The all-powerful Olorun, or Olodumare, or Odudua among the Yoruba, presides over all. As abstract as sacred, Olorun is genderless, neither anthropomorphized nor prayed to directly. The orisha, not unlike the Christian saints, are the intermediaries. They, in turn, can only be reached through the gatekeeper, Esu/Elegba. Some voudous jokingly call this formalized, almost corporate pantheon the "bureaucracy," but it is to this hierarchy that the worshiper turns, throughout life, for guidance, help, retribution and comfort, adopting a single orisha as one's personal "father" or "mother." The corporeal essence of a worshiper is but the vessel of that spirit, reincarnated through generations unending. Haitians, in a particularly descriptive phrase, refer to the experience of becoming a vessel for the spirits, the loa (or lwa), as being "mounted," thus the title of Maya Deren's lyrical study of Haitian voudou—*The Divine Horsemen*. Ava had been mounted by Oya and was changed forever by it. That was what she wanted to tell the guides, or anyone who would listen.

In her loose white short-sleeved blouse and full skirt, white kerchief tied up tight, Ava Kay-as-m'ambo had the same effect on the tour guides as she did on people on the street. Unfortunately, the thick black frames of her glasses gave her away. In the old days, under slavery, an African who had glasses probably used them for reading, and in most of the colonies or Southern states, slaves were not allowed to read. "A hundred years ago I would've been barbecued for coming here to say all this," Ava quipped, pausing at a table next to the lectern to arrange some of the herbs, charms, soaps, books and oils she'd brought. "You know what I'm saying?"

The guides chuckled, a little nervously. Probably, they didn't. White, middle-class, mostly retirees, they had signed on as explicators of the French Quarter and this was just part of the educational drill. But they listened. Some tourist was bound to ask about voudou, and this woman in white would make it clear what to say, and there was fresh French roast coffee in china cups.

She opened the lecture with a song, a traditional Yoruba chant to Elegba, for Monday was his day. It was a holy rite, but the gulf between the Africanness of what she had to say and the centuries of opposition to that race and everything it stood for made the audience react to the prayer is if it were some kind of mildly embarrassing warm-up act.

"Voudou is a way of life," she began, "not just something we do on Sunday," and went on with a brief rundown of the orisha and the culture—uncomfortably revisionist to some, judging from the crossed arms and knowing glances. "I'm a Catholic, too— oh, yes," she offered, perhaps to bridge the gap. "My favorite church is Our Lady of Guadalupe, especially the novenas. But I also believe in voudou. And when people ask me what voudou believes in, I say: we serve the same God you serve. We worship the God Force." Arms remained crossed, although many took notes.

"The orishas and the charms and the saints—all these are humanity's way of relating to this all-encompassing God Force. So I say to people, to receive good effects, you put out good causes. We do not seek to harm other people through sticking pins in dolls. Because it will come back to you. On the spiritual level, same as in the criminal justice system, you will be punished. In the Catholic Church, we say we are not punished *for* our sins but *by* them."

Some kept taking notes. Some didn't. Smiling graciously, Ava moved on with the show, picking up from the display table a small red flannel pouch, looped at the mouth with a black string. "Y'all have seen these," she said. "Now I'll show you how to make a gris-gris." Probably drawn both from voudou and palo traditions, the bags are popular throughout New Orleans; cops in the Quarter are said to carry them for luck.

Ava filled the pouch with a potpourri of the standard additives: High John the Conqueror, a common plant root usually prescribed for luck or power or money; jasmine flowers for Oshun and love; rose petals; various herbs, including frankincense for peace and myrrh and rosemary for warding off negativity. She added a pinch or two of her special potions, for love. "When teenagers come in for these," she smiled as she worked, "I tell them it's not just for physical love, it's not just to attract girls. They take the bags, say 'Yes ma'am,' and they're out of there."

We laughed, but she had a more serious point. Just taking a bag and thinking it will accomplish something on its own is wasting your money, she said. "It won't work without prayer and meditation. The psychology of the ritual is a very big part. You visualize what you want." She pressed the bag in her palms and invoked a blessing from the saints and the orishas. To make the bag work, she said, a person should hold it for ten minutes a day, preferably at sunrise or sunset ("the power times"), while meditating.

She put the gris-gris back on the table, shuffled a few of the bottles and vials, and picked up a green cloth doll—"so it will attract money." From the stir in the audience she knew she had probed a sensitive spot. But although the use of dolls with pins is the stereotypical aspect of "voodoo," it has a decidedly mixed cultural ancestry; doll-hexes are equally likely to have emanated from witchcraft brought into the South via Europeans as to have come from Africa. In the Quarter, you will see "witchcraft" stores at least half as often as the "voodoo" knock-offs.

Witchcraft and voudou are distinctly different, though frequently lumped together under the general heading of occult, a word which simply means unknown. Like voudou, witchcraft—or wicca—has enjoyed a relatively recent round of defense, especially from those who interpret its poor image as the result of social and religious persecution. The difference is that voudou was considered evil because it was black. Wicca was evil because it was female.

"I'll make this one for myself," Ava laughed, "because if it does bring in money I should get it." Chairs shuffled slightly as she anointed the doll's head, hands and feet, then lit a white candle for it and, in Yoruba, invoked the help of the gods. For nine days she said, nine being a number of change, a Scorpio number, her number, she would pray to that doll and "send out vibes into the universe to come to me." After that, "the God force" would bring change, because "you reap what you sow."

What she was doing, she said as she added a few finishing touches, was very common in New Orleans, "a city founded in mysticism," but also came out of the "hoodoo" practices she learned growing up in the southeast Louisiana Cajun town of Thibodaux, among a family of traituesses, a term for psychics or diviners. Putting an X on Marie Laveau's grave, knocking three times, and then leaving flowers and coins was a good way of asking for protection or luck. Leaving a salt cross, or a circle of salt, on your doorstep, is a way of protecting yourself; so is wearing a necklace of chicken feet, or boiling them for use in potions.

"It's a tradition more than a ritual," Ava said. "It's handed down mother to daughter to granddaughter. My grandmama still cleans her steps with red brick [dust from broken bricks] instead of Tide because it's a spiritual cleanser."

What was important, as I listened, were not the spells, but the increased attention their recitation produced in the audience. Since hexes and "black" magic were considered to be the substance of voudou, when at last Ava got to them, it was as if she'd finally reached the truth according to preconception. As if she had finally admitted that voudou was just spell-casting and pins in dolls.

A woman in a garden-club blue dress raised her hand. "How can you be a Catholic and be a voudou priestess?" There was an edge to her voice.

"Well," said Ava, "I don't agree with all the Church dogma, but if we're dealing with what Christ taught, then I'm a Christian in that sense." She let that sink in. "But if you add all the dogma, I'm not."

Another woman, who was sitting at a table next to mine and had been whispering to her friend all during Ava's lecture, raised her hand. The edge was in her voice, too, but sharper. "You've been saying that voudou is not evil. Well, how did we get that idea? That it is evil?"

Ava had heard such questions before, though perhaps with less hostility. "You got it from mis-torians," she began. "Not historians. And from movies—"

"That may be so," a gray-haired man in a yellow Polo interrupted, "but what's the difference between voudou and magic?"

Ava, nearsighted, searched out the voice. "Every religion uses or has used magic," she said, turning toward her flank. "In voudou, we have retained it. Voudou has not taken the magic, or the ritual, out of religion." Which naturally invited a comparison to the Church, and she went for it. "The Catholic Church also seeks to put ritual in the religion, so the people can relate to it."

The man crossed his arms over his chest. His face was slightly flushed. His voice rose. "Then what is the symbol of evil in voudou?"

Ava held back a moment. I could feel, it, too.

"I don't know," she said, green doll poised lightly in one hand. "I don't know if there is a symbol. Good and evil have always existed in the world. There is a criminal element who violate natural laws in voudou as well. But that part is not to be confused with the whole."

She thought for a moment, adjusting her glasses, like a college professor privately intrigued by the mystery in her students all over again. "Why is there evil? It could be a psychological malfunction. Or that there's a day and there has to be a night—"

She put the doll down. "I really can't think of a symbol, in that way. I don't really think there is one."

The man in the Polo exhaled in disgust. Many of his companions frowned, pursed their lips, shook their heads. All along, they had been trying to pry out from her the depiction of the snake, which in Christianity has come to be the symbol of the Devil. It would seem logical that if the snake is evil, and if the snake is worshipped in voudou, then voudou is really worship of the Devil.

In voudou, though, Dambada Wedo is not a metaphor for Evil but for the eternity of life. In the ancient matriarchal cultures of Asia and Northern Africa from which voudou emerged, the snake was a mighty and honored figure—the guardian-child of the earth-mother. Only in patriarchal Christianity did the serpent became the evil tempter of the Garden of Eden.

A good Catholic, of course, wouldn't have let the Christian inversion of pagan symbolism permit her to evade her intellectual and moral obligation to come up with a figure for evil in voudou, to damn the snake. But a "good" Catholic wouldn't have known anything about voudou in the first place. The problem that faced Ava Kay, in the eyes of her own Catholicism, and the minds of the tour guides, was that she had lost her ignorance.

# 4

## COUNTERTOP VOUDOU

LORITA LIVED SUCH a cash-and-carry life it was difficult for me to see how she'd managed to lease two-thirds of a brick triplex at the corner of Iberville and Dorgenois, just off Canal Street about a mile from the Quarter, as the new home for her church and the first home for her own botanica. But she'd been in business there about a year, St. Lazarus Church Supply facing one street, St. Lazarus Spiritual Church the other, her own private spiritual reading room squeezed in a narrow interior office space exactly in between.[1] The surrounding neighborhood was better than the one on Metropolitan Street, but also no stranger to gunshots, sirens, and mayhem. Still, it was lively like a Covarrubias painting, and with a fish market next door, a down-home waffle shop up the block, and a Cuban clothing boutique across the intersection, Lorita's alternative to the high-priced F&F Botanica that had weaned her seemed for all the world like a corner grocery store.

Kids, in particular, filtered in and out of the botanica, seeking not the services of a santeria priestess, or the Friday night preaching of a minister, but things on which to spend nickels

The Reverend Lorita Mitchell posing playfully in front of her former botanica and church, next to her Cadillac.

and pennies. Accordingly, Lorita had expanded her line of goods to include soft drinks, candy bars, potato chips, cookies, sour pickles, and pig's feet. The postman, too, generally picked up a daily soft drink, as did one or two of the local men, whose thirst was often as not an excuse to flirt, almost shyly, with the woman who had definitely juiced up the neighborhood. In the last couple of weeks I'd joined the regulars, going down to the "shop," as Lorita called it, almost every day; my adopted home, a place to while away the Big Easy, an invisible hole in the universe for all its contiguity to the real world. Also, she kept the thermostat on sub-Arctic. I don't know if she was amused by me or merely tolerant, but I could come and go as I wished, and could hang for hours if I didn't touch the gospel radio she kept blaring.

Some days, though, the real world closed in. I'd been reading in a corner chair up front, next to the St. Lazarus shrine. Juanika was at the sales counter, which served as a barrier to the rest of the store, selling a pickled pig's foot to a teenage boy trying to pretend he wasn't wondering just what kind of a place he'd walked into. I watched the boy's eyes make a rapid recon, starting with the ceiling-high shelves of oils, candles, soaps, superas and other items of the trade which formed an alcove around the cluttered desk on the other side of the counter where Lorita, unusually business-like in crisp tan cotton dress, sat, brow furrowed, phone at her ear. A hand-lettered poster on the freshly painted white wall said:

> All reading are $25.00 per person. If two people wish to enter the room at the same time, $25.00 per person. Except if you are bring someone who is sick are not able to understand. You are allowed to ask questions in your reading but additional information is extra. Please be prepared to pay for your services rendered. Yours in Christ,
> Rev. L. Mitchell.
> Please pay at the front first. Thank you.

The boy considered the sign a moment, looked at the woman at the desk, then leaned forward around Juanika to check out the rest of the shop, where the alcove merged into a larger room, mostly vacant except for a refrigerator and restroom. And a balsa crate containing live roosters. Plastic sacks stuffed with dead ones. A bucket of crabs parked next to a 48-quart Igloo cooler. Most of all, a cast-iron cauldron in the far corner. It was partly covered by a white cloth, but you could easily see the kettle was full of bones, iron nails and bundles of wooden branches, or palos in Spanish. In the Kongo, where the use of the palo pot originated, it is called an nganga. By any name, it is a repository of spirits of the dead.

The boy glanced back at me with widened eyes and a thin smile, declined Juanika's suggestion of a Big Red, paid for the pig's foot and made a quick U-turn out the door. Usually, Lorita would have taken care of such shyness, or at minimum called out, "Come back, baby," to any potential client who came in and left, but she was still on the phone, and it didn't seem to be pleasant.

She fussed with her gold necklace as she talked. According to her itá, gold was the only kind of jewelry she could wear. Not even diamonds. Her face had gone ashen, haggard. Rising from her chair, eyes glowing, she began to pace as far as the phone cord would allow. Her voice rose, then dropped to a growling mutter. It was Gary, and from what I could make out, it was about the car. Ten minutes later she hung up, sat down and rubbed her neck, and I knew her wrecked Cadillac Brougham, the pride of her possessions, still wasn't repaired. It was a touchy subject, so I turned my attention to the radio.

A white fundamentalist talk show preacher was healing people on the air, spacing out the broadcast miracles with recorded hymns. Lorita didn't think white people, most of whom she believed to be Catholic, could pull off gospel music—"they try, but it all sounds like, what is it, 'Old Rugged Cross'"—but she listened to white shows anyway. The Lord was the Lord, church was church, and singing for Jesus was singing for Jesus.

Presently her temper cooled and she talked to a steady stream of clients on the phone for over an hour. About five, she asked me to give her and her family a ride home. We piled into my car just as the heavy air turned to raindrops so big I could barely see to drive. All the way home Lorita tried to remain cheerful, dispensing advice on curing Antoinée's cold with goose grease and honey.

It wasn't just the Caddy. It was everything—the last three years. In some people this would be a mood; in Lorita it seemed more than that, some power, some bad thing always out there,

Shelves of candles, herbs, and other religious supplies inside St. Lazarus botanica. Candies, pop and other snacks, foreground, helped add to the bottom line.

Room behind main counter in St. Lazarus botanica. In corner under blanket, palo mayombe pot filled with bones, iron nails and bundles of wooden branches. Machete wedged to one side. Next to palo pot, Igloo cooler hides bucket of crabs to feed Elegba. In foreground, crates of live roosters and chicks.

always to be fought, not always to be defeated. Since I'd last seen her, she'd changed churches, started a new business, fought with her Cuban santeria advisors. She'd nearly lost everything when a fire inflicted heavy smoke damage on the triplex, and the insurance wasn't paying off a black woman preacher of some weird inner city religion, and the truth was going thirty days at a time right now. Forget credit cards. And now the Caddy was being held hostage by the mechanic and the whiplash hurt and the lawsuit against the taxi that hit her was a nightmare and she hated physical therapy but wouldn't take pills because they were drugs and she didn't like drugs, which was why she was dressed up; she'd been to the clinic that day.

Just before we got to her house, Lorita asked me to stop at a Baskin-Robbins. She ordered a banana split, and that was dinner, as a small can of barbecue flavor Vienna sausages had been lunch. Before I left she asked me to come by the shop early the next morning. Gary had to work at his catering job and she would need help getting ready for three "urgent" clients. I promised to be there at eight.

—=—

I had barely said good morning when she told me to take down a bunch of bananas bound by a purple ribbon tacked to the ceiling just inside the door. They were an offering for Shango, to help draw money, but had gone sugary black in the heat. I pulled them down and tossed them into a black plastic garbage bag. The phone rang. Lorita told the caller she'd try to work her in. While we waited for the first client, she finished a long over-due chore, wiping smoke film from small vials of oils salvaged from the fire.

She was still peeved about the Caddy, her neck still was achy, and she was still nursing a grudge against me for telling her last week a CAT-scan of her neck wouldn't be so bad. I offered to run down to McDonald's to get us some coffee and sausage biscuits. By the time I returned she was puttering around in her readings office, and soon I heard her singing. I took in a biscuit, but she put it to one side. In that room of her own, where the powers of Jesus and her voudou spirits worked in harmony, Lorita found the real nourishment of her life. Sitting at her cloth-covered divining table, she hummed absent-mindedly as she arranged the few things she kept on it: a thick, cream-colored Bible, three small goblets of water, a statue of St. Lazarus and another of Whitehawk (one of the Native American spirit guides popular in New Orleans), and a note pad. Like most priests, not to say therapists, Lorita kept track of the progress and problems of her clients, and referred to her notes for repeat visits.

I slumped against a wall, next to a black palo staff with a serpent carved down its length, and sipped my coffee. The far corners of the 10x20 rectangle were crammed as ever with sacrificial altars on behalf of clients. Among them were two fist-sized Elegba statues similar to one near the botanica entryway out front. The crossroads god in all three cases was rendered in the standard symbolic manner—an inverted, cone-shaped head molded of laterite and featuring cowrie shells for eyes and mouth. A pointed nail, imbedded in the laterite before it hardened, stuck up from the top of the flat crown. In all, the figure resembled the shape you'd get by filling a paper cup with sand, turning it upside down, and pulling the cup away, then sticking in shells and nails. Surrounding the Elegbas, which had been set on plain ceramic plates on the floor, were offerings of bloodied feathers, ripe bananas, and red candles.

I noticed at least one new altar, next to the Elegbas, for Ochosi. Equated with the astrological symbol Sagittarius, Ochosi's talismanic symbol is a U-shaped metal band linked at both ends by a chain and pierced lengthwise by a sharpened rod—it looks like a tautly drawn bow and arrow. Among other attributes, Ochosi is also considered the owner of all jails and traps. Lorita had set up an altar to him (the plate on which it was held also contained a pair of handcuffs) because one of her clients had a son in prison. It was a tough case, she said, and would require much sacrifice. From the fresh blood drippings on the Ochosi figure, I knew Lorita had already sacrificed several chicks, one of the god's favorite meals. I could tell by the cheeping from a perforated cardboard box that more would be required.

Not far from Ochosi was a miniature black cast iron cauldron (different from the palo pot) set up for his spiritual mate, Ogun. Santeros call the pair Los Guerreros, the Warriors. Their beads, and those of Elegba, are the first that a prospective initiate receives. Another Elegba sat nearby, also on a plate, and surrounded by sacrificial crabs, doubtless from the crate out front. Gary had set up the offering, one of Elegba's favorite snacks, for a woman who wanted to get away from an abusive husband and was asking the spirits to get her a contract for a small house of her own—her ticket to freedom.

I remembered having seen the woman come in a day or two earlier. She had been euphoric, bursting in to tell Lorita the house contract had come through, slamming down a $100 bill in tribute to the power of the priestess and the gods. Lorita had whooped with delight, picking up the money and cleaning herself with it on the spot, wiping first her "cat," as she calls it, then her legs, arms and neck, and turning to me triumphant, as if to say, "See! They believe in me. This is proof!"

But now the woman's altar was several days old, and the crab Gary had placed on it was funky and covered with black flies. You never clean an altar in any way, but you may dispose of it when it has completed its use. Lorita decided the Elegba with the crabs had fulfilled its function—or at least she rationalized doing so because of the stench. Perhaps to get me to leave her in peace, she asked me to get a small trash bag. She put the crabs inside, opened the exterior door—for clients who wished anonymous exit—and walked the bag out to a garbage can at the curb. She drew a fresh breath, chuckled a little, and came back in, leaving the door propped open. I went back to the counter.

About nine, the "urgent" clients started showing up.

A young boy was the first, bringing with him a box of chirping, yellow-fuzz chicks. Ochosi must really be hungry, I figured, and had him wait in a folding chair under the radio, mercifully not turned on yet. Right after that came a young woman and her daughter. The mother looked like Dionne Warwick—a lot, and I told her so. She was very shy, at least to a white man, but when I explained I was the temporary receptionist, she told me she'd come in about the girl, who had taken a chair in the corner, watching the boy with the chicks. Only eleven, the child was big and busty. She had started hanging around shopping malls and boys.

Before mom got much further with her story, Lorita banged open the door from her reading room. "Come over here, girl, 'case I need to hit you on the head!" she barked, striding up to the counter like she'd just been wired in to the main galactic transformer. The mother, who had been leaning languidly against the counter top, stiffened like she'd just been plugged in too.

"You run around and have different men over," Lorita snarled, "how you expect your daughter to respect you? Look at that child. She got titties big as mine. Why you let her go out alone? Juanika thirteen and I don't let her go *nowhere* alone."

The mother mumbled something about having to work and not having enough time, but Lorita shooed the pair of them into her office. Before she followed them in she whispered to me. "The kid's problem is the momma's problem. I told her she got to take care of *her* business first. But she don't want to hear that."

She shook her head in exasperation and closed the door. I could hear yelling inside. Before there were any readings that day, there was going to be plenty of "bitching out," as they call it in New Orleans, and some praying. Nobody went in to see Lorita and came out with any ambiguity. The mother and daughter emerged looking like they'd survived a hurricane, but thought that things might now be better for them. They were to return the next day, when Lorita would clean the girl and wash her hair and feet with special herbs. She was not to bathe herself before then. And there was more: while reaching across her open Bible to hold the girl's hands, Lorita had seen the spirit of the girl's dead father. Killed in a drug deal, his hovering soul was

Reading desk (with Bible) inside Lorita's reading room at St. Lazarus botanica.

filled with unrest. Lorita saw that he had been calling out to his daughter, which would account for her change of behavior.

Lorita instructed the girl and her mother to prepare a gift for the egun, and also for the father, who must be placated so he could leave the girl alone and return to his own journey through the spirit world. Until then, the girl would remain in danger. The mother said okay, but it had to be secret, because her own father knew of Lorita and feared her as the "bu-du"—a pronunciation common in New Orleans—woman. And the mother went through with her duties. Did it work? Who can say? When I saw the mother several weeks later, she said she and her daughter were getting along better, and both were attending Spiritual Church.

Altar table in St. Lazarus reading room. Pumpkin for Oshun and various other gifts and candles for saints and orisha. Palo stick against the wall.

Four or five more clients meanwhile had shown up, and the boy with the chicks left—apparently he was just delivering. I don't know which were truly "urgent," but all of them that day—most days—were at least desperate.

The next appointment was distraught because her husband was being seduced by an "outside woman." Half-sitting on her desk, listening to the story, Lorita decided the husband had been "fixed," probably with a "binding poison" of urine, underarm sweat and moisture from the paramour's "cat" mixed into coffee. The wife made a face at the thought of such a beverage. Lorita laughed and said if you mixed it right, it wouldn't taste funny. She said every time the man drank the coffee he became his lover's slave.

"It's definitely hoodoo," Lorita said, "but the greatest hoodoo is God's hoodoo, and now your man be sick in his stomach because God don't like what he do. You tell him to get rid of that woman. But to get rid of her he got to get her blood on him."

"How he do that?"

"Bust her in the mouth, or any kind of cut—but don't be cutting her with a knife or anything—and that break the spell. Any spell she got on him."

Then Lorita took the woman into her office. She gave her a scrap of brown paper on which to write the husband-stealer's name, and told her to bury the paper in a secret place. She also gave her beads and a black candle with a snake insignia—a "ward-off" votive that when burned sends the bad intentions of a perpetrator right back at her. The woman left, armed with great confidence, ready to reclaim her man. She paid $125, cash.

The workplace, too, was a frequent a combat zone, and toward the end of the long day, I met one of Lorita's greatest successes, a strong, matronly-looking, middle-aged client I'll call Dora, who was convinced that Lorita had saved her life and career. While working as a supply supervisor at the Tulane Medical Center, a huge downtown facility whose rooms are filled with the poor and uninsured, Dora had noticed strange blisters on her hands and feet. "They burst open and was black as tar," she said. "It was so bad I had to wear slippers to work."

Dora couldn't think of a medical reason for the painful sores, and therefore didn't want to waste money on a doctor. After a failed effort with a Cuban "spiritual adviser," Dora turned to Lorita, who promptly told her she'd been poisoned, probably by the young black Mississippi woman who was a rival for her hospital job. The purpose of the poison, Lorita told Dora, was to "cut off the hands and the feet so you can't work and she get your job."

Lorita bathed Dora completely, then rubbed two white pigeons over her body to draw away the spell. So strong was the hoodoo, the pigeons wouldn't fly afterwards. Even Lorita had been scared. She gave Dora a salve and said she should be okay in a few weeks. She was. She told people at work the boils and sores were the result of an accident frying chicken, and, on Lorita's instruction—"God says you don't confront hoodoo. Whoever does it, they'll get it back"—never let on to the Mississippi woman. Subsequently, the schemer lost her job, but Dora stayed on, unshakably convinced of Lorita's powers.

——

I only went through one full day's drill as Lorita's assistant, and was happy to retire. I wondered that it never got to her, that sometimes she didn't get exasperated with people's problems, with the hexing and fixing and poisons and spell-making. It was hoodoo, anyway, not even the real thing. She wasn't counseling people, she was counseling an invisible web of forces and theories and suppositions and accusations and myths in which the people were all but bit players. But it was her calling. It was her legacy, and it gave her strength.

I had been in the shop one afternoon when two young black "musicians" in flash clothes dropped by, wearing Elegba beads.

They'd heard of her through some Cuban friends and wanted a reading. There had been more and more of these types coming around, especially since word had gotten out in Miami drug circles that santeria was protection against cops and rival cartels. It was a bad association for santeria, and one that would get worse in coming years, ultimately even affecting Lorita and her family, though they would survive it. She sized up the two slicks instantly. She told them they were phoneys, looking for a quick fix, not the path to heaven. They laughed and asked for their readings anyway. Afterwards, they bought some candles, smart-assing to her—"you too fine to be worrying about us, sugar—" all the way out the door.

Lorita slumped into her chair, her face a mask of anger. "We normal people," she said, to no one in particular. "We breathe the same air as everyone else and we got the same red blood." She exhaled heavily. "Jesus!" They had made her feel like a freak. They had debased her with their attitude and she hated them for it.

---

[1] The church and botanica are now closed, replaced by Lorita's cafe, Mama Gamble's. Lorita, now remarried, offers readings from her home nearby. Though she has taken her new husband's surname, Gamble, she is still known in the community by the names Mitchell and Honeycutt. She has moved her church to nearby Eads Street, and renamed it Blessed Mother of Charity Spiritual Church. The Virgin of Charity, not coincidentally, is often syncretized with the voudou diety Oshun, Lorita Gamble's personal orisha.

# 5

# PREACHER TO PRIESTESS

CONSISTENTLY, EFFORTLESSLY, SHE strode the line between voudou and Christianity—a path so strange and precipitous I could only watch in amazement. In the end, I could barely distinguish the two modes of Lorita's spirituality, for they were as close to each other as the two sides of a zipper.

From childhood, she studied the Bible every Sunday, modeling herself on neighborhood preachers like the late Mother Fannie Bee Jorden (JUR-den) who ran the Holy Family Spiritual Church out of her own home, and took Lorita under wing, maybe saving her life. Even now Lorita refers to her own home back in the Ninth Ward as "Amityville": a stepfather who beat her, a mother who called her crazy. Brothers killed. A nephew murdered. One of her sisters killed her man for beating her and cheating on her with her own daughter.

The church gave Lorita the family she needed. Before the santeria, before the palo, before all the movement into that strange terrain that would mark her as an avatar of that which had been lost from Africa—before all that came the Spiritual Church.

Numbers are imprecise, but I was told there are as many as 3000 members in the city, belonging to a dozen or so small congregations grouped around two umbrella factions, the Israelite Universal Divine Spiritual Churches of Christ and the Metropolitan Spiritual Churches of Christ. Lorita now belongs to the former, although she was raised in the Metropolitan. Since some of the congregations are so tiny and impoverished, with no chapels of their own in which to worship, the two umbrella groups serve as guest sanctuaries, with many "churches" scheduling services in the Israelite or Metropolitian facilities throughout the week.

The Spiritual Churches grew independently of Protestant mainstays such as Baptists and Methodists, but scholars such as Claude F. Jacobs (*The Spiritual Churches of New Orleans*), point out some influences from the mostly white Spiritualist Church, a separate denomination, which developed in the nineteenth century. The names themselves have a linkage: the early Spiritual Churches of New Orleans were called "Spiritualist," changing their names to "Spiritual" in the 1940s. Both churches use the term "seance." Jacobs also believes that the doctrine of the Spiritual Church that the souls of the dead may be "materialized"—brought into tangible form—is closely linked to Spiritualist beliefs in the continuation of individual essence after death.

A Catholic connection is equally traceable. According to Spiritual Church by-laws, "communication with departed souls" through prayer or possession, as well as the use of altars and pictures to represent the dead—in voudou, the egun—is necessary "because they enliven our devotion by exciting pious affection and desires." The phrase, Jacobs has noted, is virtually identical to an answer and response sequence in the Catholic Church's well-known "Baltimore Catechism."

Yet the borrowings from Spiritualist or Catholic systems are of interest not so much because they influenced the Spiritual Church, but because they are so compatible with ancestor and spirit world tenets of voudou. The Spiritual ministers who adapted the beliefs of the white churches might well have been simply choosing those doctrines which found easy resonance with a deeply held African religious value system.

I never saw a sanctuary in which, not far from framed portraits of the Catholic saints, were photos or depictions of tigers, lions or other wild animals. Table-top altars for the dead or ill were frequently draped with animal skins and "luck" candles. Other altars displayed rows of candles and mounds of burning incense, and, especially voudou-like, offerings of food to the spirits. Almost all had busts of ancestor figures such as the Whitehawk or Blackhawk.

Often, I would observe church elders in their scarlet or purple robes and think I was watching a group of Catholic monsignors or even cardinals. Or I would notice the female "missionaries" or "ministers" dressed in white, with white kerchiefs atop their heads, and feel I was in a fundamentalist or charismatic Protestant service. Then, as the service progressed and the worshipers "fell" into possessive trances, danced in extended gospel jams, and lined up for the dispensation of prophecies, holy candles, oils or cakes—on one occasion, cornbread squares with a dime inserted inside for luck—I knew I was among true believers in a faith that had recombined its spiritual DNA into something of stunning symbolic portent.

In few other churches could a young woman bound for voudou have formed a stronger evolutionary link with the slave-assimilated Christianity of the Deep South. As Lorita became conversant and masterful in this relentlessly inventive mode of worship, she moved ever closer to what was waiting for her behind the veil of Christianity. The elements of the Spiritual Church were so compatible with those of voudou that she was able to move comfortably into the African practice without feeling she had compromised her Christianity. It took little imagination to see how such syncretization might have rooted itself,

Pulpit, center-right, in St. Lazarus Spiritual Church. St. Lazarus, left, in corner. Fan on wall is an attribute of Oshun, Lorita Mitchell's orisha.

powerfully and perhaps revolutionarily, in the generations of
tens of thousands of African Americans—but, as history un-
folded, did not.

Even Lorita's pivotal encounter with voudou spirits, which
ultimately led to her full initiation as a priestess and recognition of her African spiritual heritage, came cloaked in Christian
imagery. Worn down by efforts to find a cure for Andrew's cancer, she had sat next to his bed in the hospital "mad at God and
at the church." The stricken twin was thin, with black circles
around his eyes, and in pain. Nothing was helping. But one
morning the boy awoke with news that would change all their
lives. In a fevered dream he had seen St. Lazarus presiding over
a feast. Lorita didn't know what the dream meant, but sensed it
was important and decided to set up a feast in the saint's honor.

She wasn't sure exactly what she needed, so she went to the
F&F, at that time still owned by Ricky Cortez. Though he was a
stranger, Lorita told him of the dream. He seemed to understand,
but Lorita was a skeptical woman in matters of the Spirit. What

did some Cuban in a weird store know about St. Lazarus anyway? Cortez responded by unbuttoning his shirt. On his chest was a tattoo of the saint from the dream.

Lorita was hooked.

Cortez told her to burn a candle for St. Lazarus at her feast, and to set the candle at the rear door, along with a plate of beans and rice. Later, she used handfuls of the beans and rice to "clean" all her children of bad spirits. She saved herself and Andrew for last. But she said that when she tried to pick up the beans and rice for herself she couldn't open her hands. They were clutched tight as claws.

Disturbed, awed, she went back to Cortez and gave him $50 for a reading. He asked her if anyone had "passed the Spirit" at the services. She said she didn't know—she didn't know what that meant. He asked her to describe what had happened. When she told him of her tightened hands he said someone had. She had. She had passed the spirit of St. Lazarus. She had been possessed by a saint. Or by his voudou counterpart, Babalu Aye.

Not long after the feast, Andrew's cancer went into remission. Today he is a healthy father, a Spiritual Church prophet and a priest of Oshun. There's no satisfactory rational or scientific explanation. But Lorita wasn't looking for one. She gave thanks to the Lord, and couldn't forget Ricky Cortez. He was filled with a power, and she had to know more of it.

I understood the obsession. I, too, had met Cortez—in the days before he disappeared. By then, as an oriaté, he had initiated Lorita, very likely the first such conversion of an African American to santeria voudou in New Orleans, but he had left the city for Miami. I saw him because he had returned to New Orleans briefly to preside over initiation rites for two women from Lorita's Spiritual Church when it was still on Metropolitan.

When I arrived at Lorita's old apartment for the ceremony that evening, Cortez, who had in a brief initial meeting struck me as a middle-aged gigolo, was transformed. His gold neck chains, loud tropical shirt and cranberry slacks had given way to faded jeans, blood-stained T-shirt and sandals. He carried a sacred white-handled killing knife, the cuchillo, already used many times. Crates of chickens, pigeons, and guinea fowl were stacked nearly to the ceiling. He had just cut the throat of a young goat, and as I arrived was eviscerating the carcass for the portions vital to the spirit of Elegba, being fed on a bloody altar in the next room, which was forbidden for me to enter. He walked up to me at once, but couldn't shake hands. In one palm was the blade, and in the other a pink-gray stretch of intestine.

He gripped the knife in his fist, then pinched the membrane with his thumbs and forefingers and stretched it before his eyes, then mine. It became almost transparent. Through it, he said, you could see into the future. He said, "This, what you will see here tonight, is for the health of the people. Not for anything bad. You understand?"

What later happened between Lorita and Ricky is murky. But eventually there was a terrible falling out. Lorita's greatest fear was that one day Cortez would reappear—his last known whereabouts was said to be Venezuela—to use what is literally a secret weapon against her, the itá, the book of life readings given at the initiation ceremony over which Ricky, her original padrino, had presided.

I argued with Lorita that Ricky could have no power over her. I reminded her she had said as much to her own spiritual clients. "Don't nobody own you," she frequently told people complaining that their boyfriends or girlfriends were controlling their souls. But Lorita has never lost her fear of Ricky. Once, when I brought up the subject, she lowered her eyelids in that cold and distant gaze I had seen sometimes after sacrifices for her clients and looked at me as though I were the biggest fool on the planet.

"You don't have any idea what power people can have," she said. "They's people *can* kill you. I know you don't believe it, but it's true. You think if your spirit strong nothing can hurt you. But it can." She leaned close to me. "They people out there that can hurt you."

She was right, of course. But so was I.

—==—

In my room at the Warwick, a funky but friendly downtown hotel, I began to assemble an altar on a dressing table: statues of the Virgin of Guadalupe; laminated photo cards of St. Expedite; a couple of votive candles; a square of that blessed cornbread with a lucky dime inside and other odds and ends from botanicas and churches.

Somewhere in each of our souls lies a huge bed of energy which moves and shifts like the templates of the earth. The energy may lie dormant throughout life. Or it may find a fissure. I knew that I would sooner or later have to confront those feelings, and that I would have to do so through Lorita. I had watched her as priestess but had avoided becoming one of her clients. My hesitation wasn't caused by doubt. I wasn't worried about finding out if she really knew her stuff. I was worried about what stuff of mine she would find out. Not until I was about to leave town did I ask for an appointment. "I was wondering why you didn't want a reading," she smiled, almost as though I'd been a lover too shy to offer a kiss.

So, for the first time, I sat in the client chair in her office, on the other side of her reading table and Bible, facing her directly. She looked at me in a way that almost seemed objective, cold as a doctor's eye in an examining room. And me as vulnerable. Then she unscrewed the cap on a vial of healing oil and told me to hold out my palms. I did, and she rubbed them tenderly. I calmed. Then she gripped my oiled hands hard, looked in my eyes and recited the Lord's Prayer, a Hail Mary, and a prayer asking the spirit for success. She pushed the Bible across the desk and said to open it anywhere.

I chose a passage in the middle, somewhere between Chronicles and Psalms in the Old Testament. She instructed me to write my name on a piece of paper, which she inserted in the place I had chosen. She shut the Bible and shifted back in her chair, eyes closed behind her bifocals. When the eyes re-opened, she cracked the Bible exactly to my spot. She picked up a pencil and used the point of it to skim the page, stopping occasionally on a single letter. Each seemed to be a key to a spiritual insight, which she would tell me as though from a trance. When she felt each onset she would jolt rigid, head tilted back and eyes shut, sometimes sharply crying out "Jesus!" and always prefacing the subsequent observations with "Spirit say . . . ."

One of the things the Spirit said was that I should be careful on my trip. In and out of trance, she told me I should pay attention to my father's spirit and light candles for him in Catholic churches. I should read the twenty-third Psalm, the part about "the valley of the shadow." I should never stay in "a log cabin or something like that in a wooded area—you might get robbed." I shouldn't drive late at night. I should beware of hoodoo people, root doctors, prophets, witches—all of whom she saw as elements in a spiritual evil empire out there waiting for naive fools like me. I should refuse all offerings of food and never let myself be cleaned by any kind of meat, nor leave anything behind. I should participate in no ceremonies, especially those involving sacrifices. I would manage to violate many of her injunctions, and yet they never left me completely.

When she had finished, Lorita put down her pencil and started to close the Bible. She wondered, almost as an afterthought, if there were anything I wanted to ask about. She looked at me, fingers poised on the worn margins of her holy book.

There was, but I hadn't wanted to bring it up. Maybe it seemed too much like what I'd heard from other clients. Maybe I thought it too revealing. Maybe I didn't want to know. But I did. I wanted to know about a woman.

"That good, baby," she said at once, and told me to write her name on a piece of paper and insert it in the Bible, as we'd done before. It went the same until she looked at what I'd put down. She shut her eyes tightly. When she opened them, she asked, "Is that her real name?"

I laughed. "Yes, of course it is."

"You sure?"

I double-checked. "Yeah. That's her name."

Lorita shook her head. She closed her eyes and tried again. She looked me. "Spirit say: 'No report.'"

I smiled uneasily. Swords of skepticism unsheathed. After all this, I thought, Lorita has let me down.

"How can that be? I mean, I know her. That's her name."

Lorita didn't budge. Just sat back in her chair and looked at me over the tops of her glasses, Bible in her lap. "I don't know. Spirit say no report." I didn't know how to respond. Lorita closed her eyes again. "Nope. I just see a blank. She a shell. Nothing inside."

It got a little awkward, at least for me. A person's name was pretty verifiable. Maybe Lorita was afraid of "reading" somebody she didn't know and thus couldn't base her analysis on tricks of the trade—crafty observation and educated guesses. I couldn't believe it. She was faking it.

In the midst of this de-bunking epiphany, I had another. In fact, I slowly recalled, my friend's name was *not* her name.

I knew her as Danica, but she had been born otherwise. When her father returned from Vietnam he had forced her mother to legally rename her, so all the children would carry his initials, which began with D. I had forgotten all about it. I told Lorita.

She nodded her head and rocked slightly in her chair, but otherwise did nothing to rub it in. "Write down the name she born with," she said. "That the one the Spirit see."

I wrote "Lisa Marie" on the paper and put it in the Bible.

Lorita began to tell me about her.

# 6

# JESUS OUT OF AFRICA

BY NOW IT was late spring in New Orleans. Evenings had become thick and sluggish, precursors to the long, hot summer of Southern fame. Sticky shirts and frizzy hair were the couture of circumstance. The city was a huge, inescapable greenhouse. And I was ready to move on. At the weekend I would tell my friends goodbye, take down my altar, pack my things, load up my car. I would drive off into a world without directions, without maps, without guides, and perhaps without welcome. It seemed like a good idea to go to church.

St. Lazarus offered traditional services on Sunday, but the best sessions were on Friday nights. By 7:30 P.M. I was sitting in a middle pew with a Gideon's Bible in my lap feeling like I'd wasted time in the shower. The triplex sanctuary was air-conditioned, but the Iberville-side door had to be propped open against the sweltering night because Gary had lit too much incense and the room was choking with smoke. The cool drifted out with the sweet, thick vapors.

It was a little early, and hardly anyone had shown up, except for the regulars, maybe a dozen of us altogether. Perhaps that's

Inside the sanctuary, Lazarus Spiritual Church, New Orleans. Gary Mitchell, Lorita's son, in white cap. His wife and infant daughter, seated.

what was bothering Lorita, sitting like the wrath of who knew what in black robe and white dust cap on the pulpit dais, staring at her open Bible through her bifocals. Whatever it was that pulled her visage into a hard mask, whatever was clouding the reception of the Spirit, it was going to come out before the night was over. Nobody spoke to her at all.

A woman and her pre-teen daughter came in talking, fell silent at once, and came up the middle aisle to sit in the pew just to my right. I had never seen her and hoped she was a potential new member. She had her own Bible and gave it to her daughter to hold. Gary turned on the keyboard and started a quiet background hymn. The mother and daughter bowed their heads to pray silently, though I could see the girl's eyes peek open. Everyone was black except for myself, a young white couple who came to Lorita for readings, and Pam, who had come back to New Orleans to visit her family and had wanted to attend a service. She had been to Lorita for a reading, and had been impressed—fully willing to follow Lorita's suggestions to prepare a soothing "dressing" of fruits to place on her head, eat certain foods and, because Lorita thought Pam had a gypsy spirit, to wear a seven-pointed skirt with bells on the hem.

At a quarter to, after a few more stragglers showed up, Lorita rose and called out to a half-dozen women near the front to join her and Gary, who had stopped playing, at the small open space between the front pews and the dais. They knelt in a circle around their pastor. She brought her chair because her neck and back still hurt too much from the wreck to sit on the tile floor.

Doris, a young schoolteacher, started the praying, calling to Jesus to open her heart, help her, to help the church, to give blessings, to bring prosperity. She asked that Lorita's neck be healed, and that her own failings be forgiven, that she become a better person, that she learn to love Jesus even more. I could hear faint "Amens" to some of Doris's petitions, but no lightning was being sparked. The opening prayer, which in voudou is directed at Elegba to open the path to the orisha and in Spiritual churches is often a device to jump-start the congregation's spiritual passion, even send a member into possession, had become an aimless monologue. It occurred to me Doris may have been afraid to stop.

Lorita cut in almost cruelly, talking right over the floundering schoolteacher—or in a kinder interpretation, picking up the lead line of the straying improvisation—by launching the church's mantra-like prayer chant: "The Lord is my Shepherd, I shall not want. . . . Hail Mary, full of Grace. . . . The Lord is my Shepherd, I shall not want. . . . Hail Mary, full of Grace. . . ."

One supplication followed the other, increasing in speed until the rhythm became a hypnotic litany, at which point Lorita broke in with the fast clapping characteristic of the Spiritual Churches. It's almost as rapid as applause, except that it has a beat, and every eighth beat is accented with a cry of "Jesus . . . (clapping) . . . Jesus."

"Harder," she demanded. "Call him to come down. . . . Clear your mind and call him."

After a few minutes I was clapping, too. Gary had returned to the keyboard to lay in some rhythm and bass, but the clapping took its own direction, and he strolled outside for a break, like a jazz musician waiting out a solo. It might've been ten minutes before he returned, and we were still going strong.

"Call him," Lorita interjected, "Call Jesus. Beg him to come."

They did, voices reaching up in twining, breakaway harmonies.

She changed the chant line from "Je-sus" to "Pow-er."

"POW-er," they refrained.

"Come down with the POW-er," she led.

"POW-er."

"Money power."

"POW-er."

"Do right power."

"POW-er."

"Loving power . . . Fixing power . . . Political POW-er."

When we all were bathed in sweat, swept away in the ring-shout, when Lorita felt that all were lost in the Spirit, when the lethargy and inhibition had been smashed by her demands, by the demands of the Lord, she let us go.

"Say Amen," she commanded, and we did. "Say thank you Jesus," and we did.

We clapped fast again: "Amen" and "Thank you Jesus" spontaneous and multi-voiced, and then the prayer circle dispelled, the worshipers returned to their seats. Gary tendered a soothing gospel standard, "What a friend we have in Jesus. . . ."

Still more people had trickled in, and the pews now held maybe thirty souls. One of the late arrivals, Clarence, sat in the back, a quiet man in a conservative blue suit, an electrician by trade, distinguished and Bible-toting, who had come for the Lord, but for the minister, too. Lorita liked him, I could tell; I knew in time he would be one of the helpers and handymen she bound to her church.

As we sang softly, unwinding, resting, Lorita carried her chair back to its place behind the pulpit. But she sat in it rigid again. The mask was back; the grimace returned. The thing she had seen earlier was still there. Gary played on, filling in the dreadful silence from his mother's tight lips.

Children began to squirm and mothers hushed them. I touched Pam's hand but wasn't sure what to say. It felt like being hunted; more accurately, assessed. Finally, Lorita stood, arching her back. The pain, at least, must've been beaten down, because she moved toward us like an out-of-sorts Mick Jagger.

"God is no respecter of persons!" she cried. "Have anyone here ever been in real hard times? Times when there was no food and you didn't know where food was coming from?" No one knew where she was heading or why. "Oh, just *my* family, huh?" She walked back up the dais, and put on her bifocals, scanning her open Bible as if no one else were in the room.

"That's when you really find God. When you be praying and asking God from your heart, a time when you have no money and no bread to eat. . . . If you ain't never had times like that how you know what it's like? I was brought up eating out of tin cans and on pie plates. I know what it's like." Nearly all her congregation did, too, but that wasn't the issue. "God is no respecter of persons!" she yelled out again. "He don't care what you have or what you don't have."

She marched down to the pews to my right, where sat Doris and Lorraine and the most devoted. They seemed frozen, like quail at the approach of the dogs. Lorita searched out each face in front of her. "Do anyone here have the Holy Ghost in them?"

I could feel the entire congregation stiffen. They, if not I, knew what was coming. Doris broke first.

"Yes," she said, tremelo, standing, "because Jesus answers my prayers."

"Yes," echoed Emelda (Gary's wife) "because my body feels full with it."

"Yes," said Lorraine, still in yaguo white, "because I feel the light in my heart."

"*Wrong*," answered Lorita, her mouth twisted in contempt.

She moved down the row like a drill sergeant. First to Doris: "Something in your life is blocking it." To Emelda: "You have a hateful spirit." To Lorraine: "You think you have the Holy Ghost 'cause you have santo? Huh! When you got the Holy Ghost you need nothing else in your life. God has the power. The orisha don't change your life. God has the power."

To us all: "Some of us got the selfish Holy Ghost. When you get the real Holy Ghost nothing stops you from serving Jesus. You leave your father, your mother, your family. It's just like fire."

She started back for the pulpit, then turned so fast her robes whirled. "If you got the Holy Ghost I wouldn't have to pull the service so hard! If you got the Holy Ghost what are you doing for the Master? The Holy Ghost is power. All power."

She went up to fetch her Bible. When she came back down to the pews her gaze fell on Pam, who, like me, had been trying hard to remain invisible. "Come up here, baby." Pam rose. "Read, baby," she commanded. Pam obeyed. "What do it mean, baby?" Pam said it meant that "through Christ we are forgiven our sins."

"Through *Jesus*," Lorita affirmed. She looked straight at me. "Some people in here don't believe that. They think they can get it without the Lord. They say, 'I used to go to church but the people ain't right.'"

I looked away.

She laughed cruelly. "But I tell you that the Reverend Mitchell don't go to church for *people*!"

"Hup! Hallelujiah!" She threw her arms out, crossing them and bending double in the Spiritual Church way.

"Spirit say we tied up, wrapped up and confused. Our spirit—Hup!—a spirit of error. We confuse ourselves with the spirit of Jesus, of the Holy Ghost."

One by one, she singled out other members of her church family by name, smashing the spiritual ego of each. It was the sin of pride she was after, the proud soul that believes it contains the Holy Ghost. Lorita the Leveler brooked no pride; no one was free to set himself up as his own judge on matters of the spirit. This is what she had felt—that we were a proud and thus aloof bunch, and she was going to wipe our noses in it.

She was yelling now, furious. "Why do you think I'm like this? You think I want to? I tell you. I'm doing this so when I get to the promised land I'm gonna see you there! I'm not judging you. I'm telling you what the Holy Ghost said to tell you. When I get through fussing, you're gonna love me or hate me. It don't make no difference."

That night there were no possessions. But each member received a prophecy, queuing up for Lorita to rub oil into every mortal palm and, it seemed, restore some of the ego she had so deliberately demolished during the service. It was quiet, reflective, until the mother and daughter who had been next to me reached the front of the line. Lorita had barely taken the child's hand when she seized up tight, crying out so loudly we could all hear, "Spirit say keep this girl in church or she'll get away—Hup!"

The mother froze.

"Spirit say . . ." Lorita paused, cocking her head, as if listening. "Spirit say, 'This girl been gambling.'" Another pause. "With grownups?"

It seemed farfetched, but the mother lowered her head. "Yes."

Lorita clasped the girl forcefully to her breast and shouted into her ear, "Rock my soul in the bosom of Abraham . . ." and you could see the two of them shaking, Lorita trying to ward something off. She drew the mother up, too, and they prayed under her wings. When she had finished, Lorita cleaned the girl with some wild weeds that grew near the church and said to put the roots of the plant under the foot and head of the girl's bed and leave them for a week.

I knew Lorita saw in the girl a desperate and violent karma and knew the momma also saw it and was terrified. They would do all they could to stop it, but their resources were few. God was one resource, and now, because God came in many forms, the orisha were another. The power Lorita sought was the power to protect.

We broke with a hymn and a circle of prayer. In my left hand was Pam's; in my right, that of the woman with the daughter sinking into oblivion. Then it was over and we went outside. A pretty young woman in an aqua blue dress, clearly not a regular, wanted Lorita to read her brother and possibly clean him. Lorita took one look at the man's open-necked black silk shirt and expensive shoes and called him, to his face, a pimp. He didn't change her mind when he said he didn't want a reading, but advice on how he should bet at the track. Lorita told him that was the least of his worries. She asked him if he had made peace with his father. He threw up one hand in dismissal and turned with his sister towards their late model luxury sedan. Walking past me, he paused, looked back at Lorita, and asked if I thought he maybe should have a reading. I said it couldn't hurt.

———

The next day I left the city.

Voudou had survived here, but New Orleans was a special case, an exceptional sanctuary. Out there in the swamps, the plantation towns, the dirt roads to nowhere, voudou had almost certainly gone deeply underground, mutated, evolved into forms perhaps barely recognizable. It awaited.

I had a last cup of a thick French blend at a cafe on Magazine Street. Then I drove to St. Lazarus, in no hurry, across the town where Marie Laveau had once been an underground queen and now was buried in St. Louis Cemetery No. 1 amid the finest of the old colonial aristocrats. Lorita was on the street corner, wearing a cotton floral print dress, watching two boys chase a pigeon she had released. It acted punchy, unable to take flight. "I told them not to catch it," she said. "It full of bad spirits." Tufts of feathers stuck to her hands and I knew someone inside had been cleaned. The boys chased it anyway.

But Lorita's attention had turned suddenly to three men sharing a quart beer bottle outside the door of her church. "What you doing drinkin' in the morning?" she demanded, stamping toward them with arms swinging in wide, purposeful arcs. "Why you ain't got no job?"

She tried to take the bottle from the older of the trio, but he tucked it to his chest. "No wonder you got that gout in your knee," she said, huffing with contempt. I looked at the man's badly swollen right leg. He smiled with a helpless indifference. His friends helped him away. "That's right, sister, you tell him," they said—enough to be respectful, but probably not enough to change their ways.

"You be careful," she told me. "And if you go talking to any hoodoo or spiritual people you do what I say. You get you some fruit—oranges, bananas, some fresh fruit, and every time you go see one of those people you clean yourself. Like this"—she passed her hands up and down her body—"and then just throw it away. It take the bad spirit from you."

She turned to go and I got in my car. It was torporous hot out on the street and in the botanica a client was waiting, hoodooed by somebody nasty. "She say snake eggs growing in her stomach," Lorita had said earlier. "But she was smart to come to Reverend Mitchell. I know what to do about it." She had a special herb tea that, with prayer, would rout the invader. But a thousand more battles awaited, and Lorita was but one warrior from the ancient resistance.

PART TWO

# THE
# ROAD

# 7

## ON THE HOODOO TRAIL

IN HER CLASSIC 1953 study of Haitian vodun, *The Divine Horsemen*, Maya Deren wrote that what she had really witnessed was that which we see in every culture—the operation of a unifying myth. A myth, to Deren, was "the facts of the mind made manifest in a fiction of matter."[1] I sought both the fiction and the matter of the American voudou legacy: spirit condensed into time and place, into persons, into something I could approach.

My task was somewhat more complicated than Deren's. Haitian vodun is more or less openly practiced, and once Deren gained the confidence of the priests, she could be relatively certain that she was studying what she saw. The seeker of American voudou has no such security of observation. Rarely is anything that which it appears to be. I had certainly encountered that phenomenon in New Orleans, but that was but one city, one mutation. In the centuries of its repression in America, voudou had taken as many guises as necessary to survive. I would have little choice but to investigate all these paths: hoodoo, root medicine, spiritual healing, ju-ju, black magic, and dozens of other euphemisms and forms.

Illustrations from turn-of-the-century newspaper articles depicting voudou practices in stereotypical paradigms.

None is as authentic, that is to say, as *African*, as the parent religion, or religions, collectively known as voudou, yet all are descendants. Obviously questions of authenticity are value-laden; in this case, implying that a voudou which developed in the New World is a diluted or corrupt form of that found in Africa. But my quest was not one of comparative anthropology; rather, an on-site search for a framework amid destruction. Voudou did exist in Africa; it came to the United States with African slaves; it was prohibited, violently. It either disappeared or became something else. The search for its remains is logically also a search for origins. I settled on two basic questions: (1) how had America changed voudou? and (2) how had voudou changed America?

I had concluded, at least preliminarily, that these questions were inseparable. On the one hand, the harshness of the pogroms against voudou had warped it into practices so peculiar they seemed tied to real voudou only by the most doggedly reductive analysis. But it was equally obvious that as voudou went underground, it left its mark all around, in dance, music, medicine, folk culture, even Christianity. In outlawing voudou and forcing it into new forms, America had nonetheless absorbed many of its ways. It was as though the African religion, in disappearing, had actually infiltrated the body of its frightened and hostile host.

In wars, it is axiomatic that each foe slowly takes on the characteristics of the other. The internal American assault on voudou was nothing less than a war. And though voudou, as the religion of slaves, never had a chance on the battlefield against Christianity, the religion of the masters, it hung on in a long, covert resistance. It was my feeling that over the centuries, voudou had exerted such a remarkable staying power that most Americans, black or white, were still reluctant to deal directly with its legacies. But that didn't mean voudou wasn't endemic. Indeed, its presence was, like that of a black hole in space, all the more powerful for the inability to account for its seeming absence in the midst of highly altered activity all around. So in one sense, it didn't matter where I went or who I saw. Voudou was everywhere.

—

My plan, after leaving New Orleans, was to move randomly across Louisiana and then the South, on to Miami, eventually, on even into the South Bronx. Not a plan so much as a confession of ignorance. I can take a road map of the southeastern U.S. and say that through a hot, rainy summer I was on this highway or that road, in this small village or that big city, talking to this woman and not that man; in truth I was traveling a territory without cartography.

I figured to trace the old bayou routes westering out of New Orleans and so followed along the Plantation Road abutting the Mississippi River into Cajun country. It was as good—or bad— a place to start as any. On the one hand, Cajuns (Acadians, driven out of Nova Scotia in the seventeenth century) are notoriously insular. And racist—the region voted heavily for ex-Klansman David Duke's failed gubernatorial bid. Poking around for voudou in such a place was, at least, problematic. But I had a lead from a former girlfriend and her younger sister. Black, and Catholic, Kathy and Donna had beaucoup relatives in southwestern Louisiana. Given the historic intermingling of voudou and Catholicism, black Catholics in Louisiana—Cajun country or no—have to be one of the most likely living repositories of voudou ways in this country.

Near the refinery/chemical cancer-laden disaster of a city known as Plaquemine, across the river from Baton Rouge, I cut off the highway to the other side of the tracks—in most small Southern towns the "other" side is invariably black—and noticed a house with a hand-lettered "Reverend" sign nailed to a wall. You did not become a preacher in a poor black community without some exposure to all the spirits, not just the Christian ones. But I didn't stop. Rain fell in sheets from thick, sickly black-green clouds; lightning bounced off the Port Allen bridge.

Sarah, a writer friend, was traveling with me as far as Lafayette. She'd have to take a bus back, but she wanted to get out of the city. Four months pregnant, she was going stir crazy in her Uptown apartment. She was also a little curious. Like many of my friends, she thought I was headed into some kind of George Romero film, and looked on voudou with, at best, skepticism. But she hadn't been able to resist an invitation to go to Lorita for a reading. She wouldn't admit it, but riding with me now was a little more than just a day trip.

Sarah had gone to find out about her unborn baby. Lorita had barely gotten into the reading when she saw something bad— a binding spirit, the kind that can control. With no idea of Sarah's personal life, Lorita promptly tagged the spirit as that of Sarah's late husband, a promising filmmaker who had died of a sudden illness a couple of years earlier. It obviously wasn't his child, but Sarah had felt debilitating guilt over his death. Lorita said the spirit was powerful enough to require *ebo*, of a goat—as a four-legged creature, one of the most powerful animal offerings. But it would cost $350, and Sarah was broke. She hadn't followed the prescription. We could not know then that in the fall, her delivery would be long and troublesome, culminating in a Cesarean, and she would become embroiled in bitter fights with the baby's absent father over monetary support.

Through the downpour, we drove deeper into the bayou country, past long stretches of poverty, most of it white people living in abandoned trailers, sleeping on sofas under make-shift shelters among the cypress, children in soiled shirts and bare feet only an hour or two from the Café du Monde. During summer, at least, they wouldn't die of exposure, but in winter months, the threadbare life would likely bring disease, misery and death.

I had heard plenty of stories about root doctors, hoodoo men, prophets and traiteusses out in these parts. They weren't always black. Latter-day witches, primarily white, and frequently gypsy, usually billed themselves as psychics or spiritual advisors. I knew I'd run into them sooner or later but I didn't want it to be now.

By the time we arrived in Lafayette, it was late afternoon and Sarah was so anxious to get out of the car and jump into a swimming pool she paid for the motel. But while she was changing into her suit, I picked up a local phone book out of an old reporting habit to check anything, now matter how improbable. Sure enough, under a listing for shops selling "religious supplies," was a name I couldn't resist. I jotted down an address and guilted Sarah into temporarily forgoing the spa.

"The Shining Two" operated out of a converted bungalow at the edge of a black neighborhood not far from downtown. Middle-aged black men in dark suits waited in two cars in the gravel lot in front as we pulled up. It looked promising. But as soon as I walked in the door I felt like a kid who falls for a barker's pitch at a traveling carney show. It was no botanica;

rather, an occult shop: astrology, Tarot, Magik, psychic literature, wicca, New Age, channeling. The black-haired young white
woman behind the counter was friendly but claimed to know
nothing about voudou. My questions made her nervous, and,
perhaps to get rid of me, she wrote down the name of "someone
who did," a woman who lived nearby and who gave "readings."
She suggested, firmly, that I go there.

It had started to rain again. I wound through narrow residential streets in the black section of town where the best homes
had a carport and the worst lacked screens or doors. A dead-end
avenue led past a dilapidated frame house where two elderly
men and a woman sat on the porch drinking beer. I parked beside a muddy ditch, and walked up. Sarah stayed in the car, reading a novel. The trio smiled as I approached, but their eyes
betrayed wariness. I nodded my head in deference and tried to
explain why I'd stopped.

The small unshaven man in the fedora finally spoke. "I don't
know nothing," he said, "but my grandson might." With that,
he pointed to a modest red brick home across the street. I picked
my way back through his puddle-filled yard, and hurried across
the asphalt. I knocked on his grandson's open screen door.

Kevin Guidry, a thin, fine-boned man of about twenty-five,
was home taking care of his preschool daughter. I told him what
his grandfather had said. He smiled. So long as I understood he
was a Christian—raised Catholic—he didn't mind discussing
voudou. He opened the door and showed me to a cloth couch
next to the TV in the living room. He said his grandmother had
treated people using the "old remedies," and that his grandfather, despite what he'd just told me, "was into one of those African gods," though Kevin didn't know which. I mentioned a few
orisha names—Elegba, Ogun, Shango, Obatala—but Kevin didn't
recognize any of them. He did know his grandfather often made
medicines of garlic, herbs, roots and worms.

For a time, Kevin thought he might pick up the old ways himself, but he had not done so, preferring Jesus. Unlike Lorita Mitchell, he didn't think he could have both. Indeed, he had veered so far from the "old ways" that he had recently joined the Full Gospel Church, an independent Protestant denomination which, like the PTL Club, Word of Faith Ministry and similar charismatic or fundamentalist groups, have sprung up in the age of televangelism and cater mostly to middle-class and lower middle-class whites. But Kevin said he felt more at home there than in his Catholic chapel. He also said I should try his grandfather again, because "he knows more than he lets on." I crossed the street again. For ten minutes, I stood in the light rain trying to ignite a conversation with the old man, but all I learned was how to treat "thrash"—a throat infection—in children by blowing three times into the mouth of the sufferer.

I didn't know it at the time, but I was to spend countless days on such seemingly fruitless encounters. But you never knew until you asked, and even dead ends sometimes proved to be trailheads: the way of voudou no less than that of scientific inquiry.

The next morning, Sarah took the bus back to New Orleans. Missing her companionship as I left the downtown station, absorbed with thoughts of the long, solitary search ahead, I barely paid attention to where I was driving, and consequently got lost. Eventually I realized I was stuck in an engineering nightmare of one-way streets around the downtown square. Which is how I found the "Side By Side Bookstore." A cinder-block box building utterly dwarfed by the well-heeled, neo-colonial Baptist church across the street, it advertised itself as offering "African books and handicrafts." I slowed to make sure it was still in business. When I saw an "open" sign in a window, I pulled into a vacant pot-hole lot on the side.

I knew it wasn't another "Shining Two" as soon as I opened the door. The walls were adorned with anti-apartheid T-shirts and black and white posters depicting African scenes and African people. The front display counter was chock-full of Senegalese bracelets and green, leather neck medallions shaped like Africa—popular at that time among teenagers. A second room opened to wall shelves of books on black nationalism, Islam, civil rights, slavery, natural healing—and voudou. In a third room at the very back I found the store's sole occupant—the owner, a slim, bespectacled man in his thirties sporting a well-clipped goatee. Cowrie shell medallions hung from his neck beside a red leather gris-gris. His hair was bunched Rasta-style under a red, yellow and green banded wool cap.

He introduced himself as Lionel Brown and showed me around the store. I asked about a book on African history, and he asked me why I was interested. I told him, and he showed me some new copper wrist bracelets he'd gotten in. I bought one. We talked about New Orleans. By the time the next customer walked in more than an hour later I knew that, even if I didn't locate Kathy's Creole relatives (I never did) I was going to find what I was seeking.

Until the Louisiana oil bust of the early 1980s, Lionel had worked as a machinist. Following his layoff he tried a few other jobs until a year ago, encouraged by his wife, he decided to turn his skill with his hands and his interest in his African roots into something manifest: a store, a focal point of African tradition. Though he knew little about it, I could tell that voudou was woven into the very fabric of his life. In his family, though, it was never called that. It was just a collection of stories. While he puttered around the shop, he began telling them.

There was his aunt in Port Arthur, Texas, who had suffered a sudden but extended illness, and was unable to walk. Lionel's mother had gone to assist her, and concluded that her sister had been "fixed." She searched her sister's house top to bottom, but

Lionel Brown, Side by Side Bookstore, Lafayette, Louisiana.

found nothing. Then, in a crawl space, she spotted a small bag. She didn't open it, because of what might be inside, but she disposed of it at once. After that, said Lionel, his aunt recovered.

As he recounted other family legends stretching back generations, I remembered the tales of woe and hexing I had heard in Lorita's botanica. I was to hear many more, Louisiana to Miami. Each was unique to each family, and original in the details, but they were not unconnected. In each story, a mother, father, sister, or other relative became mysteriously ill. Conventional remedies, including doctors, were useless. Then someone—usually an aunt or grandmother—intervened and tracked down the cause, a hidden bag or talisman or similar hoodoo object "planted" by an enemy. When the object was found, and removed, the victim got well.

Whether these family tales were objectively true didn't matter. Their very pervasiveness pointed to something much more important. My theory was that these tales—what W. E. B. Dubois called "the souls of black folk"—formed an underground oral remembrance of voudou. Not of its content—that was too thoroughly banned—but its existence. Every family with a voudou story was part of the remembrance. Every telling was the myth made manifest.

Recently, Lionel had begun writing down the cures he heard from his mother, and especially his grandmother, a healer known as "Mother Brown." Each time he returned to St. Martinville, the bayou town where he was reared, he stopped along the roadside to gather plants, herbs and roots for his relatives—and now, for himself. As a matter of fact, he told me, he had just battled a high fever by brewing up "mongrea root tea," made from a local plant. He drank it boiling hot, then wrapped himself in blankets all night to sweat out the fever. The next day he had recovered. To Lionel, the method was just standard home medicine. He knew it wasn't something the doctor might have you do, but until I shared a story of my own—giving him something for what he gave me—neither of us knew that in curing a simple fever, he also had preserved a tie to Africa. He had "cooked" himself.

I'd learned about "cooking" in New Orleans from a Nigerian acquaintance named Peter, husband of a member of Lorita Mitchell's Spiritual Church congregation. But Peter wasn't a Christian, he was a voudou, initiated in Nigeria into the cult of Ogun. Before coming to the U. S. to attend Xavier University, Peter, now a journalist, had consented to the wishes of his family (his mother was Catholic, his father a worshiper of Shango) to take the traditional ritual to ward off harm. They considered America an evil and dangerous country. Ogun priests wrapped Peter in blankets, then had him sit and meditate with his head over a pot of steaming herbal potions. When they removed the blankets, the priests sliced narrow cuts across Peter's torso and rubbed herbs from the pot into the cuts. "Religion is protection," Peter had told me. "I always carry my scars and I always protect myself."

Lionel listened closely. He'd been right, after all, to make records. Perhaps the family cures *could* be traced back to Africa. I wasn't sure where all the threads lay myself, but I copied several prescriptions from Lionel's notebook. Some reminded me of things I'd heard Lorita administer, and others were similar to what I'd hear later:

—For headache: work salt and vinegar into a cloth, heat it, put it on your head and lie down.

—Measles: drink sassafras tea.

—Pneumonia: make a tea from whitened dog manure.

—Fever blister: rub it with wax from your ear.

—Ear ache: Get "Steen" syrup (a local brand), warm it on a spoon, and put drops into your ear.

—Diarrhea: Boil rice and drink the water. Do the same for food poisoning. Occasionally drinking cream of tartar in your water will also help reduce the problem. (Diarrhea remedies are common and were important in the South. The malady was widespread because of the squalid conditions on plantations; the resultant dehydration frequently led to death, especially in children. It is the world's leading killer of children today).

—Excessive menstrual bleeding: boil roots of elder plant into a tea. Also for vaginal discharge or infection.

—Sore throat: gargle with a mix of vinegar, salt and black pepper. As you gargle, stick out your tongue "almost to where you swallow, then come up and spit out, to pull out the inflammation."

Like remembering the tales of healing, Lionel's recording of the cures was an act both of creation and preservation. No wonder African-American folk healers had come to be known as "root doctors." Cutting slaves off from their own culture and religion made sense in terms of demoralizing potential rebellion, but health care was another matter. If slaves could treat themselves, they'd remain more productive at virtually no cost to the plantation. There was profit in suppressing priests, not healers. "My grandmother just learned when she was coming up," Lionel had said. "They didn't go to the doctor too much, so they had to have something for everything."

It is true, of course, that folk remedies among African Americans could have come from numerous sources, including Native Americans or European Americans. And certainly there are many such links. But the obvious point of origin is Africa. Since homeopathy is one of the most important elements of African voudou cultures, and since slaves came from such cultures, from where else would their remedies more likely have originated?

---

I drove eastward across Louisiana toward the Mississippi border, passing deep green maize fields and thick stands of hardwoods. It was a rare dozen miles that I didn't come across a church: small or grand, brick or wood—or aluminum siding—thrown up for Baptist or Methodists, Catholics or Pentecostals, blacks or whites. It was Sunday afternoon and each church was a godly beehive not only to services, but to wedding parties, prayer meetings, picnics and Bible study.

I had once read an account of a huge multi-racial evangelical assembly in mid-nineteenth-century Georgia at which an observer saw dozens of tents—whites preaching to whites and blacks to blacks, and the hills at night alive with fires around which people danced, sang, and found the Lord. I marveled at the image: probably one of the few times whites and blacks could be together uninhibited, bonded by a common thirst for heaven. A brave idea, betrayed: white churches had allowed their pulpits to be used to rationalize slavery; the separatist Black Church movement of the nineteenth century, and the lasting segregation of most American denominations, were the inexorable consequences.

As I got closer to the Mississippi River, I came to a junction. I could turn north and follow Highway 15 as it hugged the western bank of the river and led to Ferriday, Louisiana, just across the water from Natchez. Or I could jag slightly to the west, and pull into the little community of Simmesport. I slowed at the crossroads. Simmesport, close to a hundred per cent black, was a half-dozen blocks of hard-looking clapboard houses and dirt streets. If I drove up into there I would find somebody who would know somebody who knew something about hoodoo.

I don't know why I didn't stop. Time, perhaps. In a few hours it would be dark, and the closest thing to a motel here was a two-pump gas station. I also wanted to push farther, to a place listed on the map as Blackhawk—the name suggested a possible connection with the New Orleans spirit guide of the same name. But time or mission really weren't the issues. Simmesport looked like the kind of place in which you could get lost fast. So I drove on. I berated myself for miles: for lack of courage, for missing a good bet, for feeling white. It didn't help that when I got to Blackhawk it wasn't a town at all but a large and inaccessible plantation.

I turned onto a gravel lane leading up to the banks of the levee. I dug a beer out of my Igloo. I flipped on the radio and leaned against the fender. Down on the river a barge steamed by, maybe headed for St. Louis or for Natchez. The landscape was dead flat; from it, the forest line across the river rose up jagged and green like an Asian jungle. That's what this entire area was 400 years ago. A jungle. Ancestors of the people back in Simmesport carved out wealth from the jungle, but not for themselves.

I turned the radio off. There was no other sound except the engine of the steamer. Then my heart calmed. I was just a human being like everyone else. I had missed a moment but there would be others, and if I were going to follow my intuition—or listen to my spirit—I had to show a little trust.

I drove fast all the way north to Ferriday, no traffic on the lonely two-lane. It was dark and the streets were full. I passed drive-through daiquiri stores, dairy marts, muffler shops. I crossed the bridge to Natchez, found a cheap motel and went to sleep thinking about the last time I was at Lorita's house. Her Caddy was still in the shop and I'd driven her and Juanika home again. She was bone-tired but invited me in for a beer. I wandered towards the back porch to look at her Oshun shrine, but Lorita stopped me. I couldn't enter the room, she said, because all her superas were not in their usual places up on the shrines or cabinets, but were spread out along the floor. Lorita said she'd been so low she had to put the spirits down, too, so they could come back up and lift her with them.

---

[1] Maya Deren. *The Divine Horsemen*, 1953, reprinted 1970, McPherson and Co., New York, p. 21.

# 8

## SPIRIT WARS

AT A SMALL corner grocery in Natchez the owner's wife listened to me with bemusement while her teenage rapmaster son looked on like I was an escapee from some honky nuthouse. I wasn't connecting, but was honing my approach. When asking around, I would only mention voudou if someone else did. If not, I would rely on a preamble about researching traditional Southern medicines and healings, and say I was seeking anyone in the area, probably an older person, who might have such knowledge or know someone who did.

People generally got the drift, but I had to be aware of another possible impediment—they might think I was a cop. There wasn't much I could do about that one, except rely on my looks. I was white and all, but I think people know how cops look—and I don't look like one. It wasn't so much that a cop would be investigating voudou, but that he might be looking for drugs, or trying to bust some preacher/hustler on a minor vice rap. Who knew with what imagined social ills America's police busied themselves?

The woman in the grocery store said she'd heard of somebody, "an Indian," she thought, to whom people went for readings. I traced the tip to a Romanian palm reader, not unlike some I'd run across before, and decided to skip it. They were three-card monte players, con artists with zero connection to voudou, although I am sure they allowed that association to work in their favor in the black communities, from whom they drew a high percentage of their clients. It was too ironic. An Asian Indian or Romanian psychic could set up shop and advertise with big signs on the highway, but with the exception of certain parts of New Orleans and Miami I've never seen any above-ground voudou shops, let alone billboards.

It's understandable. The Black Codes of colonial and antebellum America so regulated African culture and religious practices that any activity that even smacked of voudou, such as singing, dancing and drumming, was outlawed. Blacks in some states could not even worship as Christians without a white master present. Even today, although anti-voudou laws have vanished, it is widely assumed, among both blacks and whites, that practice of the religion is illegal. Not ineffective—illegal.

I decided to abandon Natchez. It was becoming apparent to me that either big cities or small hamlets would be the best places to make contact. Mid-sized towns lacked either quick familiarity or urban anonymity. I was anxious to explore Mississippi, but something tugged on my senses to return to Louisiana. I hadn't covered the top half of the state, a big agricultural area relatively white and Protestant, compared to the black and Catholic bottom. But the region had also been home to plantations filled with slaves and their descendants. Isolated from the urbanity of New Orleans and its influence, African Americans in the northern half might have steered voudou along a different path. I thought it was worth a slight backtrack.

I re-crossed the Mississippi River and gradually aimed northwest toward Grambling, home of mostly black Grambling University, and maybe a good place to touch down. But my mind wasn't completely set. I was open to anything. Lafayette had taught me to trust my impulses, take chances. So even as I drove, I was wondering if maybe I should change plans. At any number of the highway junctions, I considered zipping off on a totally different route—perhaps head farther into western Louisiana near the Texas border, for example, or veer sharply up into the Arkansas flatlands. After all, I could go anywhere. It was a burden more than a liberation—the possibilities of choice, the anxiety about narrowing them to one spot, one town, gave me a light-headed feeling, not unlike vertigo.

About midday I came upon an unmarked blacktop—most Louisiana roads are poorly marked—at a T-junction next to a beer 'n bait store. I drove it a few miles into woods and farmland until I thought it might be a waste of time. So I went back to the T-junction. By then, three black laborers, or farm hands, had assembled to drink beer on a pile of boxes back of the bait store. When I asked for directions, one of the men got surly because I couldn't understand his thick local inflection. He was looking for trouble, but I wasn't, and drove on. In a few miles I came to a patchy asphalt highway, also unmarked by directional signs. I followed it northwest until I saw markers indicating that it was about to fork off. One way led towards Jonesboro, Arkansas, and the other to Ruston, Louisiana, which is adjacent to Grambling.

I was really uncertain which fork to take, but as I downshifted on the approach, a black mechanic standing outside a repair shop walked towards the Ruston side of the shoulder, wiping his hands on a red work cloth. I looked over at him and he was looking directly back at me. He had a mustache. Short hair. Smooth skin and even teeth. He smiled. I turned his way.

It's hard to know what to make of something like that. A voudou priest would've said I had been guided by Elegba: once to warn me off at the bait stand and again to to lead me through the junction. Maybe it was just a fluke, the "significance" based on the questionable logic of imputing desired effects from selective causes. How odd, given all we know, that no one can say, finally, whether one answer is true or another false. I do know that if I hadn't turned towards Ruston I wouldn't have met Sarah Albritton.

—▬—

Anyone within a hundred miles, black or white, who knew anything about good food, knew about Sarah's Kitchen. The owner's northeastern Louisiana cooking had won awards and acclaim and been served at official folk festivals as far away as Washington, D. C. Set back off a tiny, easy-to-miss street not far from the Ruston Vo-Tech school, the Kitchen was a one-room house reborn as a cafe, spruced up with green paint, white trimming and lace curtains on the two front windows. Regulars liked to eat outside under the big cedar trees, on park benches brightened with red tablecloths held firm by Mason jars filled with condiments.

Inside, three formica tables provided seating for maybe a dozen if you crammed in, and you did. A lace-covered wooden counter accommodating a half-dozen more people bisected the room, with the plain-view cooking area on the other side. Iron frying pans, assorted stainless steel pots, and all manner of vines or flowering plants hung from the cedar ceiling and walls, along with spices and drying hams. It really was like eating in a kitchen, maybe your own grandmother's if you were lucky, about the homiest place on earth.

I showed up about 9 A.M. the second morning after arriving in town, the first day having consisted of a fruitless, maddening search for "Mother Butler," an elderly, and probably deceased, healer last seen in the Ruston HUD projects. Both Sarah and her husband, Robert Lee, were already hard at work—had been

Sarah Albritton, Sarah's Kitchen, Ruston, Louisiana.

Inside Sarah's Kitchen.

since 5:00, cooking up chicken, bread, greens and roast beef. They were in their fifties—she oval-faced, caramel, thin; he stocky, dark, white-crowned—but both seemed fit and strong. I knew at least one reason. The interior temperature was at least ten degrees hotter than it was outside. They spent their days working out in a steam bath.

I didn't particularly want coffee, but it was a way to keep the conversation going. After my second cup, and a biscuit, and questions, it got obvious I wasn't just a sales rep killing time.

"You're talking about voudou," Sarah said matter-of-factly, looking at me as she bent to extract a pan of cornbread from the double oven. I thought she'd ask me to leave. Instead, she smiled proudly. "I taught voudou for six weeks at my church," she said. "There's thirty-three verses about voudou in the Bible."

I must have looked slightly stunned.

"I don't believe in it," she said quickly. "I study it to help people who think they've been hoodooed. I've been hoodooed myself. There's some people in Chatham who made a candle against me 'cause I preach against the hoodoo." She placed the cornbread on a counter and wiped her hands on her white apron. I asked for a refill.

For three days we jousted. I'd drop in to eat—chicken, turnip greens, squash, potato salad and sassafras tea ("good for your sex life"). While she was kneading dough or fixing take-out platters or dictating the next day's menu to her son, or sitting down to coffee—she drank huge amounts—she gradually revealed to me the tormenting confrontation in her soul. She had joined the great spiritual battle. She was a warrior for Jesus against the evil of voudou. She always had been.

When she was six years old, she now realized, she'd had her first encounter with it. Her family lived in Clay but she'd gone over to Ruston to visit her cousins. They'd heard some money had been lost out in the woods and went to find it, using a silver spoon dangling from a red string that would "point to the money." Deeper and deeper they ventured into the forest. "Then we saw a light," Sarah said. "It was the spirit of the person who lost the money. Everybody was afraid to go any farther and we ran back. We buried a root under the doorstep to keep away the spirit. But I went back that night and saw the light again . . . and I decided never to go back."

Spiritually, she never did. What she had seen was Magic. It was not God. From then on, what Lorita learned to embrace, Sarah passionately rejected. "God might have said, 'Sarah Mae, you become a voudou queen.' But He never did. Why would he? I don't believe in those gods of Egypt and Africa. Why should I? In my heart I know I serve the one true God. I don't want no hand-me-down God. Why would a person go back to those African gods? Why choose to go back into darkness rather than choose the light?"

Robert Lee, washing dishes, listened. I began to defend voudou, explaining about the orisha and their ways. Sarah was unfamiliar with the names of the deities but seemly keenly interested in what I was saying. To Robert Lee, it all came down to one question. He asked it over his shoulder. "But do you believe any of it works?"

I said I didn't know. I could see him smile.

But Sarah knew.

"Those gods cannot heal one thing," she said. "Only God can heal. You see, voudou is really Satan . . . and Satan has power. He was an archangel. He rule the earth right now, so he can give the power. On the whole, voudou have a good name around here, but Satan can make a sinful thing look good."

"What make it look good," Robert Lee observed, "is that if you can tell people something to tickle their mind, it's good." As for himself, he remembered the time he'd stepped on a nail while fixing a roof. "A prophet [spiritual healer] said some holy moly stuff and rubbed my foot. When I got home I couldn't hardly walk on it."

Sarah wiped her hands on a dish towel and laughed. "You could spread the word a prophet was in town and people would come in from all around. They used to stay in motels—they stayed in that one you're in—till they run 'em out of town."

It was getting close to the lunch rush and customers were driving up. Sarah invited me to come back and study the Bible with her. She said she'd also send me to some of the local hoodoo people so I could see for myself that they were "counterfeit." She even knew of a "white voudou lady." Name of Margaret, out in the country.

—▬—

The two-story wood cabin was set in deep piney woods so thick even the half-regulated clear-cutting didn't faze the relentlessness of nature. I drove by it twice. It looked more like an upscale lake lodge or weekend getaway cabin than a hoodoo shack. Late model sedans and fresh-washed pickups were parked in the dirt driveway, and just back of the house was a small outbuilding the size of an office at a construction site. But that's not what it was.

I pulled in and set my handbrake. I remembered Lorita's advice to clean myself with fruit before meeting spiritual people and regretted not having any. I went up to the front porch and knocked. An elderly black woman opened the door halfway. I could see by the expression in her eyes—she was scared—that I was at the right place. She said Margaret wasn't home.

Then a white woman in a muumuu came out to say Margaret had left town and to call back "next Tuesday." I said I wouldn't be around that long, explained that I was the one about whom Sarah had called, and proffered my card. While she scrutinized it, I leaned forward a little to recon. I could see an entry foyer with a table, around which sat four or five women, all white except for one. That was probably the friend Sarah had told me about who had bought some "blue water" from a traveling prophet for $150, hoping to kill the wife of a man with whom she was having an affair. The potion hadn't worked. Later, the woman had gotten a job with Margaret, after which the husband left his wife. Now he lived with the woman.

My mind said: Witches. Maybe they were just clients, but I said goodbye, left my card, and drove back to Ruston. En route I stopped at a roadside stand and bought peaches, tangerines, apples, and bananas. I wouldn't be caught unprepared again. As soon as I got back to the motel I cleaned myself.

At four that afternoon, uninvited, I drove back out. This time I went directly to the small shed. I knocked on the door and someone said to come in. When I did I saw two women facing each other across a small desk flanked by votive candles. One, black and middle-aged, was the client. The other was Margaret, a statuesque, white-haired, part-Cherokee of about fifty. Both seemed startled, but Margaret more so; after all, she was supposed to be out of town. I didn't stay, but agreed to meet her two days hence. "I don't usually use cards," she said, referring to the deck in her hand, "only with clients who find it helpful."

—=—

Sarah spread her color-coded Bible before us on the kitchen counter to show me how many times she thought the Bible revealed the use of hoodoo. First there was Exodus, in the tale of Moses casting down his rod and it turning to a snake—hoodoo magic. There was also Saul's reliance on prophecy, which Sarah considered a type of hoodoo, because prophecy was too often the work of man, not God. And did not Jesus cast out demons? She turned the pages rapidly, her finger like a pointer in a military briefing. There: spirit healers in Corinthians, more prophecies in Acts, and magic and occult symbolism in St. John's Revelations.

To Sarah, each of the thirty-three hoodoo passages was there to show it up as evil. I made a contrary claim, that references to snakes, magic, divination, prophesying, etc. merely emphasized the historical influence of African religions on Christianity. She would have none of it.

"I stand firm," she said, patient indulgence over her bifocals. "I don't care what denomination you are, if you're not serving our God the Saviour, you got to be serving Satan." The Bible backed her up in dozens of passages—thou shall have no other god before me, cannot serve two masters, shall abide by the one and true way. "He that is not with me is against me," said Jesus in Luke 11:23. The Bible is pretty unequivocal about who's the boss.

I shouldn't have been surprised at her intransigence. The equation of African religion with evil had been a long-standing Christian theme. According to Ishmael Reed, the "magicians" in the Bible were really African priests. Condemning them and all they represented became an obsession, fully elaborated once the slave trade began. In *Black Religion and Black Radicalism*, Gayraud S. Wilmore observed the seeds in the first European missionary contacts along the African slave coast:

> The Protestants, much more than the Roman Catholics, were horrified by the native religions . . . saw nothing vaguely representing a preparation for the Gospel. The use of charms, magic, ghosts and witches was deplored as nothing less than Satanism and superstitition. No religion that was basically polytheistic, that countenanced polygamy and made so much of ancestors, spirits and the phenomena of nature, could provide

an acceptable ground for Christianization. It
had first to be stamped out.[1]

Little in that perception has changed over the centuries. The
question put to Ava Kay Jones by the tourist guide in New
Orleans—"What is the devil figure in voudou?"—had long ago
been specifically answered for Sarah. It was voudou itself.

These were not idle theological matters. All around Ruston,
in her view, people were making wrong choices, listening to
healers who thought you could serve two masters. Such healers,
to Sarah, were false prophets, among the most virulent and
sneaky of all Satan's minions.

The longer we talked, the more perplexing I found Sarah's
fascination. Then it came to me. It was exactly as she had told
me on our first meeting. The conundrum wasn't whether she
believed in voudou—she obviously did—but what to do about
it. Sarah Albritton thought it her Christian duty to maintain
vigilance, and, where necessary, to intervene.

---

[1] Gayraud S. Wilmore. *Black Religion and Black Radicalism*, 1972,
Doubleday, New York, p. 21.

# 9

## TWO-HEADED MEN AND GHOSTS

THE TWO-HEADED MAN, the Reverend Allen Buckley, was a prophet from down near the Quarters, the old slave section. He was a hoodoo man by reputation, but also, like Lorita Mitchell, a charismatic minister. Buckley's New Freedom Faith Center, part of a bootstrap alliance called the Interdenominational Affiliated Ministries, was one of hundreds, or even thousands of independent Protestant churches which seemed to fall around the big trees of God like acorns on hard red clay. I don't know if Buckley had found root or not. His ministry was a plywood annex to his own unpainted clapboard house on an unpaved street in an unwanted part of town. I'd heard his name in the course of looking for Mother Butler, and thought his "Divine Healing," which he described as "a cross between hoodoo, spiritism, and mediums" might be exactly the thing Sarah Albritton, who didn't know him, would've said the Bible condemned.

I pulled in next to his old pickup and shook hands with him in the driveway. A handsome man in his mid-thirties, he wore a white shirt and dark trousers, giving him the appearance of a modestly appointed Baptist preacher. He led me around a grassless yard full of car parts, toys and cast-off bits of machinery to show me the sanctuary in which worshipers were "slain in the spirit," spoke in tongues and washed each other's feet. The white walls were virtually unadorned: other decor limited to a lectern, floor fans and a couple dozen unmatched chairs from yard sales.

His wife, a pretty, demure woman, invited us into the kitchen and made some hot tea. I wondered what her life was like with him. What did it mean to marry and raise children with a man whose very presence struck spiritual revulsion or fear into most of the community? Yet in their demeanor, the tidiness and discipline of their home, I thought of the spareness of Islam. Another religion that hadn't worked out well with Christianity.

Buckley had left the Baptists over a decade ago to become a "two-headed man"—like Ricky Cortez, able to see into the future—because of his past. In his mid-twenties he had been arrested in Ruston for carrying a stolen gun across the state line to Arkansas. "Guilty as everything," he spent about six months in jail in El Dorado. There, he said, he was like Paul, reading the Bible till midnight and preaching from his cell, getting put in solitary for it, coming out and preaching again. When he was released, a jailer told his mother, "You have a prophet up there."

Divine Healing was his way of converting his ability to do "supernatural things, which can either help you or hurt you" to the uses of the Lord. The difference in helping or hurting, to Buckley, "defines the line between Christians and the spiritualists who just do negative work." Around town, his use of oils, herbal potions, special teas and "annointments" with poltices— what Lorita would have called "cleaning"—earned him a tag not only as a two-headed man, but a prophet, root doctor, hoodoo and worse. Hard shells condemned him as a blasphemer, what Sarah would have called a usurper of God's powers, a false magician.

Their heresy, of course, was his act of faith. "The power to heal is a gift of God," Buckley insisted. "Witchcraft and sorcery are gifts of God that have been mis-used. But a lot of plain folks don't know the difference, and so they say, 'This guy must have voudou.' They're more apt to believe in voudou than in Divine Healing because that's what they've heard about." He glanced knowingly at his wife. "If I put up a sign outside with a hand painted on it and wrote 'The Prophet Wonder' underneath, some people would pay their last dime to come in and see me. They'd think it was voudou."

An intense man, committed, passionate in his own defense. It occurred to me that perhaps Buckley hadn't left the Baptists, but had been pushed out. At about the time I met him, another maverick who wanted Christianity to be more closely tied to Mother Africa was starting on his own breakaway path. The Reverend George Stallings, controversial priest of the Imani

The Reverend Allen Buckley, New Freedom Faith Center, Ruston, Louisiana.

Reverend Buckley's home in the Quarters, Ruston, Louisiana. Faith Center in room at far right.

Temple in Washington, D.C., had accused the Catholic Church of racism and demanded that his Mass be permitted to incorporate Africanized elements of worship, including the ring-shout, dancing, and display of spiritual possession. For months the Bishop of the diocese ignored Stallings, who not only began performing an Africanized Mass, but continued his denunciations of the Church, drawing considerable media attention. Eventually the Bishop responded: Stallings's actions were condemned and he was ordered to return to orthodoxy.

But by then Stallings had gone too far to turn back. Defying his Bishop, he not only continued Africanized Mass, he also authorized divorce, birth control, and abortions. He said it was okay for women to be priests. His parishioners gave him overwhelming support, believing, as he did, that "no Church, no Pope, no power can separate anyone from God." But Stallings exhausted the patience of Rome. In February 1990 he was excommunicated, as were some of his parishioners.

It was more an old story than new—too old, in the black churches. But each version was of the common web, and the web reached into every corner of America.

"I have to be careful not to be associated with being a two-headed man, because that's not with the main line," said Buckley. "For a time I wouldn't even have a candle, because they'd think I was two-headed. They even said we drink cow's blood here." He looked at me with a kind of vulnerability, or frustration—a look I'd seen in Lorita's face. "The two-headed man is isolated. Through fear he is respected. Everybody knows he's there but no one confronts him. But he's a gifted person. He can work wonders."

—==—

When Tuesday lunch rush ended, Sarah asked me to drive her over to the home of a troubled friend—I'll call her Yolanda—who had been "hit." A former prostitute, Yolanda lived alone in a modest frame bungalow in a lower middle-class black residential area. Now in her late sixties, she could barely see and was mostly house-bound. Sarah had taken it on herself to check on Yolanda from time to time, and help arrange for grocery deliveries, trips to the beauty shop, checking account balancing. And, as I was about to see, much more.

We parked near a side porch. Sarah noted the grass needed cutting as we walked up through the screened patio and into the living room. My eyes took a moment to adjust—the blinds were closed to keep the un-air-conditioned house cooler. It was modest but not run-down, almost grandmotherly, full of the totemic still-lifes of the elderly: ceramic cats and kitschy knicknacks, lumpy naughahyde couches, slightly soiled arm chair doilies, phalanxes of photos of relatives, a gilt-framed print of "The Last Supper."

Yolanda hunkered in an overstuffed armchair in one corner, watching a soap opera on an old TV. She wore black shorts, tennis shoes, and a short-sleeved sweatshirt with a leopard's face on the front. Her head was bound in a scarf, to hide her baldness. She barely acknowledged our entry, other than to spit tobacco into a green-bean can beside her chair. Her face was an unhealthy yellow, and when she forced a smile of greeting, I could see that age or disease had taken most of her teeth. A heavy woman, she also was diabetic with high blood pressure and heart trouble.

We began to talk, generally, about her health. She took insulin twice a day, which she said was the same number of times she read Romans from her Bible. She said she was also very depressed, and never seemed to have any energy. But she didn't think the cause was physiological. She'd been to two doctors and they hadn't found anything other than the obvious. Then she just came out with it.

"I been hit. That's what wrong with me. I been hit lots of times."

She looked to make sure I was listening. "I'm hit right now," she said, her thickly drawled voice so loud—she was a little hard of hearing—I would've been listening whether I wanted to or not. "Sometimes I feel crazy and sometimes I can talk to you—" Her tone trailed off into the quietness of a child getting ready to pout. "But I might not want to talk to you all the sudden, though." Her head dropped back against her chair.

"Yolanda," said Sarah, "he came here because he wants you to tell him how it happened."

Yolanda leaned forward, looking at Sarah, then me, and spat. "You mean about T.?"

Sarah nodded. She was ramrod straight next to me on the couch, her hands folded atop the white kitchen apron covering her lap. She reminded me of a cat waiting to pounce.

Yolanda exhaled heavily. The thought of her unfaithful ex-husband made her scowl. I wasn't sure she'd go on, and started to get up, thinking we'd be leaving. But she shook her head, as if throwing off some muzzle of the past.

"I was having—you know how ladies come around," she said, leaning forward. "Well, I didn't wash myself right and I put my things up on a shelf till I could wash them later. I had a little bath towel there, too, and later when I went to look for it I asked T. about it. He said he didn't know where it was.

"But I didn't believe him, so I went to look for it. When I opened up his clothes trunk he had two of my sick clothes. I knowed it was mine—it was a big diaper and a blue sheet. It was coming so bad I was using anything.

"I got it out and burnt it up. Then I run out of the house. I couldn't stay there. I went to Bastrop looking for a house. Then when I came back I looked for T. down in the Quarters, and he was in bed with Alice." She paused to spit. "But I knew I'd been hit because I was feeling bad."

Sarah's hands moved slowly from her lap, gently gripping the sofa cushions on either side. "Yolanda," she said, her brown eyes flashing knowingly in my direction, "why people hoodoo you?"

Yolanda tensed. She looked away. It took a while to answer. "I don't know."

Sarah pressed. "You know why."

"Sure I do."

The room was silent again. I pretended to scribble something on a notepad.

Yolanda spat. Sarah didn't flinch. Yolanda fussed with a doily on her chair. When it was exactly so, she continued her story. She and T. got back together, she said, but he never admitted he had hit her, and she didn't tell him she knew. Then she went to a hoodoo man to get the fix off, but he told her T. came from a family that knew "the secrets" and had concocted something too powerful to break.

Then, she said, T. hit her again.

It happened one evening at dinner. "I'd put on a pot of greens—honey, I'm a greens lover. But you know, the pot liquor was white and had, like, a skin on it, you know? The liquor should have been green. But I let the greens cook down. Even the meat wasn't right."

At the table, she whispered to her daddy, "Don't eat none of them greens if T. don't eat 'em. If he don't, you don't eat 'em either." She looked at me. "You know where they went?"

I shook my head.

"Outdoors. I didn't eat 'em and Daddy didn't eat 'em and T. didn't eat 'em. After that time we started sleeping in separate beds."

Despite her tale, Yolanda wouldn't say for sure that her present afflictions were still lingering from the hit from T. To do so, of course, would have been to acknowledge the very thing

"Yolanda," inside her home in Ruston, Louisiana.

she knew Sarah had come to torment her about, that she had been going to the faith healers. To the voudou.

One, she said, called himself a prophet, but "all he had me do was read scriptures" from her large print Bible, especially the twenty-third Psalm and Romans 10:8 ("But what saith it? The word is nigh thee, even in thy mouth, and in thy heart: that is, the word of faith, which we preach.") She read them, she said, "but neither one changed me."

Sarah listened with an almost beatific smile. Actually, she was just waiting for Yolanda to stop talking. It wasn't that Sarah was bored. She just wanted her friend—her depressed, ailing, and, very probably, bedeviled friend—to see the broom.

Earlier, Sarah had winked at me and slipped into the kitchen, returning with a big straw broom, placing it flat on the wooden floor. I thought the action odd, and Yolanda's failure to comment on it equally strange. But given the dynamic between the two women that afternoon, who knew what was going on? Then I realized it wasn't that Yolanda hadn't seen the broom. It was exactly the opposite.

As soon as Yolanda finished a long and dreary tale about a healer known as Reverend Gray, who had been known to have people soak their feet in Clorox and had humiliated Yolanda by demanding she take off her wig so he could rub her head with expensive oils, Sarah called out, sweetly, "Hand me that broom, will you?"

Yolanda tightened instantly.

Sarah repeated the question.

Yolanda looked at the broom and then, as though the sweep of her vision were the edge of a cutlass, at Sarah.

Sarah turned to me. Loud enough for Yolanda to hear, she said, "She won't pick it up."

"Why?" I resigned myself to playing straight man.

"She afraid to," Sarah said sarcastically. "She superstitious."

Yolanda glared at both of us. Defiantly then, she got up and hobbled with difficulty over to the broom. Halfway there, she snapped off a deep frown and returned to her chair. "Don't you do that to me, Sarah," she breathed lowly.

Sarah shook her head, got up from the couch and picked up the broom herself. She'd made her point. But there was another of which neither of the women was aware. The broom is a symbol of Sonponna, a.k.a. Babalu Aye, the feared orisha of diseases. "Superstitions" about it might have run deep, indeed.

"If I told you I could heal you, would you believe it?" Sarah asked, returning to stand in the center of the room, relentless.

Yolanda frowned, angry now. She shifted in her chair. "I don't know, Sarah. Explain yourself."

Sarah crossed her arms. She looked at me, then at Yolanda.

"Do you believe I could do it?"

"Well . . . no."

"Then why you ask me?"

"The way you said it, like you could do it."

"You believe I could?"

"I know when you put your foot down . . . I think you could."

Sarah didn't answer right away. When she did it was with an almost stern confidence. "Well, the first thing is, Gray has you reading the wrong scripture. That's about Holy Spirits, but you need to study *evil* spirits."

Yolanda looked at her, then away.

"Why you go to Gray?" Sarah asked. "You think he's out to get you."

"I don't."

"You lying to me when you say that. You're more likely to trust a stranger than me."

"I didn't say that."

"Then who would you go to around here if you wanted to get some help for being fixed?"

Yolanda stared at some photos on a shelf. She spat. "If *you* can, then you do it. There's your answer, sister."

Sarah glanced at me, then looked full upon her charge, and gave us the plan.

She would heal Yolanda by going through all the Scriptures to find out about "voudou, hoodoo and sorcery." She would show her how Satan, or the Devil, is actually behind all three. "We gonna start with the Devil and pick up Christ at the end," Sarah promised. "With Christ you don't believe Satan can win. But first," she said, "we got to know what spirits we dealing with."

"Whether with Christ or with the Devil," Yolanda said slowly.

"'Cause there are two sets of spirits in the Bible," Sarah replied. "The only thing that save you is if you believe Jesus Christ is Jesus. You got to separate Christ from the Devil."

"The Devil is in all of us," Yolanda affirmed, biting down on each word. "So is Christ."

And so they would work it out. Yolanda, like Sarah, like most African Americans, would come to believe that voudou—the true legacy of her own African soul—was the work of Satan. At least that was what Sarah wanted Yolanda to believe. But as I left the house, I knew that there was a place inside the broken old prostitute that would never completely let go.

—

The last place Sarah took me was to visit Uncle Clem. He was going to be 103 that week, and lived a few miles out of town in one of those ramshackle, tin roof, weather-beaten places you drive by all the time in the South and wonder who lives there. Clem Wright did, and had for the last seventy years, with his wife, Annie, ninety-three. Though now small, frail and bent with age, as a younger man he'd built the house himself with hand-hewn logs. They'd raised nine children and had outlived them all. Now Clem and Annie, who was mostly bed-ridden, tended the small farm around the house and kept one cow, one chicken, one dog and one mule, with which Clem still worked his garden.

His parents had been slaves, brought in from the Carolinas to work and die on the northern Louisiana plantations. "They'd set their hoes up in the field and pray for them to do the work," he smiled, then didn't. "They worked 'em so hard." As a boy, he had seen fires out in the woods. That was where the slaves went for dancing. He said his daddy had been to some of those dances, but wasn't allowed to say much about them, or about voudou, or even where he had come from before arriving in Louisiana.

But Uncle Clem had seen plenty for himself. "There was a man named Kandolo. He come in and stayed around here four or five years, I guess that was back in 1897 or '98. He taught people and showed 'em how to pray. But he called himself a preacher man. I stayed away from it.

"I been hearing about it all my life," he said, "but I never did believe in no hoodoo." He pronounced it in a variant I hadn't heard before: "hoe-doe." That would be consistent, perhaps, with an adaptation of the Fon word vo-du.

Sarah and I rounded up a couple of straight-back chairs for the bare living room, where the tarpaper walls were decorated with yellowed newspapers and old advertising prints. "They used to have a lady, Aunt Jenny, who did hoodoo work," Clem said. "But I used to take all them hoodoo people to the Lord. I watched people a pretty good while. You can tell when they call themselves fixed. I can tell."

He looked toward the bedroom, where Annie lay sleeping. Three nurses had been in earlier in the day. Sarah explained that I'd come to hear about the "old healing ways" used by Clem and his family. He'd only been to a physician once; most of his life it hadn't been an option. As a younger man, Clem had fallen while working and split his rib cage open so far, he said, "I could see my liver." There was no doctor, so he and Annie smeared coal oil over the wound and it healed. Another time he slipped while feeding some hogs and broke his collar bone. He rubbed himself with coal oil, jimson weed and turpentine and waited for the fracture to mend. It did, though it must have been wildly painful. He opened his shirt to show me a large, disfigured knob on his collar bone.

Ordinary illnesses, he said, were treated mostly with teas brewed from mullein weed, sassafras and "hoe-how"—I never learned what that was. You could also boil hog's hooves into a tea for a cold. Jimson weed was effective for diarrhea, which Clem said was "awful common" when he was a boy. Jimson weed and brown cow manure ("depending on what you feed your cows") was good for pneumonia. Mistletoe, when boiled in an iron pot with four or five square nails, would take care of arthritis.

After a half hour, Clem tired, became distracted; anyway, Sarah had to get back for the evening meal. I was sorry; he was one of the last living links from "home remedies" to the primary culture which had generated them. Mixing herbs with iron in an iron pot, the stock-in-trade of Osanyin and Ogun, was but voudou under an assumed name.

Before leaving, Sarah had a final question of her own. "He wants to know"—she winked at me—"if you know the secret to life? Is it because you live in the country, drink spring water and all that?"

Clem sat bolt upright and stared at his niece. His voice, sometimes barely audible, fairly thundered. "Well, I will tell you girl. *Jesus!*"

He rose to fetch his 'bacco. A smoker all his life, he came back holding a hand-rolled, half-smoked butt, and some fixings.

As ever, Sarah had one more question. She looked at me as she asked it. "Uncle Clem, how do you know there is a God?"

"You get on your knees," he said. "My Lord showed me last night. You can call him, ask him for things. If you worthy, he turn it over to you. Don't worry about that." He sat back at his chair, rocking. I think he lost track of us. He said, as though to himself, "It shall be like another world."

———

I had a cup of coffee and blackberry pie back at the cafe, then told Sarah goodbye. Mounting I-20, I sped eastward through the rain, the inescapable June rain. I listened to the noises around me. The drops striking the windshield, the whirr of the wind in the half-cracked ventilator, the tires spinning at 80 mph, ancestral ghosts in my mind.

I had gone back to Margaret's a couple of days ago for our third meeting. This time she had let me into her house, not just the outside shed. We sat very close to each other on wooden chairs next to a low, dark-stained coffee table. Her teenage daughter stood near a piano, watching. Another woman was also in the house, but kept back.

Margaret made no secret, now, of her acquaintance with voudou—including the names of the gods. "I was raised in it and around it back in North Carolina," she said, her voice sultry, warm, beguiling. "I remember seeing people in bed being chanted over in African tongues." Brought up Pentecostal, her spirit guide now was Marie Laveau, who gave her "second sight"—the same thing the Reverend Buckley meant by having two heads. She said she believed in the god Jehigi, and the lost Book of Moses, from the so-called twelve lost books of the Psalms, and in the works of Allan Kardec, Edgar Cayce, the Books of Seth and others in the mystic genre.

She was clearly more suited to "The Shining Two" than a botanica, and yet she had a powerful personal charisma. As she talked, she dropped into momentary trances, her head rolling back slightly as her green-brown, almond-shaped eyes fluttered upwards. I had seen that look. In and out of states, she told me

Margaret, the "White Witch," on right, with her daughter. Outside Ruston, Louisiana.

she had a channeler who had played classical music through her hands, though she herself didn't know how to play. And she had performed strange tasks. She had mixed potions to help people who came in with maggots in their backs. She had laid on hands to excise frogs from a man's arm. Women with black warts she would bathe in "Hebrew salts" for relief, and for difficult afflictions, she said she would kill a black or a white chicken and drop the blood on the troubled parts of the client's body. She broke brown eggs in quart jars and chanted Psalms over the water.

Yet of all that, the only thing that stuck, except in my notes, was one recurrent remark. Despite holding my business card in her hand the entire time we talked, she consistently referred to me as "Don." I had puzzled on the mistake driving the winding two-lane farm road back into Ruston. At a Catholic church, as Lorita had counseled, I stopped to light a votive candle.

I was nearly at my motel exit when it hit me. My father's name was Don.

I braked hard off the highway into the lot of an E-Z Mart. I fumbled out a quarter for the graffiti-scarred phone. "Did you know you called me Don the whole time I was there?"

"I know."

"Oh."

"I mean I know that's not your name but I couldn't stop myself. I saw a spirit ghost standing behind you. He had gray hair, thinning, and wore glasses."

"Except for thin you're right."

"I meant his hair," she corrected. "His body wasn't thin. His body was medium, kind of stocky. It was his hair that was thin."

I could feel my voice crack. "Oh," I said. "That's him."

"Well"—as if it were routine—"he must be there to protect you."

I forgot what I said after that and thanked her and hung up. In a bar late one night on Magazine Street, my friend from New Orleans, the other Sarah, had told me, "If you get in too deep we're going to have to pull you out." But I was thinking I was finally beginning to find my depth.

# 10

## ELVIS AND DR. KING

OUT OF JACKSON I took Highway 3 north to Yazoo City. The moon alongside the Yazoo River was only a sliver, and a thick lowland fog made the countryside seem like a Yorkshire moor. Off to my left lay the Delta National Forest and Panther National Wildlife Refuge but all I could see were clumps of roadside mailboxes and the occasional porch light. I pulled to the side a couple of times to check my map. I got on a long stretch of blacktop as the mist cleared, and in the dim moonlight the moor had become an enchanted forest, a verdant kaleidoscope, the kind of place in which apparitions might beckon at the end of a silver spoon hanging from a red string. What appeared for me was the back of an old green Ford pickup traveling without any lights and not much speed. I braked hard, swerving into the passing lane to miss it.

Soon I began to see a glow of yellow light to the west, and then I could smell what I'd been watching for miles grow out of the horizon: a big chemical plant along the river, smokestacks coughing out flames like hell's own dragons. Texas to Florida, the rural South has become home to giant backwoods industrial plants, refining chemicals or sugar or petroleum, turning tim-

State highway, rural Mississippi.

ber to pulp to paper, making defense parts and plastics. It was the New Plantation Economy. It doesn't buy slaves these days; it pays wages. It substitutes bank loans for chains and it admits whites. Prefers them. Part of the illusion. Black or white, though, everybody drinks the water; everybody breathes the air. Everybody gets the cancers.

I got to Yazoo City about 10 P.M., plenty tired, but I couldn't find a motel. I don't know why. I drove around a half hour, which is a long time in Yazoo City; there wasn't much to do but press on towards Greenwood if I wanted make Memphis early the next day. I continued up Highway 49, past farmland and through small towns, blowing off Lorita's warning never to drive late at night or when fatigued, and by that point willing to pass up her other proscription, against staying at an isolated tourist court set amid the woods.

I could've camped but it kept raining and I wanted a bed. I passed more flame-lit chemical plants, more night monsters. At Tchula, I pulled into a convenience store for a drink and to use the phone. It was a very black town, except for the white cop cruising. Across the tracks, the roadway was lined on both sides with parked cars—older American models. I saw a few black men walking towards a roadhouse. It was a Friday night and I figured there was plenty of music and action. I would've liked to go, but in my jeans and T-shirt I looked too much like a bubba. At a little after midnight, I finally stopped at Winona, where I-55 led to Memphis. It was a rotten motel—I had to switch rooms because the sheets on my bed hadn't been changed. It took me a long time to fall asleep.

Next morning in Batesville I nibbled on a sausage 'n biscuit breakfast next to a table where two local white good ol' boys joked with a black woman who repped for Mary Kay cosmetics. They were telling her about a man who got rid of a Mary Kay saleswoman by telling her he wouldn't let his wife wear "anything but Estelle Lauder." At the table on my other side a black woman was helping her teenage son fill out an employment application for Piggly Wiggly.

I left with a plastic cup of coffee and got on the big highway, turning my radio to the Mississippi classical music network—there is one, and it's good. I knew why I wanted to go to Memphis. Two American icons had died there. One had taken a lot from African-American culture; the other had given. I didn't know what, of voudou, I expected to find at Graceland or the Lorraine Motel, but I was pretty sure whatever it was would reveal itself.

When I crossed the Tennessee line I stopped at the tourist station for directions. Elvis's memorial was marked clearly enough on the maps, but not Dr. King's. "I can't seem to find the Lorraine Motel," I said, spreading a city guide open before the white desk attendant, referring to the place where the civil rights movement was stunted on April 4, 1968. He seemed surprised but recovered fast and politely excused himself to find the hostess. He said she would know. A black woman in her thirties, she knew exactly where the motel was. "They're going to raze it, though, and build a museum," she added.

I went to Graceland first. If it was a bust, I'd have the rest of the day free. No lack of signs directed me how to get there most efficiently, and I parked in the crowded lot next to the *Lisa Marie*, the King's private jet, named after his daughter—the same name with which my friend Danica had been temporarily christened. I walked down to the main ticket hall, dodging most of the souvenir shops (okay, a coffee mug) and waited for the tram with my ticket group to ferry us across the road to The Mansion.

Too much has been written and sung about Graceland to add anything, but at the end of the tour, I understood the purpose of *my* visit. I had come not to see how Elvis was praised, but the manner in which he was buried. To see him as egun. Perhaps it was the virulent Elvis cult, the "sightings," the semiserious denials of his death, like Jim Morrison's, whose Paris grave had more offerings than Marie Laveau's. Perhaps it was the occasional celeb-speak, like a black reggae singer saying, "I always wanted to be like Elvis," or the white Florida rock 'n roller, Tom Petty, describing his boyhood idol: "Elvis didn't look like the people I'd known. He had a real glow about him, like a full-body halo. He looked like a god to me." In my head had formed a notion, and because it had formed, couldn't be ignored: that Elvis, the poor white boy with the black music, might have been some unaware—or whimsically disguised—avatar of Elegba, or Shango. Over the top, maybe, but compared to what?

A sidewalk path and black wrought-iron fence curves around the graves, so tourists can walk up pretty close. The flat tombstone is capped with an eternal flame enclosed in protective glass. All day every day, mostly white Americans amble slowly past the grave. Some pray, some leave flowers, some take pictures, some say blessings. Some cry, some talk to him.

For white people to worship the dead, create gods of them, is not considered evil. Odd, perhaps, even camp, but not sacrile-

Elvis's grave, at Graceland, where white America worships the dead.

gious. Conversely, since the landing of the first slave ship in the Caribbean, that form of reverence has been in one way or another prohibited or taboo for Africans. As for their ritual of sacrifice—all the altar to an orisha requires is replenishment with fruit, water, candies, from time to time the blood of a fowl or perhaps a goat. Natural and straightforward. The altar of the dead god of commodity culture, on the other hand, requires the ongoing spiritual consumption of thousands a day: humans, in buses, with tickets.

***

The Lorraine Motel, 406 Mulberry, isn't far from downtown, surrounded by enclaves of black urban poverty simmering like ongoing affronts to Dr. King's dream. I drove over amid light showers cloaking the hot streets with hazy vapor, blocking the sun just enough to cast a dispiriting grayness over the city.

Sometimes history is forged in banal places. The protective barbed wire fence keeping out vandals couldn't hide the disrepair and disrepute into which the motel had been sinking even before it closed for good several years earlier. But wreaths of fresh flowers in front of room 306 on the second floor bore continual witness to the plain brick building's role in American life. But how did it figure in the life of voudou? Graceland was an analogy; The Lorraine was something powerful and direct. Dr. King was standing on the balcony in front of that room when James Earl Ray shot him dead from a window of a rooming house across the street. A preacher had been slain, for preaching. In that violence lay the answer. I didn't have it yet, but soon I would.

It was still possible when I was there to enter a side gate and, with the permission of an on-site caretaker, not used to seeing that many people, to walk up to the second floor. Outside room 306 I paused to read a plaque on the door bearing a quote from Genesis 37: 19–20: "They said one to another. Behold, here cometh the dreamer . . . let us slay him . . . and we shall see what will become of his dreams."

Back out on the street I took some pamphlets from Jacqueline Smith, a thirtyish woman sitting under a tent shelter among a mottled row of sidewalk vendors. She'd been living there for over a year, protesting the impending conversion of the motel into the $9.2 million National Civil Rights Museum. Smith's idea was that the motel site should be honored, but as a "living tribute" in the form of a daycare or a drug rehab center, or homeless shelter. Ultimately, Smith was to lose her battle. The museum opened in April 1991.

I ambled around Mulberry for a while, getting drenched. I stared up at room 306 for some time, tried to trace the line of sight back to the killer's flophouse. A homeless black man spinning a red yo-yo walked past me, nodded, and went on to the protest tent. Then he walked off, talking to himself. I glanced up the street. Two white policemen in a patrol car watched me. I hoped they were protecting Ms. Smith, but who knew? Beale Street revival notwithstanding, Memphis was still not dealing with the King assassination so well. McDonald's had nearly drawn a boycott from the NAACP in January because a sales promotion calendar circulated to sixty-five franchises in the Memphis area listed January 16, the designated date for celebrating Dr. King's birthday, as "National Nothing Day." I sat on the hood of my car while the cops watched.

---

In the morning I turned south, vaguely in the direction of Meridian, a fast-growing military base city of about 50,000—large for Mississippi—on the southeast side of the state, near the Alabama border. I wasn't sure how far I'd get before nightfall. By noon I was in Oxford, home of the University of Mississippi. I was always ready to stop if the feeling was right. But I didn't get the feeling.

Tupelo wasn't my town either. Less pretentious than Oxford, but a little too much on the hustle. So I thought maybe I would get all the way down to Meridian after all. About an hour away, at Philadelphia, I turned off the main highway for some coffee. It was a classic small town; winding, tree-lined hills, a traditional city square, a tacky retail strip out on the main highway, a gas station where the locals hung out. But it had the feeling.

There was more than one black neighborhood, of course, as there was more than one white, and I cruised until I came up a gentle hill onto a plateau of modest frame and brick homes with freshly mown yards, scattered tricyles and plenty of shade trees. I glided slowly up and down the quiet streets until I saw a middle-aged black woman standing in her yard. I parked and approached her deferentially, smiling, offering my business card, lamenting the heat—a normal Southern introduction. I told her I was looking for old people who knew about folk medicines. She didn't know anything about that, of course, but there was an old woman up King street who did. I thanked her and walked up to a tidy, two-bedroom frame house. It took some knocking, but at last Miss Eddie Lee Mason answered.

Half-Choctaw, her nut-brown cheekbones accentuated by gray hair pulled back into a tight bun, she was in her mid-eight- ies and now lived alone as a widow. She was cautious at first, but when she saw that some of her neighbors were watching, she said it would be okay if I stayed in sight on the screened sitting porch. It was nearly two hours before I left. I was begin- ning to find out that although many people didn't want to talk about voudou, when they did, they wanted to tell everything they knew.

"All that used to be bad way back yonder," she said. "People in the old days could get you down just by putting something down. You didn't even have to be near it."

Her most vivid memory reached back to early childhood, when her own mother had gotten "down." Miss Eddie's daddy

Miss Eddie Lee Mason, Philadelphia, Mississippi.

earned extra money calling breakdowns at "frolics." At one dance, a stranger took an interest in Miss Eddie's momma and tried to follow up. She spurned him, and he vowed revenge. First, the family's house caught fire, nearly trapping one of Miss Eddie's sisters, who tried to run back in for a china doll. After that, Miss Eddie's mother took ill. Every time she walked down to the pea patch, she got faint and had to be carried home. The father called the doctor, who could find nothing wrong.

The illness continued. Some of the older people in the area concluded Miss Eddie's momma had been hoodooed. They reasoned that since her illness occurred when she went to the pea patch, something along the route must be responsible. Miss Eddie's daddy searched the area. Finally, looking at a log footbridge over an irrigation ditch, he found "something," possibly a small bag—she never found out what it was or what it had contained.

"The older people told poppa to tell momma to cross further down from then on," Miss Eddie said, rocking slightly in her chair, absorbed in memory of the old days. "And somebody told momma to wear two silver dimes around her left ankle. As long as my momma lived she wore it. She never crossed at that place no more, and she never got sick again."

Sometimes the hexing could backfire. Two of Miss Eddie's neighbors, one married, one not, had been locked in a triangle over the husband of the former. To save her marriage, the wife went to a root woman known to make poisonous hexes out of snake scales. The root woman gave the wife a handful of the scales and told her to crumble them into a glass of whiskey, then serve it to her husband's paramour. Something went wrong, however, and the wife accidentally drank the hoodooed potion herself. Apparently, it was effective. When the wife was found, "She had a spoon in her mouth and she'd chewed her tongue up with fits." Eventually, Miss Eddie said, a snake grew in the wrathful wife's stomach and she died.

I listened with what I hoped was not obvious skepticism. Hoodoo was full of these kinds of snake stories. I've never been sure if the symbolism derives from unconscious ties to the cosmic voudou serpent, Dambada Wedo, or to the Bible, but I rarely met or heard of a hoodoo man or root doctor who hadn't seen a snake growing in or out of a body. In one case, I was told that a snake had burst right out of a woman's big toe, "and after that you never saw her barefoot." Nonetheless, it seemed likely that there must have been at least some basis for the accounts. For example, there is a type of tropical parasitic worm that attaches itself to the bones in your ankle and works its way up the femur; a remedy I had seen in a medical text when I was in the Army was to dig out the tail of the worm through the ankle hole, wind it around a matchstick, and twist the worm out bit by bit. That could be a snake growing out of a foot.

Similarly, a glass with snake scales might, like the legendary zombi potions in Haiti, also contain some other pharmacologically active ingredients. The scales of a snake are not necessarily toxic, in fact are unlikely to be so, but if those scales are mixed in with a real toxin, for example tetradotoxin, a poison common in certain types of toads—said by Wade Davis in *The Serpent and the Rainbow* to be the practice in Haiti—then you'd have a drop-dead Mickey Finn. But the idea of the magic coming from a serpent is altogether more terrifying than saying it's from a frog—or a mushroom, or a plant, or fish, or any other of the plentiful natural sources of lethal chemicals. Hoodoo, like any kind of hexing, is a magic of the mind.

Miss Eddie has just begun to tell me about a phony root doctor who came around during World War II using his "cures" to seduce women when we are interrupted by a black deputy sheriff dropping by on his lunch hour. No reason, he said, looking me over good, he just wanted to be sure she was okay. She told me she had lots of friends who checked in on her now that she's on her own. But she didn't want to live with relatives or in some nursing home. She'd lived in that house since 1926, birthed all eight children by her two late husbands, there. It was her home, her life; it was her memories. She drifted off into some of them, such as the time her son came back from the Air Force with a white friend from the service in the fifties and they got thrown out of a segregationist cafe, and later got the cafe declared off-limits to servicemen by the Pentagon, effectively forcing it out of business.

And then, she said, there was the civil rights trouble.

I could feel my head jerk up as if I'd been shot through with lightning. Of course. That's where I was—Philadelphia, Mississippi! I was so absorbed in looking for hoodoo I hadn't realized that the place I'd been drawn to on the way to Meridian was ground zero for Andrew Goodman, Michael Schwerner and James Chaney, who had been hijacked and executed on a lonely highway one summer night in 1964 by Ku Klux Klan thugs. The bodies of the three young idealists, two white and one black, were eventually found buried in an earthen dam, following an intensive FBI manhunt. Although the killers drew only light sentences, national outrage was so intense it helped recruit thousands of young white activists to the civil rights cause, gave great moral fervor to black organizations, and, it could be argued, was one of the racist outrages that influenced Congress to pass the remainder of President Lyndon Johnson's civil rights legislation.

What Miss Eddie remembered of that time was being very afraid, for herself and for her children. When one of them came home with an NAACP lapel pin she "beat and beat" on it till it couldn't be worn. "Whites were shooting at coloreds and coloreds were shooting back." Then the stores stopped selling ammunition, at least to blacks. It was a time when she found out a white man she liked was in the Klan and churches were burned and bombed and when she was afraid to shop for groceries because NAACP black activists knocked the bags from her arms if she bought from white merchants. The most dangerous area, she said, was "across the tracks."

I said goodbye, and drove over.

The poverty was worse than I had seen in Memphis. Among these same semi-paved streets and clapboard houses, Klan nightriders—carloads of beer-drinking, redneck bigots, winked at by local police—had tried to stop the civil rights movement through relentless terrorism. The churches and homes they left in rubble and flames had long since been rebuilt or razed; nonetheless it felt like entering a former war zone, and my color marked me as the enemy.

I spotted a group of old men under a shade tree drinking wine from a paper bag. They were friendly, but they had been on the hard life too long—a couple were drifters from farther east. I felt awkward and out of place not so much because of my white skin, but my clean clothes and car. Before I left, though, one of the men, a thin waif of a man with yellow teeth and torn, dusty brown trousers, told me of a hoodoo woman on a nearby street, and pointed the way.

I drove up a gentle hill to a cluster of small stores, mostly boarded up, on what had once been the main street of "colored town." I approached a group of men and women in their twenties enduring the afternoon heat by relaxing in the shade, drinking beer. Children played on the porch of an abandoned store. One of the men said he'd heard of a hoodoo woman in town and thought I'd find her a few streets farther along. I followed his directions to an asphalt street deeper into the ghetto, but all I found was an extremely old woman—I guessed she could have been 100—sitting alone on the porch of a brick HUD house. She wore a yellow and red head scarf and brightly colored patchwork skirt. When I got close, I could see a milky film over her eyes. I'm not sure if she really heard my words, or could see me, but either way she said she couldn't help.

On the way back to the railroad track demarcation line, I stopped at an intersection—a crossroads—abutting an incongruously suburban one-story brick building with a white steeple. A sign identified it as the Mt. Zion Baptist Church. It looked new, I later learned, because the original church had been blown up by the Klan. The parking lot was empty—it was a weekday— and the yard needed trimming. I almost drove away before I noticed, in a grassy patch near one wing, a gray tombstone with what appeared to be three photos along the top rim. I decided to have a closer look. The use of photos, as well as pieces of glass or tin foil or other shiny objects—considered by art historians to be based on African tradition—is not uncommon in black cemeteries. But art wasn't what I found. It was the grave of the three civil rights workers.

Of course. Shunned even by white morticians, where else could Goodman, Chaney and Schwerner have been buried but in a black church yard? For all the heroism of their lives, and

Gravestone for slain civil rights workers, Goodman, Chaney and Schwerner, Mt. Zion Baptist Church, Philadelphia, Mississippi.

historic impact of their martyrdom, their gravesite, somewhat like the Lorraine Motel, was practically a local secret. Millions had journeyed to see where Elvis lay; I wondered if a single Graceland visitor had even considered paying homage to those who had died here.

I leaned against my car. It was wrong. It was all wrong.

I decided to make an offering. I didn't have anything except the fruit and vegetables I now routinely kept for cleaning, but they would do. I set two ears of corn and an orange at the base of the headstone, near two pots of white flowers. Then I made a silent prayer—I guess it was a prayer. I didn't ask for anything. What to request? Justice? Equality? Vengeance? I looked at the three photos, crossed myself and drove back through the cross-roads.

—==-

That the path of voudou crossed the path of racial struggle was no more an accident than my repeated stumblings across the juncture. Many writers—Thomas Gray, William Words-worth, for example—have come to their senses among the tombs of the dead. In Philadelphia, I realized I had, too. The synthesis I had been seeking in some corner of my mind now seemed so apparent I couldn't believe it had ever been opaque. Except that it flew in the face of everything my culture had taught me. Except that linking voudou with black liberation bordered on the taboo.

Yet it was undeniable. The long, incessant attack on voudou, from pulpit to newspaper, from university to statehouse, was not simply a reaction against foreign gods. Other, stranger, religions have survived here, even prospered—Mormons, Amish, cults such as the Oneidans, Shakers, for example. But those belief systems did not arrive with slaves. They might have been different, and often were markedly at odds with mainstream

America, but they were not black. Nor were they revolutionary. Voudou in America was never anything else.

Although it now seems difficult to imagine, the true religion of the slaves was once the most subversive and feared ideology in the New World. As the quantity of Africans in the colonial New World began to swell in the eighteenth and nineteenth centuries, so did concerns about revolt. On the eve of the Civil War, the 1860 census listed 3.9 million slaves in the South and 8.1 million whites, making slaves about thirty-three percent of the population, though the numbers seem likely to have been undercounted. But in the major states, the proportion of blacks was significantly higher: Fifty-five to fifty-seven percent in South Carolina and Mississippi; forty-seven percent in Louisiana; forty-five percent in Alabama; forty-four percent in Georgia; thirty-one percent in Virginia. In the Caribbean basin the ratio was almost improbable: ninety percent in British Guiana, eighty percent or more in Haiti, Saint-Domingue and many other islands, and probably that high in Brazil.[1] Control of slaves became an ongoing obsession of the plantation societies. The well-known cruelties, the Black Codes, the very cultural and moral tone of colonial culture but attest to the bulwark of fear in white society.

Nor were the fears unfounded. The United States alone generated at least nine major revolts or conspiracies, principally: New York City, 1712; Stono, South Carolina, 1739; Point Coupée Parish, Louisiana, 1795; Richmond, Virginia (Gabriel Prosser), 1800; St. John the Baptist Parish, Louisiana, 1811; Charleston, South Carolina (Denmark Vesey), 1822; Southampton County, Virginia (Nat Turner), 1831. In the Caribbean basin, where conditions were even more brutal, but also more remote, large-scale plantation work units increased isolation from whites, and diminished security. Outbreaks were incessant. Bahia, Dominica and Jamaica were so volatile that bands of runaway slaves—

known as maroons, or dreads—were able to escape into remote terrain and live as permanent guerillas.

Despite the frequency and pervasiveness of the New World uprisings, the results rarely varied, especially in the southern United States. Rebels were whipped, hanged, shot, drawn and quartered. The spontaneous and ill-led St. John the Baptist Parish revolt, in which 500 or so slaves marched on New Orleans, was perhaps the bloodiest in the U. S., stemmed by U. S. troops and local militia. Nearly seventy of the mutinous African slaves were killed in the battle and many more executed—severed heads were mounted on pikes all along the road to New Orleans. The symbolism of the butchery was not just for the benefit of the Africans—mass decapitation had a way of making revolt seem manageable to white society.

But against all the failed insurrections was the shocking—to colonial powers and slave-owners everywhere—success at St. Domingue (Santo Domingo), now known as Haiti. Beginning in 1792, slaves from the maze-like hill country and rural plantations on the western side of the island of Hispaniola began a bloody twelve-year rebellion against Spanish, English and French expeditionary forces, and defeated them all. Spurred by the leadership of Toussaint L'Ouverture, who perished at French hands before the final victory, the rebels in 1804 proclaimed the Free Republic of Haiti, the first and only independent black nation in the New World. The defeat so disturbed Napoleon, who lost 60,000 men, that he gave up on a planned expedition to the Lower Mississippi Valley, subsequently under-selling valuable French holdings to the U. S. government: the Louisiana Purchase.[2]

Panic and backlash spread throughout the American South. Haitians—slaves or citizens; black, white or creole—were refused entry into the major seaports of the U. S. coast. Even Cuban slaves who had once been in Haiti were barred from

American auction blocks. Everything Haitian was bad news. Haiti was the worst thing that could happen. The blacks had risen against their white masters, and destroyed them. At least one of the black leaders of the St. John's revolt, Charles Deslondes, was a free mulatto from Saint-Domingue.

But there was another element to the spectre of black vengeance and victory—less tangible, more disturbing. Voudou priests—houngans and m'ambos, had played critical roles in the Haitian revolt, recruiting and rallying fellow Africans who, even after several generations, continued to look to priests as community and social leaders. To anyone knowledgeable in African culture, the involvement of voudou was ominous. African slaves, almost all of whom came from a contiguous area along the western coast, had lived for centuries in the theocratic tradition. All laws, all ethics, all morality, all social conduct derived from religion. Priests were communal leaders, often kings, and kings were the vestibules of the gods.

If the voudou priests had become active in Haiti, and if Haitian slaves had succeeded, where the other rebels had failed, then any slave society with vast numbers of unassimilated Africans—no real contact or interaction with the culture of their masters—was in serious danger. As the South proved, the converse was also true. Any society which had co-opted its slaves had already made it impossible for them to break out.

The plantation economy in the South was far different from that in the Caribbean, resulting in smaller work units and closer supervision. Instead of being left to their own devices and beliefs, rarely even seeing their colonial overlords, as was the case in the islands and Latin America, the North American slaves were drawn to the very bosom of Southern life. In that bosom, they were, like Miss Eddie's grandmother, converted to "the religion of the master." In the antebellum South, slaves became Christians at a rate estimated by the influential, pro-slavery journal *Debow's Review* to be five times higher than anywhere else in the world.

Direct repression of the slaves' real religion—voudou—further enhanced the binding of Africans to the culture of the masters. Every law forbidding dancing, singing or drumming, forbidding social gatherings, even at Christian services, put Africa at more distance, brought slaves more into the fold. In the fold, they came to believe they shared an interest with their captors: Christianity. It would be entirely missing the point to see this process of conversion, coupled with repression, as a matter of saving souls. It was an issue of military and political security.

Slaves allowed to practice their own religion could not be so easily disoriented, deprived of leaders, shorn of purpose. They would not be plantation zombis, working like cattle, their spirits stolen along with their gods, but would be instead African prisoners of war—temporarily held under force of arms. As prisoners, not slaves, they would constantly be thinking of escape and revolt. Through the common culture of voudou, they could communicate one plantation to another, even one colony to another. They might find a religious bond that stretched from the cotton fields of Texas to those of Virginia, the swamps of Brazil to the tobacco and sugar plantations of Cuba. They might find the strength and will to resist—successfully—and even to overthrow the white minority, perhaps carve new nation-states in the New World to which they'd been hijacked.

Just as in Haiti.

And then suppose the African usurpers—no longer slaves but a full-scale, disciplined force of armed warriors numbering in the millions and occupying huge swaths of the Americas—forged an alliance with opportunistic European powers, or with the white working classes also suffering under colonialism and mercantilism?

Class war. Holy war. Hemispheric revolution.

A world we will never know.[3]

But in voudou nothing is all bad or all good, and in the horror of one thing may lie the glory of another. History is no more a vacuum than is nature. Squash something here and it pops up later, as most colonial powers learned in the nineteenth century, and as the imperial ones did in the twentieth. Even amid wholesale destruction, ideas and cultures have a way of surviving.

I knew, of course, that voudou had survived. I was seeing it all around me. The gods had not given up. They had altered form. In the Caribbean, the orisha had learned to syncretize, to align themselves with Christian deities. Africans who wanted to worship Shango but couldn't under law could pray to a Catholic saint who reminded them of him—St. Barbara. Babalu Aye could be St. Lazarus. Jesus could be Obatala. That was working well. Perhaps prevailing.

Hiding "beneath Mary's skirts," a folk idiom for syncretization, may have begun as camouflage, but in time the orisha showed their real faces. The resultant Afro-Christian hybrids known as santeria, candomble, obeah, macumbe, Shango Baptist and so on became strong evidence that, given the right socioeconomic conditions, voudou could not only cloak itself within Christianity, it could dominate it.

At least in the Caribbean.

In the United States, African voudou was not syncretized, or hybridized, or even sanitized. It was eradicated. The smaller, more closely controlled plantations of the American Bible Belt never gave the orisha a chance to become saints or to create spirit world fusions like those in Cuba or Haiti. Yoruba slaves forced to worship in an icon-hating Baptist Church in Mississippi couldn't praise Oshun by calling her the Blessed Virgin. They had to give her up. They had to give them all up.

As I was seeing with my own eyes, the crushing of voudou in America proved so pervasive that almost all that remains in any indigenous form is hoodoo. In fact, I could not see voudou directly at all. I was observing it as though watching a solar eclipse through a pin-hole in a piece of cardboard, catching nothing more than its reversed shadow on the ground. Even with persistent scrutiny, the best I could make out of the originating shape was voudou's distinct, but ghost-like outline in music, dance, poetry, folk medicine . . .

And the church.

That was where American voudou had hidden—in plain sight.

The descendants of the slaves are Christians now, at least in name, but that makes them no less African, no less inclined to seek their leaders in the African way, from those who knew the gods. Even if voudou ritual vanished from slave communities, the ancient emphasis on priests as social leaders has not.

It is true, the leaders are no longer called priests. They do not speak of Elegba or Obatala, and they do not cast the opele or peer through the gut of a sacrificed goat to see the future. It is true that they have abandoned the horsetail whisk and the wooden staff for the Bible, and that their words of praise fly up to Jesus, Mary, and the Lord Jehovah. It is also true that the leaders are now called preachers.

It is true that, as DuBois said, the preachers are the priests.

Not that the modern day preachers—or ministers, or reverends, or bishops—themselves will fully acknowledge their voudou lineage, except perhaps in terms of a vague, scholarly, historical link. That's not what I mean. I mean the preachers are the priests. Directly invested. Unlike the Caribbean model, where syncretization allowed voudou to retain much of its ritual and religious essence, and where the priests could continue to function as such, voudou in America turned political. The priests *became* the preachers.

Lacking the opportunity to function even in a cloaked version, the faith withdrew into the bones of its leaders. The hiding place is almost too good. In Cuba, you may look upon a santeria ceremony or visit a babalawo and know you are seeing the legacy of voudou. In Haiti even more so. And in America?

Let them talk of Jesus and Mary. Were not preachers the leaders of virtually every struggle for black liberation in American history? Denmark Vesey, Gabriel Prosser, Nat Turner, Martin Luther King, Jr., Jesse Jackson, even Malcolm X—all based their power on religious vision. Perhaps the religions they invoked were no longer called voudou, but their role among the people was the same: to bind society, to provide a forum for the spirit, to produce leaders, to lead in struggle if necessary.

If the martrydom of Dr. King is seen as deriving from Jesus Christ instead of Ogun, Ochosi, and Obatala, the misconception is but a passing quirk of mortal interpretation. Or so I thought, driving away from the quiet graveyard in Philadelphia, my mind at one with what the snake knows.

---

[1] Saint-Domingue is now called Santo Domingo. The population figures are from Eugene D. Genovese, *From Rebellion to Revolution*, 1979, Louisiana State University Press, Baton Rouge, and from various almanacs.

[2] Of the many excellent histories and analyses of the role of slave religion in the American experience, the most pertinent to my perspective, and from which I draw heavily here, came from Genovese and Alfred N. Hunt's *Haiti's Influence on Antebellum America*, 1988, Louisiana State University Press, Baton Rouge.

[3] See Appendix 2 for an extended discussion of voudou's revolutionary potential.

# 11

# KINDRED SPIRITS, LINGERING FOES

I SET UP a temporary base in Meridian. Instead of constant driving, I thought I'd try a hub and spoke strategy. The small towns and rural roads of southeastern Mississippi teemed with spirits. As usual, I relied on hunches—the look of houses, the feel of the streets, the tone of the woods. The new strategy had its moments, but also, and far more often, frustrating clots of plodding tedium.

Walking up to total strangers with questions about voudou can be hell on your self-esteem. I'm glad my eyes weren't cameras so I can forget some of the expressions. At one apartment complex I yelled up to two young women in tank tops and shorts on an upstairs balcony at dusk. I couldn't tell if they thought I was flirting or just crazy. They didn't know anything about hoodoo—surprise—but suggested I ask those two guys in muscle shirts just leaving in a late model Buick; they had an auntie who did. But the guys didn't know anything either. What they had was pressing business that didn't involve strangers.

Later, traversing a thick Southern pine forest en route to Lake Claude Bennett, it came to me that I wasn't just frustrated, I was a fool. What was I seeking? The presence of the orisha. And how did one contact the orisha? By "hunches," word-of-mouth suggestions? Wrong. Through prayer and sacrifice. I had performed neither. No wonder my path was so often blocked. A few months earlier, before setting out on this journey, I might have ignored the urge. I would no more have considered asking a supernatural power for aid than rubbed a rabbit's foot or prayed on the Bible. Now I was turning off a Mississippi blacktop with Elegba on my mind.

I drove slowly up a narrow access lane to the lake until, under the canopy of the pine boughs, I spotted a public campground along the shoreline. A few families had pitched tents or parked camper-trailers at one end. I doubted if any of those folks would want to see what this white man was about to do, and I knew I didn't want them to, so I drove on until I found a spot all to myself.

I parked and looked around again to be sure I was alone. I was starting to feel jittery, like I'd had too much caffeine. I'd seen much of voudou, had left memorial offerings and cleaned myself, but this was different. I rummaged around in the rear floorboard until I found my fruit sack and dug out an ear of corn and a banana. I was completely improvising the ceremony. I didn't know any of the real African worship words or real protocol, but I thought I could make a reasonable guess, or at least an honest one. For some reason, it came to me that I should add something from the immediate area to my ersatz offering of fruits. I picked up a pine cone. Then I selected a sturdy young conifer, and arranged the offerings into a kind of pyramid altar at its base. I took a deep breath and knelt before it on one knee.

At once, a cold wave of fear rushed over me. I felt myself smiling, as I always do for some reason in moments of personal danger. For a long, terrible moment, I was wracked by deep, unexpected Christian guilt at bowing to a pagan god. But I remained kneeling. I was all alone in that clearing—just me and any gods who chose to rip me asunder or transport me to glory. Lorita had said to remember Psalm 23 in times of peril. Just then, I didn't, though I was in some kind of valley of the shadow. By any Christian standards I was blaspheming.

But as quickly as the fear had settled on me, it vanished. Just like that, as fast as the snap of your fingers, I felt as though my spirit had moved on. No apologies, no remorse, no guilt. Chains of whose constrictions and weight I wasn't even aware had snapped. I knew, as I knelt, that my instincts had been good. I was here among friends, not enemies, and certainly not devils. I was still a little nervous, but with anticipation, not dread. I asked the god of the crossroads for help in my search.

—===—

On a nearly deserted southeastern Mississippi state highway between Meridian and Hattiesburg, I passed a cluster of black homes set back from the road, a community without a name. I thought: This looks promising. I should stop here. But I didn't. Instead, I drove a mile farther, into the town of Paulding. As soon as I got there I knew I had made a mistake, had passed something up I shouldn't have. As if the realization required punctuation, abruptly a thundershower fell with such intensity I could barely see. I pulled into a gravel parking lot which turned out to be that of a Catholic Church—the second oldest in Mississippi, according to a sign. Speaking of signs. I sat in the lot with the windows fogged up and my shirt damp against my skin. Fuck it, I thought, I'm going back.

At the nameless community I took a red dirt lane to a trailer home where I saw a young black man on his plant-laden porch arranging fishing gear. I trotted through the drizzle to ask him about local healers. He said he didn't know anything—but his wife did. She sat inside watching a TV game show and tending an infant. I took a chair at the coffee table. These days, she said, people around here usually went to see Sister Plummer, over in Heidelberg, or Mother Adell, who had gone to Raleigh.

Tracing Mother Adell was tracing a spirit itself. As with Mother Butler in Ruston, I could find nothing of her except a memory. At last, at a service station in Raleigh, one of the mechanics lolling against a tool shed drinking RC told me I was probably looking for Sister Marks, who used to be around. He didn't really know about her, but the station manager did. When I asked him, he frowned, "Why you want to see her? She done hoodooed everybody and skipped out of here one night." Walking back to my car I passed two local black men who'd overheard the conversation and said if I was looking for a hoodoo what I really needed to do was go to Laurel. Sister Mary, that's where everyone went now.

Before adding any more names to the list, I decided to run over to Heidelberg to see if Sister Plummer existed. There wasn't much of a crowd along the two-block main street, but a couple of oldtimers on the corner drinking from brown paper bags seemed open to the questions of wandering writers. The first man didn't know of Sister Plummer, of course, but, passing the bottle, said his friend did. The friend took a short swig and said that was true. When I asked where she was he said he couldn't give me the directions but if I'd give him a ride he'd just show me. We made our way up a hilly road past a farm equipment store and turned into a driveway for a house and a converted trailer. "That's where she is," he said. I parked next to the trailer and he walked over to the house to join a group of his buddies drinking beer. They all waved.

Sister Plummer wore purple culottes and a purple blouse, had curlers in her hair and was frying chicken for lunch. A thirty-eight-year-old black woman, with Asian-Indian blood from her mother's side, she had been brought up in the Holiness church,

Sister Plummer's house, rear, Heidelberg, Mississippi.

a fundamentalist Protestant denomination. We sat at her kitchen table while a teenage son took care of a younger child and watched TV. She said she knew people called her a hoodoo woman but she really only counseled, mostly women and mostly about love, though she also gave readings using the Bible. She felt she had psychic abilities.

Her line on hoodoo was not far from Sarah Albritton's: "It's just like it is with sin. You either for God and have faith in God or you're in with the Devil." It was true, "people with weak minds" did come to see her, thinking they had been fixed, but she considered them more with pity than concern. "If you believe and have faith and trust, how you gonna believe someone can hurt you? That mean you really don't trust God."

I asked if business were good. She said it was mostly drop-in clientele, and not that much of it. There wasn't a fee, but people usually left something as a gratuity. She laughed. "But if they left a lot I wouldn't be living in no trailer park."

—=—

In Laurel, a sleepy railroad town of 21,000 just above the boot heel, I tried to find Sister Mary. It didn't take long; she advertised. But as soon as I saw the characteristic red out-turned palm on the big sign in her front yard, not far from the airport, I regretted having made the drive. Nothing ventured nothing gained, I parked in the driveway next to a half-dozen late model pickups, probably belonging to clients.

A graying white woman, possibly part-American Indian, barely opened the front porch door. I had to introduce myself like some kind of vacuum cleaner salesman. She gave me a cold once over. I showed her a business card, elaborated a little more, and requested a brief interview. When that failed, I asked for a reading at her regular rates. "Maybe next time," she said, closing the door in my face. I left and swore I'd never visit another palm reader.

But Laurel looked to me like a hoodoo town, and I remembered one of the friends of Reverend Buckley, the two-headed man back in Ruston, saying he'd grown up near Laurel and that there was plenty of hoodooing. So I drove around, past Depression-era storefronts downtown and pre-fab retail strips on the highway. Clearly, the place I had to go was across the tracks.

The town instantly descended into ghetto. Unpaved streets, uncollected trash. Many of the homes, from turn-of-the-century farm houses with the farms long gone, to tarpaper shacks, seemed abandoned. Broken windows and rusty cars everywhere. Each time I went up to a house where someone lived I was utterly rebuffed by walls of silence and suspicion.

Further efforts seemed hopeless so I got back in my car and was driving away when I passed a taxi stand/barbecue joint— not a bad entrepreneurial idea. I needed a lead and sandwich, so I decided to take a chance on both. The dispatcher, a large man cooling in front of a rotary desk fan, suggested if I wanted to find "spiritual healers" I'd be better off trying the "other colored town" down past the fork near the railroad underpass. The chopped pork I could get right there. I took some with me.

I eventually found the place he meant, a modest black working class area of shotgun style houses and narrow, but paved, streets. I'd gone down about two blocks when the deluge resumed. Exasperated and cranky, maybe from hunger, I pulled over to the side and ate, and waited. From time to time I rubbed condensation from the windows to see, but what was there to see? Noah had better weather. I slumped back in the seat. My luck, if any, seemed to be stretching awfully thin—could it be Elegba was sporting with me? The Divine Trickster was known for that. He kept you in line. Humble.

Then, as fast as it had turned on, the faucet turned off. The late afternoon sun popped out and the steaming streets were alive with children, dogs, cats, caterpillars and everything else in creation pent up by the storms. Directly across the street, several couples in their twenties emerged from a green frame house to fire up a charcoal grill. They were drinking beer and unwinding from the workday. I felt bad about carping about Elegba. Maybe he was going to give me a break after all. I walked over through the drizzle to introduce myself. Maybe they thought anyone going to that much trouble ought to be heard out, or maybe they were especially convivial from the beer, but they invited me up on the front porch.

All of them had heard hoodoo tales but nobody admitted to believing in hexes: "It don't work unless you got a weak mind," said the handsome, muscular man in a gimme cap tending the charcoal, echoing Sister Plummer. "I got a strong mind." His wife, a pretty woman in a red striped T-shirt, said hoodooing wasn't all that common, really, though she did recall one man she knew who'd gotten very sick because his girlfriend had been fixing him by putting menstrual blood in his food. The husband and the other two men on the porch nodded; they remembered that. Other than that no one knew anything about hoodoos or root doctors. But they knew someone who did.

"Go talk to Miss Maidie," said the man with the strong mind. "She can tell you about it. She's been around here a long time." He pointed to a house three doors down. I could barely see it because of thick bushes and plants growing all around the front screen porch.

Miss Maidie was shelling snap beans into a bowl when I walked up, but quickly put her labors down to open the door, glad to have company. A small woman in her mid-eighties, with light chocolate skin and hair so gray it seemed to have been powdered, she bore the signs of a long-past beauty; like Miss Eddie, she also was part Choctaw. Pointing to a chair next to her own on the small wooden porch, she invited me to sit—a welcome invitation not only because of the chance to talk but because it had started sprinkling again.

She said I was wasting my time if I wanted to ask her about voudou because she didn't know much about it. I believed her, but I had learned to put disclaimers in context. Like Uncle Clem, Miss Maidie wouldn't have known an African god from apple juice, but she, too, had lived her entire life influenced by the unacknowledged traditions of such gods. Clem had stories of farm life and home remedies; hers were of a natural way of eating. "What makes us sick today is the food we eating," she told me. "It's all that fertilizer. When I was growing up we didn't have that. Now you get sick from buying food at the store." She pointed out a half-dozen plants, tomatoes to parsley, she maintained in her front yard.

I smiled, thinking of the "new" natural food stores. Black people, especially in the South, have long based their lives around a vegetable-heavy diet, and shunned store-bought ingredients. Down-home cooking, or soul food, is really based on purposeful combinations of home-grown produce or livestock. Poverty has altered that wholesome, natural diet, especially for those in the cities, who have come to rely on cheap starches and drive-through junk, leading in turn to a high incidence of heart disease, obesity and related problems. Older African Americans, at least the ones like Miss Maidie, who haven't been trampled beyond repair, still think of food as "good for you" in the most fundamental sense. The white society which once enslaved them has not yet poisoned them. Like the Rastafarians of the Caribbean, they have stayed close to the earth, which they can trust, and which is, as the ancient priests of voudou knew, the source of mortal power and health.

It had gotten into twilight by the time we finished talking. I decided to drive back to Meridian for the evening. En route, the June rain turned to pelting sheets. The radio talked about tornadoes in Alabama, which wasn't that far away. I got stuck behind a line of pickups and we slowed to ten mph, barely able to see through the downpour. Chunks of pine branches blew out of the forest to litter the highway. Tornado bank clouds of black and green rolled up, filled with lightning flashes.

I didn't quite outrun it. I got back to my motel tired, wet and hungry. Talking to Miss Maidie had deterred me from grabbing a quick greaseburger en route. Another Sarah's Kitchen would've been perfect but I was too exhausted to look for one, so settled on a Thai restaurant called Faraway Places, only four blocks down. I sat at the bar, studying the many Buddhist statues and altars along the walls. Kind of unusual in Mississippi. I said so to the owner, a Thai woman named Tim, as she took my order for lemon grass soup. She laughed and said she was aware of that. We talked a little, and I asked if she knew anything about voudou.

She said she just knew it had something to do with spirits in Africa. I asked if she thought it was satanic. She shook her head. People told her the same thing about Buddhism all the time. She said there were many different ways of believing, and to her, voudou was just one more. It didn't bother her. She was the first person I had met of any gender, race or nationality for whom the mention of voudou did not trigger even the remotest unease.

Just as I was feeling good about that, a thirty-ish blonde holding a highball glass came up to stand next to me. She and her husband—their khaki, madras and loafers marked them as Southern gentry—had been eavesdropping from the corner of the bar. She said she was interested in voudou but didn't I know it really *was* a form of satanism? I said that was the kind of remark I'd expect from a Baptist. She laughed aggressively. She was no Baptist. She was Catholic. She turned away and ambled slowly back to her husband, who had just punched in a Jimmy Buffet song at the jukebox.

That night I slept fitfully, thoughts of Buddha, the orisha, of philosophers and poets, and thoughts of Tim's curvy beauty and even thoughts about the blonde's legs, Southern nights being what they are, but mostly thoughts of how and what and why I was where I was. If Elegba was helping me, was this the best I could look foward to?

Some time later, a professor of anthropology challenged me to justify my meanderings. He wanted an empirical methodology. I understood his need, but the spirit world is immune, even hostile, to systematic inquiry. Paradigmatic research produces paradigmatic truths. That is, if you know what you're looking for, you'll certainly find it. So, yes, I was inefficient, random, foolish. Truly, these faults weighed on me. But the hunt was taking its own shape. Voudou in America: So close I could breathe it; so chimerical it evaporated like that same breath on a mirror.

The next day I left Mississippi and crossed eastward into Alabama. I can't say I ever felt comfortable there. It's a beautiful state—lush rolling hills tapering off from the bottom of the Appalachian chain, acres of blue lakes, endless evergreen forests. It boasts important military bases like Ft. Rucker, the Army aviation school, and has attracted some of the New Plantation Economy industry, and yet it's another country, was even home to an infamous right-wing mercenary training center for awhile. I felt I had crossed not only a state line, but a psychological one. Of all the southern states, Alabama has always been the most intransigent to integration and acquiesent to racism.

My route would take me through several towns which once stretched across the front lines of the civil rights movement: Demopolis, on the western edge of the state, and then across to Selma and Montgomery. For a change, I had someone to contact—Julia Mae Haskins Foster, a forty-four-year-old African-American school teacher who had settled in Demopolis. A friend of mine had had an unrequited crush on her when he, a white college student, was working on voter registration in the mid-1960s with SNCC (Student Nonviolent Coordinating Committee). She'd also been an activist, and had joined the famous fifty-mile protest march from Selma to Montgomery. Her older brother Jim Haskins, now living in New York, had made numerous contacts among local healers for *Voodoo and Hoodoo,* his thoughtful 1978 account of hexes and spell-making.

I crossed the Tombigbee River on Highway 43 and drove through the Demopolis town square, complete with its Confederate monument and quiet perimeter of family-owned retail stores—the kind malls destroy. As in many small towns, the white section lay to one side, the black, known here as the New Quarters, to the other. Which was where Julia Mae lived with her father and children.

I could see why my friend had been smitten. Less obvious was why the Haskins had taken him under their roof. A movement house—one committed to providing refuge to civil rights workers—it was already a twenty-four-hour-a-day target for the Klan. But the movement involved all colors, and in those days more than one white person took shelter with this remarkable African-American family. Nor was the danger ever underestimated. It was not uncommon for the Haskins place, where Dr. King, too, had once stayed, to pass the night under armed protection. In the worst times, up to twenty people had lain outside the house through the dawn to fend off terrorist bombers and snipers euphemized as "night riders."

But civil rights work wasn't the only thing in the Demopolis air. One of the most famous of the Alabama hoodoo men had lived in the block just behind the Haskins. Cars with out-of-state licenses, black and white folk, had for years lined the street late at night waiting to see Dr. Holloway and receive his cures and readings. He had since died of cancer, although at least one of his sons was said to still do work out on Highway 80.

That seemed a good place to begin, and I tried to reach him through one of Dr. Holloway's grandchildren, now living in the home behind the Haskins, but she was unable or unwilling to provide a phone number. Shifting plans, Julia and I went into the projects to search out a woman who reportedly did some hoodoo, but after making the rounds we decided it was probably just a rumor. That only left Miss Patsy.

Julia's older brother Alfred wanted to go with us and later that afternoon we drove deeper into the New Quarters, where the pavement turned to dirt and the houses hung together in disrepair. Heat had forced most people inside in front of fans or, if they could afford it, air conditioners. I saw almost no one except a few children lounging under a shade tree and heard nothing save the intermittent yelping of a hound dog. We pulled up to a brown clapboard set back amid a muddy lot, surrounded by a few big hardwoods. An iron kettle and some yard junk had accumulated to the side of a cluttered front porch. So had two huge dogs—a snarling black Lab mix and a dirty yellow mongrel the size of a bear. As a replication of the prototypical little hoodoo shack on the wrong side of town, it was without peer.

Ignoring his sister's caution, Alfred got out of the car to go knock on the door. As soon as he did the Lab leapt forward to attack, tearing at his jeans until Miss Patsy came out on the porch and called the animal off. Julia yelled out an introduction through her half-cracked window but it seemed useless. Not budging, Miss Patsy said she didn't want to talk to "no white man," and went back inside, slamming the door. Alfred scrambled back inside the car unhurt but shaken by the attack. We took him back to the Haskins place. I asked Julia if we might try again.

We drove up slowly and parked in the same spot but this time made no attempt to get out. Miss Patsy came down to the car. Her dogs followed. I rolled down the window and told her what I wanted. I don't know what changed her mind, but she said it would be okay after all to come sit on the porch "if all you want is to talk." I looked at the dogs. She said they wouldn't bother me if I didn't act up. Julia, though also invited, stayed in the car. I wasn't sure why she wanted to minimize her involvement until later.

Another part-Choctaw, Miss Patsy had been doing "spiritual advising" for nearly forty years, and I judged her for about sixty. She learned much of her craft from the late Joe King, her former common law husband and a locally famous hoodoo man. As stipulated, she wouldn't let me into her house to show me the small room where she gave occasional readings, at $15 per session, but told me there wasn't much in it except a table and the Bible. "My power comes from the Lord," she said. "Hoodoo spells must come from the Devil."

But spell-making was clearly part of her repertoire. As we talked further, she opened up enough to admit that her clients commonly suffered from hexes, usually about romance. And although it was true that she used the Bible, she told me she also frequently prepared potions, teas or other concoctions. Taking a chance, I asked if she performed animal sacrifices. She didn't answer. The silence—which I took as a yes—lasted so long I thought the interview might be over. Trying to direct the subject away from an area in which she obviously seemed threatened—animal sacrifice was illegal, for whatever motive—I asked if she had ever heard anything about the African gods. I dropped a few names—Elegba, Shango, Obatala—but it was obvious she'd never heard of them.

By now she'd received me for about fifteen minutes and that was at least fourteen minutes longer than she wanted to. She sat tense and tight in her chair, her pursed-up lips concealing a strained, gap-toothed smile. A teenage boy, perhaps a grandson, came out of the house, looked around, then went back in. The two dogs had settled a snarl away on the porch steps. We were done. I stood up and gave her my card. I said I'd like to come back. She said goodbye.

Julia drove me back to her house. On the way I invited her to have dinner with me, in gratitude for her assistance. Her face flushed a little. She appreciated the offer, but she didn't think it would be a good idea for her to be seen with a white man like that. I told her she must be joking. It was a small town, she said.

I went to my motel and changed into my shorts and Nikes. I tried to run a few miles at least every other day, no matter where I was, a practice which more than once made me look even stranger than merely being a traveling white man looking for hoodoo doctors. Jogging in Demopolis, Alabama, or Starkville, Mississippi, isn't exactly like going around a hike and bike trail in your local community park. I headed up the grass-filled median along the highway to Selma, past tractor sales lots, barbecue stands, convenience stores and all the familiar landmarks of retail strip ugliness. Later that night, I ate alone.

In the morning I went back to the Haskins's to say goodbye. Julia Mae was going to work but wanted to tell me something. Someone had called her and told her to "be careful no one throw some powder on me for taking a white man 'round." I didn't say anything—no wonder she'd sat in the car. "I hope nothin' happen to you, either," Julia Mae added. We both laughed, mostly because we both knew such hexes were ridiculous, but just a little because we weren't completely sure. Then I went to the hoodoo shack again.

It was bothering me that Miss Patsy had been so secretive. It was making me mad. I found her house without much trouble and parked by the porch, but before I could get out, the hounds from hell were at my window. I had no choice but to wait for their master. When she came down from the porch she let the dogs circle and growl and told me to stay in the car.

I said okay, but that I'd come back not just to talk but to pay for a reading. She shook her head. "I'm pretty busy." I said I could come back when she was free. She shook her head again. "I don't know when I'll have time." I asked if I could pay her just to have a look at the room in which she gave readings. "That's not to show," she said.

"I'm not out to steal anything or any secrets."

"I know."

"I just want to help make of record of your work, put you in history." It sounded lame to me, too, especially delivered through a half-open window guarded by junk yard mongrels. I sighed and told her I'd leave. She and the dogs walked toward the porch but watched to make sure I really drove off. And I did, cursing that snaggle-tooth mean old lady halfway to Selma. I didn't know why it had gotten to me that much. It didn't seem to be about race or even fear—or the cautions Julia Mae had exercised. Miss

Patsy had shut me out cold. In my pique—at that moment—I could only see two reasons for her doing so: (1) she had some heavy stuff in there and didn't want me to see it, or (2) she didn't. The more I drove, the more I dwelt on the latter. A hoodoo practitioner who's any good doesn't live hand to mouth—he or she has a list of clients to fill a book, and does not shrink from contact but welcomes it. Obscurity is the ally only of those who deal in ignorance. And voudou is nothing if not knowledge, especially self-knowledge. Five and dime palmistry and shotgun shack root doctors were for the foolish and the gullible. How I had tired of spiritual shell-games! I felt myself sinking more than ever in the diminution of the voudou legacy, in despair at the endless ways it had mutated, contorted.

To be a priest of voudou one must prepare, study, sacrifice, devote oneself to the spirits. To be a hoodoo one might get away with a simple bent towards bunko. A hoodoo woman simply confused and distracted those who came to her, teaching them not the path to power, which is the path of self-revelation and devotion, but encouraging the idea of quick fixes, literally and figuratively.

The hell with hoodoo, I decided, driving through the flat farmland and pine forests. I should just leave it to its own chicanery. Hoodoo is the worst kind of lie, what the academics call a simulacrum, a contrivance substituting itself for the real thing. How useful to the old anti-voudou campaigns to have the great African religion thus reduced to snakes in your stomach and menstrual blood in your coffee. Who, black or white, could take something like that seriously?

I passed a logging truck like it was standing still, and noticed I was going about eighty-five. I slowed down; my foul mood was translating too easily into bad driving. Not once in my trip had I seen a shrine, or an altar, or heard a minor conversation about the orisha, or seen the slightest recognition of a connection between the hexing to the ancient knowledge. Maybe I would never find the missing links. For several miles I weighed that possibility. Maybe my theory was just plain wrong. What wishful thinking or arrogance had made me think I would find voudou inside the trappings of hoodoo? I was nothing more than a crazy prospector, a seeker of pyrite.

In my funk, I drifted back to a telephone conversation a couple of years earlier with Luisah Teish, whose *Jambalaya: The Natural Woman's Book of Personal Charms and Practical Rituals,* recounted her own journey into the African spirit world. She, too, had encountered stonewalling, ignorance and fear. But she'd seen it more objectively than I seemed to be able to do.

"You had people having to pretend they were Christian while holding on to their African ways," she had told me from her home in San Francisco. "The next generation remembers the ways, but doesn't remember the reasons. The next generation . . . keeps some of the ways but all they remember of the content is that it's dangerous to identify with the African race. They've lost the theology, but they've kept the practice." Teish had paused a moment. She herself had embraced the danger—her search for the theology had led her to initiation as a daughter of Oshun.

"They've also kept the fear. The fear is righteous in that there's no reason for people to trust the Constitution when it says there's freedom of religion. So now you'll get people who, if you say the word 'voudou' to them, they'll say they're damn good Christians and want nothing to do with it."

Recalling the conversation slowly brought my anger under control.

Ranting against hoodoo was ranting against history.

Of course hoodoo was a debasement of the real thing. Slavery was a debasement of real people.

I had become lost in my own ego.

In Selma, I stopped for coffee. The town was now clean and relatively prosperous—even had a black mayor. It seemed to be trying hard to overcome its image from the 1960s, when police used dogs and cattle prods and fire hoses on marchers and the name Selma was synonymous for violent bigotry. Watching the people come and go on the sidewalks outside the small cafe where I sat, I felt my anger and frustration dissolve. I stopped feeling contemptuous toward Miss Patsy. I remembered what a voudou priest once said to me: "It's true, some of these people working out there might not have the knowledge or even be aware of the spirit—they don't know any of the orishas or anything—but that doesn't mean the orisha aren't working through them."

"We have a saying among the Yoruba," he had said. "Those people that are born in it, those that are selected for it, and those people who out of their own desire would like to be part of it—the most effective are those who are born in it."

—=—

The next fifty miles of highway, the one the protest marches had taken, led to Montgomery, where the young Martin Luther King, Jr., had preached from the pulpit of Dexter Avenue Baptist Church. The highway became a traffic-clogged artery leading past suburban shopping malls into the antebellum gentility that is the capital of Alabama and at least a sentimental holdout of the Old Confederacy. The Stars and Bars flew at the Capitol.

I had a fast-food lunch near the capitol complex downtown and used the pay phone to call the Southern Poverty Law Center, a nonprofit group which specializes in suits against hate groups. I had thought perhaps someone over there might know of a possible lead in the area. I wasn't expecting much, but I did expect at least to be able to visit. I couldn't. The telephone receptionist, quite politely, refused to tell me how to find the Center. Nor would she make an appointment for me with the director, attorney Morris Dees. Finally she told me it would be better not to come over at all, as I wouldn't be admitted.

I said, "What is this, Beirut?"

"You never know who might come over," she said. "Our old building got bombed."

I tried to visit anyway, and she was right, I couldn't get past the electronically locked entry doors. I remembered Julia Mae Haskins worrying about having dinner with a white man. This was three decades after Rosa Parks ignited the twentieth-century civil rights movement by refusing to sit in the back of a Montgomery bus.

The fear remained, and remained righteous. For a slave religion to have survived it in any form was evidence of a valor and steadfastness that reduced my critiques of hoodoo authenticity to Monday morning quarterbacking. I drove away eastward toward the Georgia border humbled and awed, and also a little sad. There was too much to learn, too much already gone.

# 12

## · CROSSING THE LINE

THE RELENTLESS RAIN that had dogged me had been no stranger to Atlanta, either. A curtain of gray steam, punctuated here and there by torrential cloudbursts, almost obscured the downtown skyline as I came in from Montgomery. The Georgia capital felt much better to me than had the one in Alabama. Here, blacks had moved into positions of real power, politically and socially. Legions of unsolved problems remained, as they do in every American city, but on the whole, Atlanta was known as a progressive town, a magnet for ambitious young people, black and white. The colonial and antebellum gentility of the older parts of the city often segued into the upscale shopping villages and refurbished homes of the city's yuppie contingents in the north and east. Along with Dallas, Atlanta was the hot place to be in the New Plantation Economy.

I had come to find two voudou priests. Not hoodoo men or root doctors. The real thing. I longed to be back among the true believers. I missed my conversations with Ava Kay Jones, priestess of Oya. I missed my visits with Lorita Mitchell, priestess of Oshun. It was time to accelerate my movement into the true world of the orisha. I wanted to know more of the complex Ifa divination system, its name derived from the god who bestowed it, of the ritual of voudou life and practice, of the intricacies of the theology. I missed the gods.

The two priests I had come to see were cousins, Panamian-born but U. S. residents for years. The older, Baba Oshun Kunle, was a babalawo, the highest priestly order in voudou, interpreter of Ifa. The other, Baba Tunde, was a priest of Obatala. I had originally met them in New Orleans, where they had flown in to give readings for a week—it is a common practice among priests to maintain a clientele in various cities. We'd had a pleasant conversation in the patio garden behind Ava Kay's botanica, Jambalaya, and they had offered to see me if I ever got to Georgia.

Approaching the southwestern Atlanta neighborhood where they lived, I thought I must have had the directions mixed up. A busy, ugly exit off the interstate descended pitilessly into a blighted tract of duplexes and apartments grisled with corner liquor stores and tough guys hanging out looking for action. It seemed to me the two priests had a good business and could have done better for themselves. And then I considered the nature of their business. Practicing voudou priests would be noticed, but in a bad area, nobody cared what you did for a living. Even the black middle class was a long way from accepting voudou as a valid option, and it would scare hell out of most New Age white people, who probably wouldn't live in integrated parts of town anyway.

I turned right at the street name I'd marked on my map and the scenery got a little better. Weekly rentals with underpowered window units and beer bottles in the yards gave way to sturdy, almost stately wooden homes on sprawling lots full of moss-covered trees. Probably a turn-of-century neighborhood that had hit the skids and, looked at in the right way, might be rebounding. Then I spotted the spacious, robin's egg-blue two-story house Baba Tunde had described.

Rear view, home of Baba Oshun Kunle and Baba Tunde, Atlanta, Georgia.

I parked and walked under droopy oaks still dripping from the rain to the chain link fence gate at the side—"where the clients go." As soon as I saw the back yard I could see that the unassuming front really was a façade—the action was all in the opposite direction. How voudou-like. What you see is the reverse of what you get. The yard was about a quarter of a football field deep, covered on each side by trees and fence. A driveway connecting to an alley ran the length of the left side. An old sedan was parked up close to a small concrete patio near the house. Most of the right half of the yard was given over to a garden, laden with vegetables and herbs, and a stock pen, filled with pigeons, chickens and goats. Everything was flooded.

Breaching the gate, I stepped rock to rock through ankle-deep puddles toward the two screen doors at the back of the house. The one on the right was at the top of an exterior wooden staircase, and most likely led to the upstairs living area. The other seemed to be the entry to some sort of basement, perhaps

Basement of Atlanta home. Marcus Garvey Centennial poster on wall. Ibeji likenesses on top shelf. Pies and pastries on table for bimbé.

an office. I was pretty sure it was for me. The lower door was partly open, but I thought it best not to just walk in, so I knocked and waited. Presently I heard the mellifluous Caribbean tones of Baba Tunde. When he saw me he smiled broadly and, apologizing for the effects of the rain, showed me into a spartan waiting room.

In Yoruba, "baba tunde" means "grandfather returns," and one thus born is considered to bear the traits of his ancestor. Baba Tunde had been born within twenty-four hours of the death of Baba Kunle's grandfather, and in the same hospital. That not only bound the two cousins, but, according to Tunde, accounted for his psychic sensibilities. He listed himself on his business card as both a priest and a "trance medium," although, strictly speaking, the latter wasn't voudou nomenclature. I think he thought it would be something clients could more easily comprehend. And "trance medium" sounded more professional than saying he was easily possessed by spirits of the dead.

Water had collected in sloshy pools where the floor slanted down, but the second-hand sofa and coffee table were dry. Glancing around what reminded me, oddly, of a graduate student's living room, I noticed a statue of the Ibeji on a metal bookshelf. Also several earthen and wooden pots, and a sign that said, "Prosperity." A shakeree lay on a chair. A discount stereo unit was tuned to a classical station. Among the wall posters was a Senegalese print celebrating the Marcus Garvey Centennial (1887–1987).

Baba Tunde explained that he had to go back upstairs because he and Baba Kunle were seeing a client, a mortician from Alabama, who had been there all morning. Besides that, he said, tomorrow they were traveling to Jamaica and had to pack. He asked if I could wait, apologized again about the flooding, and excused himself. An hour later, when he returned, apologizing for the delay, he told me that he and his cousin had decided the best way to start our visit was for me to have a reading. It would cost $35. This was slightly unexpected, but I agreed. Later I would learn that an up-front reading with a stranger was virtually de rigeur among priests. It was, if nothing else, a way to screen unwelcome or untruthful visitors—cops, for example.

Baba Tunde led me down a white hallway to a maze of other rooms in the lower level. We passed several orisha altars before ducking under a white hanging drape into an all-white ceremonial chamber the size of a small bedroom. A white sheet had been stretched across one corner behind a slim white statue, stylized as an old man, representing Obatala, to whom the room was consecrated. Because the deity is revered for wisdom and intellect, his priests often become arrogant. But there is no justification for it in the religion itself. All the orisha have different qualities, and none is considered "superior" to the others— except Olorun, the supreme being.

There wasn't much in the room other than the motif of purity. A low wooden table toward one side held a clear bowl, candles, a photograph of an unidentified man, and eight glasses of water. A plain mat of woven grass, the kind you can buy for the beach, was positioned opposite a single wicker chair. Between the chair and mat was a shallow basket for cowrie shells and next to that a small bowl of water, some sea shells and small stones.

Baba Tunde offered me the chair, and sat himself cross-legged on the mat at my feet. He began the reading by asking me to fold the $35 and hold it in my right hand. As I did, he began the invocation to the orisha, speaking in the Yoruba language. He then instructed me to put my money on a tray, and gave me a stone and a shell to shake in my cupped hands. After that I took one object in each hand and made a fist, enclosing each. Baba Tunde proceeded to throw the sixteen cowries—the principal divining instrument of a babalorisha, or iyalorisha, father or mother of the spirits, respectively, a senior priest one rung lower than a babalawo. According to legend, the cowrie secrets were obtained by Oshun through seduction of her husband, Ifa. She had complained that iyalorisha were not permitted to cast with the palm nuts (ikin) or chain (opele) used by male babalawos and thus could not share the secrets of divination. Ifa relented to her charms and imparted his secrets, but only if she restricted their use to the cowries (caracoles in santeria), leaving the opele and ikin exclusively for the powerful, cliquish, and territorial babalawos. In a way, Oshun became a feminist hero of voudou mythology.

Baba Tunde made several throws. I could see by the expression on his face that the reading was not going well for me. He saw waves, he said; he saw difficulties. He marked the odu figures, determined by how many shells in each cast fell "face up" or "face down," in a spiral notebook, and then leaned back against the wall.

Because he was also a trance medium, Baba Tunde frequently dropped into a possessed state. As though speaking from another body, as the psychic Margaret had done, he began to tell me of problems within my family about which I had told him nothing. He knew of this, he said, because of a spirit which had been speaking very strongly through the reading—the spirit of my father. Baba Tunde's eyelids opened as the trance passed. Perusing his notebook, he returned to the exegesis of the shells.

I was "very close" to Obatala, he said, and should consider his ways. "His pace is very slow. He takes care of things one at a time. You study the snail. It takes its time in its moves. If there's going to be danger, the snail is going to stop. He's going to think before he makes a move. So that any time you make a move it's a sure move. Your reading is speaking strongly of Obatala. He is one of the forces that is close to you.

"You have to thank Obatala for making it possible for you to be receptive, to be allowed in different houses and to meet the people that you have met. It's not a coincidence . . . and it's very unusual. It's very seldom you see white folks seeking the knowledge. Somewhere back there your ancestors had some connection with this."

He stopped, as if something had come to him. "In some time another way back, in some incarnation, you was black. You understand? And it happened to be you came into this incarnation. That's why that spirit is there. It's speaking of a black female spirit that is there, that was into all of these things, a black woman, a black spirit. It could be many generations back, you was a black woman who used to deal in this, was a priest but used to deal in this. And you come into this existence as a white person and you don't understand the attraction and the pulling that you have for this whole thing."

I told him my ancestors were all Welsh, German and Irish, which though not a bad pool for the spirit world, nevertheless were not African. Curiously, it was not the last time I would be told this, and the psychic association raised some fundamental questions about divination, especially subjective projection. Was it so unfathomable that a white man sought familiarity with an African religion that the only explanation was the presence of an African ancestral past? Or was there an ancestry of which I was utterly unaware? Certainly there was nothing within memory of recent generations. But reincarnation did not necessarily follow strict family genealogy. In the world of voudou, a spirit waiting to be reborn petitions to Olorun, who then assigns it an earthly vessel of life. Baba Tunde himself is a reincarnation. In my case, perhaps a black woman from Nigeria had come back as a white boy born in Ohio and then reared in the South. I guess that would explain one or two quirks in my personality. But, if one accepts voudou theology, such a possibility is far from unusual, and no less strange than the idea of the Holy Ghost inhabiting the souls of preachers, prophets, warriors, or messiahs.

Another possibility, raised later by someone else, was that the African spirit guiding me might belong to that of a person that someone in my genealogical family had helped at some time in the past—possibly a runaway slave. I was never able to corroborate that through any knowledge of family history. Baba Tunde also said I was giving off strong indications of an American Indian background, another link of which I am unaware.

The question of lineage became as pointed as it was crucial. How should I interpret divination which seemed as farfetched as a cross-racial background in the world of my ancestors? And yet that was what the odu had indicated to more than one babalorisha and babalawo. Of course, priests have been wrong—the odu have been interpreted incorrectly, and no, I don't think or presume that I am in any way or in any sense African—but why *was* I doing all this? Could I absolutely dismiss the possiblity of an African spirit in my past? Logically, I could not. To that extent, I could not *not* believe in Baba Tunde's intuition, nor anyone else's.

As Tunde spoke, Baba Kunle quietly entered the room to sit cross-legged on the floor near us. Tall and elegant, like his younger cousin, he wore only a white caftan and sandals. He was more powerfully built than Tunde, and his mid-forties voice much deeper, and although his air of authority intimidated me in a way that his cousin's more easygoing manner did not, in truth he was a kind man.

He studied the sequence of odu in Tunde's notebook. He, too, saw a spirit guiding me, and said it might lead me to eventually want to undertake full voudou initiation rites. I knew that some of the most authoritative of the white voudou scholars— William Bascom, Maya Deren, and Robert Farris Thompson— had all been initiated in the course of their encounters with the religion, but I told Kunle I was not yet sure if I could take that step. "Anyway," he said, "you have a spirit about you that possibly welcomes you or makes it possible for you to enter certain quarters." He told me to guard against having my research used for disrespectful ends.

Tunde, reviewing his own entries, interrupted: "Obatala is saying you have to organize your life. Everything is in the air, is like at a standstill. It's frustrating you, playing a mental thing with you, playing tricks with you. You have to be careful not to feel that you're losing your mind. Strong Obatala here. He is the one who will help you to put this in order." He said my personal, emotional life was not being taken care of, a topic he'd addressed in his trances. I was alone too much, he said, and needed recreation—a woman. No kidding. "Your life seems to be going too much one way. My mother always says, 'Too much of one thing is good for nothing.'"

Kunle nodded. It was now time for the parable, the symbolic tale to illustrate the cautions they had seen in my reading. Known as apataki, parables are an intrinsic element of a true reading. They are both voluminous—thousands of them—and formal, each parable linked to a specific odu pattern. Priests must memorize the stories in the parables as well as the proper pairing with the odu. Thus priests become not only diviners, but storytellers. Usually, the parables involve animals, or even plants, which act like humans, whether for good or ill. It wasn't much of a stretch to re-see Uncle Remus (Br'er Rabbit, Br'er Fox, etc.), despite his "creation" by Joel Chandler Harris, a white author, as another footprint along the voudou trail.

My own apataki was about a pig.

"There is this farmer that raised pigs for slaughter," Kunle began, as though narrating a movie I couldn't see. "He would fatten up his pigs, pen them off and when it's time, the fattest one would go. And there's this one pig that is a little bit wiser that refused to eat because he saw all the fat pigs going for slaughter. In the meantime, he was being thin and not fat like the other pigs. He was digging a hole in the back of the corral so that he could sneak out and not be a candidate for slaughter."

He paused to let me consider the tale. Now it was his duty to interpret it for me. "So the oracle is saying to you, number one, be careful where you eat, who feeds you. . . . Be very discreet about what you're doing. Let no one know what you're doing."

I could tell that Kunle saw something in the casting of the shells that troubled him. "Your reading says osobo (a blockage). There is some loose ends, some waves in the path."

I wasn't sure what that meant. He told me.

"When there's osobo, we do ebo."

I breathed in a little. So there it was.

Baba Kunle picked up the shells and cast again. He wanted to determine the exact nature and cost of the sacrifice. In ancient Africa, the price was precisely denoted in terms of cowrie shells—for monetary units, a larger kind than in divination. Now, like Latin Mass, the final tally is stated in the vernacular. I would require both sacrifice and a cleaning, and it would cost $150.

I was asked to leave $60 as a deposit, with which they would purchase, with a substantial professional mark-up, the necessary ingredients: honey, palm oil, gin, and a rooster. Baba Kunle said to come back about nine that night. That would give them time to prepare for Jamaica, and by then it would be dark. It was June 21, the summer solstice. Baba Tunde showed me out, but at the gate I walked right through the puddles, soaking my shoes and pants.

———

Back in my motel, waiting, I tried meditating on the particulars of my reading, but mostly I was not wanting to think about the ebo. This was a line I had not crossed. Yet the more I considered it, the less it bothered me. It was something I had to do, and something I wanted to do. I felt drawn to it. Compelled. I had already stepped through the looking glass; of course I wanted to experience all the wonders. Not as a voyeur, though. That would never work. Whatever happened would happen. I knew sacrifice was holy, and I would accept it as such. I would cross the line and not look back.

I packed up my suitcase and checked out of the motel. I had decided to drive on later that night to Athens, a college town about ninety miles east of Atlanta. Athens didn't have much to do with my voudou search—it was mostly a nostalgic detour, or so I thought at the time. I'd gone to high school there. There, too, I'd fallen into apostasy. I had been baptized at age twelve in a small sect called the Christian Church in Bryan, Texas, and, after moving to Georgia, had switched to the Methodist denomination along with my family. In Athens, for a couple of years—in high school, no less—I had turned evangelical. I kept a Bible by my bed and read from it each night, went to church and Methodist Youth Fellowship, tried to convert friends. Then I stopped.

I can't pinpoint the moment, but I remember it had to do with segregation. I couldn't understand why blacks had to have their own churches, or schools, or drinking fountains. I couldn't understand why black students couldn't enroll at the University of Georgia, where my father taught. I couldn't understand why my minister and deacons let it be that way. Most of all, I couldn't understand why they insisted that the Bible itself believed in keeping the races apart. So I stopped believing in Christianity and in the church. I never went back. Nor had I ever been back to Athens. For the first time in years I thought it might be okay to return.

<hr>

It wasn't yet dark when I got back to the home of the priests. In the indigo and burnt orange dusk I could see neighbors moving in adjacent yards and the occasional car pass down the alley. The chickens in the pen were pecking about for the final bits of grain before bedding down for the night. The lush summer garden glistened like green velvet. The rain had stopped and the evening was cool, fresh, alive. I might have been in a painting by Rousseau.

I didn't want to go back into the basement—it seemed too claustrophobic—but Baba Tunde instructed me to do so right away. He wanted me to take a few moments to write down the names of all the people I wished to influence or gain access to as a result of the sacrifice. The point of the ebo was to remove what was blocking me. I should therefore know who or what I wanted to find as the result of the cleared path. This wasn't a game. Something would die for me in a few minutes and the gods would be asked to intervene for me. I'd better have a reason.

As I wrote names on a blank piece of paper, I could hear African music from a stereo and the priests singing upstairs. Outside, the skies passed purple into opaque until night provided the requisite cover. When it was completely dark, Baba Tunde came downstairs. He said it was time.

He led me outside past the patio to a tree at the edge of the yard. Kunle was already outside, leaning against the sedan in the driveway. Even in the dark, I could see the altar he had prepared for me at the base of the tree. It was a simple plate, adorned with candles and fruit, tucked in among altars and offerings for other clients and various gods—I recognized the conical, stylized head of Elegba next to my own prepared spot.

I also saw a human skull, I think, but I really couldn't make out everything in detail because of the glutinous, yellowish-orange residue that covered most of the tree trunk and entire altar collection. Oozing wax dripped from thousands of multi-colored candles would have created the same visual effect, but what I was seeing was more accurately the accumulation of months worth of dried blood (red), palm oil (orange-red), honey (yellow) and feathers. Soon I would add my own contribution.

Baba Tunde told me to take off my shoes and socks. When I did, I felt the cool wet mud rise through my toes. I took the remaining $90 for the ebo and wrapped it in a brown paper, folding it three times towards me, silently telling the ebo what I wanted. I gave the folded paper to Baba Kunle. He touched me with it on the forehead, used it to make the sign of the cross on my body, then put both the paper and the money in one of his pockets.

When that was done, Kunle turned to his stock of ingredients on a nearby chair and seemed to be emptying something into his hand. He turned and opened his palm, revealing what looked like birdshot but were actually peppercorns—a total of sixteen, the same as the number of cowries used in divination. He told me to open my right hand and when I did he gently poured the peppercorns into the cup of my palm.

"Chew them," he said, "but be careful not to swallow. Keep them in your mouth from now on. It's okay to swallow your spit." I ground them slowly with my molars. They were a little spicy but mostly just grainy. I salivated a lot and though I tried not to, I eventually swallowed most of the slush.

Baba Tunde told me to face the altar and asked for the paper with the names—I had come up with about a dozen. As soon as I gave Tunde the paper, Baba Kunle put a small, gray-flecked rooster into my hands. I hadn't even seen the bird. It wasn't just the darkness. So many things were happening so fast, and much of it through the Yoruba tongue, that each new command seemed to come from nowhere. I was never sure which of the priests would speak next, or what they would ask of me. But I knew I would accede. I knew what that meant for the young rooster, trembling in my hands.

I held it carefully, trapping its wings and feet so it couldn't get away, and continued to face the altar, silently repeating the favors I wanted from Elegba. I really did pray. When finished, I extended my arms to return the rooster. Baba Kunle accepted it, said a prayer in Yoruba, and moved up next to me.

Taking the bird between his hands as though it were a chalice, he began to clean me, rubbing the perimeter of my head, then all down my body, just as Lorita had used pigeons on her clients. It seemed as though something were being drawn away from me. The bird was motionless as a feather duster.

The two priests faced the altar and prayed in Yoruba to Elegba, Ogun, Obatala, Oshun and the other spirits. I turned to face the altar, too, thinking it best. Just as I did, Baba Kunle held the rooster away from his chest with his left hand and with his right deftly twisted the rooster's neck. In another quick motion he pulled off its head.

He dropped the head to the ground and held the body over the altar. Blood dripped across the god of the crossroads like rain on dry land. Then Kunle passed the decapitated torso over the paper with the names I'd provided. I watched blood slide across something I'd written. I felt an unwanted smile on my face, but then, I always laugh when I'm really frightened. Both priests continued to pray.

Kunle fell silent, turned, and stood directly in front of me, the headless rooster in his left hand. He brought the body up in front of my face and dipped the middle finger of his right hand into the neck socket. In the African way, Kunle placed his bloody fingertips to the middle of my brow, and traced a line to the back of my head. He then anointed his finger in the blood again, knelt at my feet, and marked dots of blood on both my big toes.

He rose, stepped over to the altar, and lay the carcass at its base, offering more prayers to the spirits. He pinched out some feathers and scattered them across the offering, then retrieved the bottle of gin—a favorite drink of Elegba—from his sack of ingredients on the chair. He took a mouthful and spewed it out over the headless ebo. Baba Tunde did the same. Then Kunle spewed another mist on my bare feet and the top of my head. It was cool, astringent, its juniper odor refreshing amid the sweet smell of blood and the tartness of my own sweat.

Baba Tunde knelt to wash his hands in a small container of water. Floating inside were four coconut shells—the obi, the divination implements I had encountered in what seemed light years ago in the French Quarter. Before casting the husks, Tunde cleaned me with them, as Kunle had done with the rooster. The first throw came up all black—husk side up. Oyekun: Danger. Of the five possible variables, oyekun was the worst—the ultimate negative.

Both priests fell silent a moment. They exchanged what sounded to me like dour intonations in Yoruba. Baba Kunle went immediately into the house. Tunde prayed. I just stood there.

Baba Kunle returned with three white candles. After cleaning me with one, he told me to hold it in my right hand. They lit the other two and planted them in the sticky mud around the altar. Tunde again cast the obi, several times.

I couldn't see which configurations came up, but on one cast, one of the shells flipped up against the ebo carcass, making the reading two black, two white—ejife, a very good sign. But because the husk had fallen against the ebo, the reading apparently was compromised. I could see the two priests were now even more bothered. Kunle bent down to pull more feathers from the ebo and throw them against the Elegba.

Baba Tunde cast again. I couldn't make out what it was, but it must have been at least a little more favorable. Neither priest spoke. As if something had finally been settled, Kunle leaned down to pick up the rooster's head and then its carcass, and put them in a brown paper bag. Instead of folding it shut, however, he set it on the ground, then poured palm oil and honey all over the remains of the ebo inside. When finished, he spewed out another mouthful of gin. He picked up the sack and brought it to me. He told me to spit everything from my mouth into the bag. Then he handed me the bag and told me to seal it shut.

While I did that, Kunle reached down for a gallon plastic jug—one I hadn't noticed before—filled with a thick, grayish liquid. I knew it wasn't palm oil. I took it in my free hand while Kunle gave me instructions for the completion of the ritual. Once I had left their house, I was to go directly back to my room and shower, then clean myself by pouring the liquid from the jug all over my naked body. I was not to wash it off until morning. Meanwhile, I was to throw away the paper bag containing the ebo. I was to leave the line of blood on my head until I showered.

That was it.

I looked at Baba Tunde—Kunle seemed too distant to approach. That didn't make me feel very serene. What about the four black shells, I asked. What did that mean? Tunde said, "You may be taking your R&R sooner than you had planned." He said I was overtaxed—this was the warning of the ebo. In such condition I could make a mistake. Take some days off right away, he said, preferably near an ocean.

I was planning to drive toward Oyotunji, a voudou community along the South Carolina seashore, after visting Athens, but I wasn't sure if this was a warning to skip Athens and head to the sea without delay. Baba Tunde shrugged, as if to say he'd said all he could. He told me goodbye and walked towards the house after Baba Kunle, who had left in complete silence.

I carried my jug of cleaning potion through the puddles and out to my car. I leaned against the bumper and put on my socks and shoes. I eased into the driver's seat and, while the interior light was on, glanced at myself in the rearview mirror. The blood on my head was vivid—a bright, wide stripe of red. I didn't know who was looking back, and yet I did. He came from some time that found its door in the mists of the spray of gin from a priest's mouth. He was a spirit, a spectre, a demon and a holy man, a blooded creature that felt at one with the heavens and with the flesh. He was invincible. He had dilated pupils and a smile.

I started the car, wheeled around in the street and peeled away back out onto the boulevard of liquor stores and desperadoes. They didn't faze me. They had no idea where I'd been. Near the freeway entrance I spotted a dumpster next to, what else, a fast food chicken outlet. I threw in the bag with the ebo.

Alive, the rooster had been a kind of spiritual sponge, a conduit whose life would gain the most meaning through service to the gods. Now, its own spirit had gone to the gods, and lived in them the way any food becomes part of those who eat it, or as communion crackers convey the spirit of Jesus into Christians. Now the rooster's carcass was just a toxic container filled with all my bad energy. I felt no more for it than for a dead chicken at Safeway. I was glad to be rid of it.

I headed towards Athens. I didn't see why I couldn't go to the ocean later. As I drove through the upscale enclaves of northeast Atlanta and out into the green, hilly, gorgeous and unre-

pentant Dixie that was rural Georgia, I rebelled against the undue caution of the two priests. I didn't feel *that* strung out. Maybe
they just weren't used to seeing writers on a long assignment.
You get wired in this kind of work; it's not unusual. But maybe
it was unusual to them. They had probably just subjectively pro-
jected their feelings onto me.

East of Atlanta the vicious heat-storms of summer came
again. Fierce this time, as they'd been in Mississippi. Ground
lightning popped around me until I could barely see to drive.
Then, from the front of the car, I began hearing a rhythmic clunk-
a-clunk, growing ever louder, ever more grinding. I knew it was
bad.

I just wanted to make it to Athens. I had blood on my forehead and a gallon of mysterious liquid to pour over me and it
was nearly midnight and it wouldn't be good to stop anywhere
broken down. I asked the spirits to keep me going, and tomorrow I'd take time to fix a lot of things.

I reached Athens, and spent an uneasy half hour trying to
find a motel. Rooms everywhere were filled because of a convention at the University of Georgia. I settled for a seedy inn
whose spotlit marquee advertised budget rates and XXX in-room
cable. The parking lot was filled with muddy pickups and old
clunkers. I checked in, forgetting the blood on my head. The
clerk didn't say anything.

I wasn't sleepy, so I went to the tavern next to the motel and
drank a couple of beers. I guess I must have looked odd, or maybe
smelled pungent, because nobody sat anywhere near me. I went
upstairs to my room. I stripped down. Actually, rain and perspi-
ration had cleared most of the blood from my brow, but my big
toes were still brightly marked. I carried the jug of Baba Kunle's
cleaning potion into the bathroom and put it on the toilet seat. I
got in the shower and turned the water hot as I could stand it.
Lorita had said not to let anyone put anything on me. Yeah, well.

When I'd washed off the blood and sweat of the night, I turned off the water, reached out around the mildewed shower curtain and grabbed the jug. I had no idea what was inside, but it smelled sweet, like apple juice. I turned off the shower, then held the jug over my head and poured.

Mostly, it was *cold*. But my flesh warmed the mixture fast. I watched it trickle down my shoulders, my chest and stomach, over my groin, down my thighs, across my toes. It was gray-brown, filled with chunks of various herbs.

I examined myself in the mirror. Bark and seed pods all over me, my whole torso light gray, as if I'd evolved from the mud. I waited a few minutes for the mix to dry, then sat naked and shivering on a towel on my bed. I turned on the TV. Satellite soft-core. I watched. I don't know for how long. I fell asleep.

In the morning, the sheets were damp and tacky and my head was still wet. I showered again, as I had been instructed to do, then dressed. I checked out, leaving the empty jug in the motel room trash can. I went to get my car fixed. CV joints out, about $300. While waiting, I caught a city bus into downtown Athens and walked past my old haunts alongside the UGA campus. I ate something. Then I took the bus back to the repair shop and headed for the nearest coast —Savannah, a half day to the east. On the way storms blew in so fiercely the traffic on the interstate came to a complete stop, and then my muffler burned out. Another $120.

I got the message. I backed off. I found a nice Savannah motel. I went to the clubs along the river and listened to music and ate oysters. I spent a day at the beach. I saw *Batman*.

# PART THREE

# THE
# WAY

# 13

## AFRICA IN AMERICA

IT WOULD BE easy to miss Oyotunji—and although I'd been there before, three years ago—I almost did. The I-95 exit halfway up from Savannah to Charleston dumps directly onto South Carolina 21, a two-lane blacktop with the traffic load of a New York thoroughfare. Day and night, cars and trucks connecting Beaufort, Parris Island, the Gullah Islands or the tourist resorts of the South Carolina coast to the rest of the state thunder along as though in transit from the earth to the moon. It's dangerous, distracting, and sometimes deadly to drive—that much worse if you're looking for a faded, hand-lettered wooden sign, half-obscured by brush, proclaiming, "African Village—As Seen on TV."

I zoomed past it the first time, doubled back, and barely picked it out on my second pass, braking down hard for a sudden right turn into the red-dirt entry road reaching out from the high weeds. Too hard, too fast, for the eighteen-wheeler barreling up my rear bumper at least twice my velocity. Figuring I had maybe two seconds to get off the highway and live, I steered sharply to the shoulder. Loose gravel and slick mud carried me into an uncontrollable rear-end skid toward the lip of a deep rain gulley. Only because my tires found some small salvation of traction did I right the wheels and pop into the side road inches ahead of the semi's massive oncoming chrome grille. The passing air horn was deafening, and righteous.

My hand had knotted on the gear shift knob so tightly it hurt to loosen up. I was okay, though after I had taken a few deep breaths and moved down the rutted lane I had been seeking, I was still trembling from the adrenalin. Perhaps that heightened my next impression, the gradual transformation, as I drove, of the curtain of semitropical forest I had seen from the highway into a living tunnel of vines and trees, an unsettling, ambush-quality density of every hue and shape of green. Then, abruptly, I rounded a curve and the foliage parted. In the clearing before me was an almost unbelievable tableau that had changed little over the years.

Road coming into Oyotunji village.

I paused at the untended and mostly symbolic sentry gate, where a half-fallen sign warned, "You Are Now Leaving the United States," and parked in a grassy clearing just outside. I could see up ahead several young boys, clad only in red waist-wraps, running down one of the dusty trails that laced the compound. A woman in white robes and white head scarf followed them, shouting something I couldn't make out in the Yoruba language—likely a scolding.

The air was wet and thick as in New Orleans. I was already sweating as I walked through the gate and angled over to a shady patio within a quadrangle, or bazaar, of five or six stalls offering African clothing, jewelry, potions and wood carvings. Beyond the bazaar, Oyotunji stretched out for several hundred yards in every direction. The living quarters, open-air temples, dancing pavilions and shrines were off to the left. To the right, past an Elegba altar and a wake-up drum fashioned from an oil barrel, rose the walled enclosure known as the Afin—the royal compound. Within the Afin were the homes of the king and some of his wives and a half-dozen or more individual altars to all the major orisha. Everything had been built by hand, over the years, exactly as it would have been done in Nigeria or Dahomey.

To my surprise, no one was out. I walked into the main crossroads at the center of the village, then back to the patio and plopped into one of the molded plastic chairs. Not a soul. I thought about the afternoon when I'd first seen the place. I'd only stayed a few hours, just enough time for a quick tour, a visit with the king, and a cowrie shell reading by a haughty female Shango priestess. But the memory had stayed with me, like a glimpse of Xanadu, and I knew even then I would someday be back.

"It's a curious feeling just coming in here," the man who ruled the ten-acre medieval compound had told me. "You leave the highway and you twist and turn down a dirt road and then suddenly, you're here, in another context altogether. Everything

Oyotunji village children.

is very different. Then you go back on the highway. You wonder if you were really there."

The heat made me drowsy and I nodded off for a half hour or more, awaking to the voice of a young girl, about nine or ten, who wanted to know if she could help me. On her forehead were three parallel scars—the sign of a member of the royal family. I told her I was the man who had called the Oba—the king— about staying in the village for awhile.

The Oba wasn't there right now, she said, he had gone to town with her mother, Iya Orite. She said I was welcome to wait and that she'd tell the king I was there as soon as he got back. I could get something to drink at The Horseman, the girl said, and pointed to a small hut that served as the village's Carib-

Oyotunji village Elegba shrine.

bean-style bistro. Then she excused herself to get ready for the
festival. Of course. That's where everyone else was, too.

Throughout the year, the village honored the various orisha
in rituals ranging from a day to more than a week. Last month's
celebration had been for Shango. This month the honoree was
Yemonja. A heavy schedule of events would play out all week—
a walkabout to all the shrines of the village for Elegba, then an
even larger parade for the egun, the dead ancestors, and then a
procession and dances for Yemonja, to be followed by a trip to
the beach at Hunting Island to present the goddess to the sea.
The public was invited to watch some events—tourists and education were important sources of income—but other ceremonies, particularly the sacrifices, were closed to strangers.

No one was in The Horseman to sell me a coke, so I went
back to the bazaar and waited. As usual in the village, things
seemed to be running late. But I didn't mind. In truth, my presence for the Yemonja festival was coincidental. I hadn't known

of its timing until I had called the king from my R&R in Savannah several days earlier. I stretched back in my chair and relaxed. I had nowhere to go, nobody to badger. I was where I needed to be.

—=—

Although the culture of the orisha in America has survived and in some places today thrives anew, nowhere else has it been so devoutly and comprehensively preserved as in Oyotunji. Life is an African voudou village from dress to manners to food to laws. Yet Oyotunji is not an African village, for Oyotunji is not a place that grew in Africa. It is a place in which Africa grows. "Oyo" is a Yoruba word for horseman and also for a famous Yoruba city. "Tunji" means return. Oyo-tunji is the return of the horseman, the return of African civilization—in America.

It is also the result of the vision, perhaps the obsession, of the man I was waiting to see again. And I finally did, as the afternoon stretched out and a late model gray Nissan sedan emerged from the blind turn of thick trees up the lane. "It's the Oba," said one of the teenage boys I'd seen earlier, this time not being chased, but hurrying through the patio carrying a ceremonial conga drum.

As the car reached the sentry port, I could see the boy was right. Oba Oseijeman Adefumni I, formerly Walter "Serge" King of Detroit, a Harlem artist who had virtually reintroduced orisha voudou to black Americans and was now the country's preeminent African-American priest, eased the car to a stop and rolled down the driver's side window. His currently favored wife, Iya Orite, dressed in wrap-around lapa, coiffed with powdered gray dreadlocks, sat in the passenger seat. She looked good and so did he, although he was more than twice her age. At sixty-two, the Oba was still virile and handsome—goateed, strong, square-jawed, light-toned face and solid body under his brown dashiki. He had taken five wives altogether, who had born him twenty-one children and grandchildren, all of them consecrated to the orisha.

Miwa, the king's twenty-year-old daughter by Iya Orite, emerged from the Office of Tourism—the thatched roof hut used to distribute books, pamphlets and guide materials to the all-too-few visitors. When she got to the driver's side window, the Oba gave her a Burger King sack. He and his wife drove away before I could catch his eye.

———

You only had to think about the incredibleness of Oyotunji to understand the scope of what the Oba had accomplished—the creation of an American mecca for the worship, study and contemporary living of orisha voudou culture. Before Oyotunji, any black Americans interested in the religion had to learn the mysteries and rituals in much the manner Lorita Mitchell and Serge King had been forced to do—through Cubans, through the half-remembered distortions of hoodoo. Oyotunji changed everything. Its emphasis on strict adherence to Yoruba ritual and the exclusion of Catholic syncretization—voudou without Christianity—shook the American voudou community to its core and separated it, not always happily, from its Cuban mentors.

By the time Serge King, who had changed his name to Efuntola and become a priest of Obatala, journeyed to Ife, Nigeria in 1981, the purposefully distinct identity of Oyotunji as an African bastion was well entrenched. In Ife, an ancient and holy city of the orisha, Efuntola was invested with royal lineage and instructed by the King of Ife to return to North America to perpetuate a true voudou kingdom. He took the royal title, Oba, by which he is known even to rivals in the santeria community.

When the Oba began his singular journey toward the African grail, however, he had little more in mind than finding out more about his own roots. Trying to make a living as an artist and dancer in Harlem in the fifties, he began to run in circles which included Cubans who had come to New York in the pre-Revolutionary decades when the trade routes of art and commerce to Havana were vibrant and well-plied. Some of the Cubans he met were especially fascinating. They bore more than a foreign tongue and nationality. They bore foreign gods. The young King wasn't sure at first what he thought of santeria, but he was excited about its overwhelming African content. He began attending ceremonies.

In 1959, King and artist Chris Oliana journeyed to Matanzas, Cuba, to become, or so it is believed, the first African Americans in recent memory to be fully initiated in African voudou, even though it was technically santeria. King returned a priest of Obatala, and Africanized his name to Baba Oseijeman Efuntola. Oliana became a priest of Shango.

Returning to New York, the two pilgrims opened the Shango Temple on East 125th Street in Harlem. During the next decade, Efuntola began to develop not only his own expertise as a priest, but his idea for an African-American renaissance of orisha voudou. He was sidetracked in the sixties by politics, and for a time served as minister of culture to the Republic of New Afrika party, a black separatist organization. But Efuntola didn't believe the solution to the cultural dislocation of African Americans could be resolved through politics. It went deeper than that. It went straight into the loss of the soul. The loss of soul came from the loss of voudou.

By 1970, he was ready to leave New York. Quarrels had been increasing between the Cubans and the African Americans. The Cubans demanded too much; for instance, that the Americans worship African deities through Spanish names, calling Elegba down as Elleggua, Yemonja as Yemaya, Shango as Changó and Ifa by an altogether different name, Orunmila. It wasn't that Efuntola and the group which gathered around him were anti-Cuban. They knew that had it not been for the Africans in Cuba, powerful secrets, especially Ifa divination, might have been lost to the New World, so completely had they been stamped out in the U. S. And Efuntola maintained strong ties to Matanzas.

In the thick of the disagreements—by some accounts, potentially violent—Efuntola drove down to South Carolina with friends to look over some rural land one of them had inherited. It was in the middle of nowhere, but Efuntola knew he'd found the place for Oyotunji—the return. Within a few months he'd packed up and left Harlem for good, and, with like-minded spiritual adventurers, began to cut trees, clear brush, build roads. Within a few years, word began to get around that an African revivalist village was being created down South. People interested in hard work and spiritual renewal were needed. For the most part, those who came to the village stayed and saw their lives transformed. Over the years, a thousand or more became full voudou initiates and have subsequently spread throughout America, setting up bookstores in Dallas, boutiques or botanicas in Oakland and San Diego, temples in Washington, D.C., Miami and the Bronx.

There was one casualty. In 1972, a fugitive Black Panther showed up, just after the settlement had moved from its original location, across the highway, to the present ten-acre site. Nobody minded he was a Panther, but they did mind that he was wanted on several warrants. The last thing the fledgling village needed was a reputation as a hideout—just the sort of thing local authorities could use to bust up the strange "cult" which had moved into the county.

Tensions grew, finally boiling over into a shooting in which the Panther was killed by one of the villagers. It was ruled self-defense and no one was ever tried. The true meaning of the killing, however, lay outside South Carolina courtrooms. In Yoruba tradition, the founding of a new city required human blood sacrifice, which in ancient times meant the killing of a captured enemy or a criminal. "As we thought about it in hindsight," the Oba recalled, "we thought, hey, maybe that's how the gods arranged that, cornered this dude like that, and then he got killed on that land and we'd already started building the village by then, so we construed it as, hey, look how the gods had worked that deal."

In the seventies, the village reached a peak population of about 200. Homes were built, sewer lines and wells dug, temples erected by hand. There were even plans—at least talk—of great expansions, to make the village a 100-acre theme park, a Six Flags of African culture, "to bring the best of Africa to America," according to a poster distributed by the African Theological Archministry, Inc., the corporate structure through which the village does business. But the eighties saw most of the great plans dwindle. The population steadily declined, an irony given the upsurge in interest in voudou in America that began about mid-decade. I could not help feeling sad that the mecca had become so hard-pressed after twenty years of heroic survival. But the Oba took it in stride, as a cyclical turn of the mandala. Maybe even a weeding out.

"At first, the people poured in here full of enthusiasm," he said. "They were full of interest in their race and all excited about being voudou priests. They thought, 'Africa!' You sit down and you castigate white people and you don't eat pork and you walk around in robes or something all day long. And they thought that was Africa. But what they found out is that you didn't just become a voudou priest and learn a whole lot of magic over-night."

———

About suppertime, Iya Orite came to my squatter's patio to formally greet me and show me the windowless hut, about the size of a supply shack you might see alongside a landing on a seldom-traveled bush country river, in which I'd be quartered. It anchored one side of the bazaar and went for $10 a day. Fur-nishings consisted of a narrow cot, a small table, and an auto-

The author outside his guest hut in village bazaar.

Inside the guest hut.

mobile battery for a portable TV. I could camp out if I preferred, for $2. I said I'd take the luxury route. I reminded her that I'd like to see the king. She said he was busy because of the festival but that she'd try to set it up in a day or two. It was a mañana pace that at first nettled me but which I soon learned to accept.

I passed the evening drinking a few beers in front of the box fan in The Horseman, where I was the only customer, and retired early. The king and his family remained sequestered in the Afin. The other village residents—altogether about two dozen adults and children—were closed away in their homes.

I couldn't sleep. The only sounds of the night, except for nature, came from a radio in the sentry house. According to long-time procedure, the village's adult males took turns standing armed guard each night. The hut was hot, too. Until I bought my own box fan from K-Mart, there was no air circulation. The only window was stapled over with plastic storm sheeting, and I kept the door rigged shut with a plastic wire. That kept out most of the mosquitoes, but more importantly, the pair of chicken snakes some of the village boys released from a cage just outside my door as a prank (and got scolded for the next day). Yet even with the door shut and a pillow over my ears, I couldn't block the piercing, cat-like cries of the peacocks. Two of them, favor-ites of Oshun, prowled the grounds at night. Worse, they favored a roost in the big tree directly above my quarters.

I thought about walking down to the new shower stalls, about 100 yards away, to cool off, which would certainly happen, since there was no hot water. Of course then I'd have to choke down the strong smell of sulphur from the new well, and I wasn't sure if the showers had lights. Electricity had only come two years ago. But mostly I didn't think it wise to wander around late at night. And I didn't feel like putting on my shoes. And maybe it would cool off.

About four in the morning I was still awake. Staring at the plaster ceiling had grown boring, so I turned to my side, funky with insomnia. Across the dark room, I noticed a small, screened, triangular opening in a corner near the ceiling. It was an odd architectural touch I never figured out, but was one of the few places a breeze could enter. It also provided a strange view.

It was while gazing through the triangle at the boughs of the dense trees of the surrounding forest that I saw them, first as seeming coalitions of shadows, and then as solid objects, and then as more than that, as energies of unmistakable definition. I remember a phrase coming to my lips in a whisper: "the Ibeji." My lips were smiling in self-mockery, and yet they were speaking the truth. I was looking at the the orisha known as the Twins, among the most complex of the voudou manifestations, and one of the ultimate symbols of Yoruba theories of linked duality.

The Ibeji connote both the unity of opposites and of their binding contradictions; indeed, the worship of twins is itself an inversion of an ancient Yoruba belief that twins are extremely bad luck, which belief for many years encouraged twin infanticide. I stared hard. The image did not go away. The Ibeji were exactly as I had seen them in sculpture in museums and botanicas and in the half-flooded basement in Atlanta. One twin was male, one female, with oversized, erect penis and pronounced breasts, respectively; both had sleek black hair and wore golden necklaces. The figures were stylized in the ancient manner—elongated bodies, almost oval in shape, with hair piled conically. They were looking at me. At first they lay horizontal, as if in repose—in the next instant they were standing upright.

I ran through the standard dismissals: I was projecting, I was seeing Rorschach shapes in the branches, I was dreaming. But I was awake. I closed my eyes a half-dozen times. I looked away and changed my thoughts. But when I looked back the Ibeji were always there.

The next day I mentioned it to some of the villagers. No one was surprised. The place was full of African spirits. It would have been odd had I not seen something. So I eagerly looked

through the triangle every subsequent night I remained at
Oyotunji, but I never saw them again. At each daybreak, I could
see that the branches in the trees weren't shaped like the Ibeji at
all.

# 14

## THE DAY OF THE LIVING DEAD

I AWOKE SURROUNDED by Baptists. Several dozen of them had come down by bus from Durham on a church-sponsored outing, and I threw on jeans and T-shirt hurriedly to get out of my hut before they all congregated in the patio. Most were over fifty, about evenly mixed by gender, but all black—I continued to be the only white person in the village. As they began trickling into the bazaar after an introductory tour of the grounds, most of them looked like they were having serious second thoughts. Trying to be unobtrusive, I perched like a disheveled sprite on a log back near the parking area, sipping orange juice from my Igloo. I heard one woman say she had "always been curious about that African stuff," but most everyone else was fidgety and silent.

Then Chief Elesin showed up. A lanky artisan from East Texas who had been in the village almost from the beginning, he was, by title, "keeper of the king's horses," and in practice the royal bodyguard. But now he was decked out in one of the more salacious "aspects" of his already ultra-flamboyant deity, Elegba: barefoot, in fish-net red shirt, grass skirt, bells on his ankles, a leather pouch more or less covering his crotch and, atop his head, a bead-draped skull cap with ebony cow horns. He lacked only a tail to be the worst nightmare of everyone present.

"Hi y'all," he said, throwing candies and gum, bumping and grinding his way through the literally open-mouthed, figuratively pole-axed crowd like a Chip 'N Dale stripper the size of an NBA forward. I nearly did a spit take with my Sunkist. But Elegba kept it up, mooning anyone in proximity, laughing and cat-calling for sixty-year-old women in sun bonnets to "get off your booty" and join him. It really was unbearable to watch. Then, like some ancient levee giving way, whispering led to titters to open laughter and then a couple of the men started shaking their butts back at Elegba, others egged him on. An impossibly proper matron in floral print dress and white gloves said to her friend, "You can see his ding-a-ling," and they still may not have cared for Oyotunji but they were no longer afraid of it.

Perhaps on cue, perhaps just seizing the moment, a curvy, dark-complected Trinidadian known as Iya Ghandi ("Iya" means mother; Ghandi was the name of her youngest son, which she took for reasons I never understood) suddenly strode into the quadrangle and, waving her arms with exaggerated theatricality, shooed the satyr off, mocking him as a "bad boy who needs to grow up."

When they had settled again, she briefed them. The festival for Yemonja was in progress, she explained, and it had been Elegba's duty to greet the new arrivals, and the thing about Elegba was that you never knew what he'd do and you couldn't control him if you did. It was his nature. Now, though, it was time for the egungun, a ritual for the spirits of the dead. Soon, a procession of villagers dressed as various of the orisha, like the one who had just welcomed them, but "nicer," would dance and sing their way through the village grounds, stopping at each of the altars to pay homage. They would see worship just as carried

A royal residence at Oyotunji. Ogun and Elegba implements left of the door.

Visiting Baptist group in the village bazaar.

out in a true voudou village in Africa. Everyone was welcome to watch, and ask questions, and take pictures.

"I won't have nothing to do with no blasphemy," said one of the Baptist women who had not been amused.

"Amen," said a couple of others.

"We have no wish to offend anyone," Iya Ghandi replied calmly. "This is the way we worship here."

No one said anything else. The levee had re-formed. Seizing another opportunity, Iya Ghandi excused herself.

She had not said so, but the next time they would see her she would not be herself. Like an actor assuming a role, she would have transformed herself into her patron spirit. Only she would not be acting. Yemonja would inhabit Ghandi's body. Like Elesin, she would be possessed.

—=—

The egungun began, hours later than scheduled, with the thunderous beating of the main village drum. The Baptists had long since gone away, but a half-dozen new visitors had driven in, some from as far away as Washington, D.C. As the procession finally started, we all joined as spectators, following the three drummer boys, now clad in scarlet tunics, toward the village center.

The rhythm of the saints echoed off the Afin and the forest, and Iya Ghandi re-appeared, this time all in white, save a blue seahorse embroidered onto her skirt. She carried a white staff adorned with blue spirals, and a white scarf was wrapped around her head. She was Yemonja: mistress of the oceans and queen of the witches.

Let the ceremony be late. It was Ghandi's patron orisha, and things would happen when and only when she was ready. Even the Oba yielded to her wishes regarding the pace and timing of events. And on the days when Yemonja seized Iya Ghandi like a rag doll and sank her into deep sullenness or paraded her bare-breasted in exultation, no one would cross her. She had grown up in the Caribbean and in her thirty-four years had become an initiate of all that came her way—santeria, palo mayombe, Shango Baptist (from her native Trinidad) and orisha voudou. You did not defy Yemonja, for she was the ocean, and ruled the tides of life. And you didn't mess with Iya Ghandi either.

As the drummer boys reached the first shrine, a phalanx of the other village adults appeared, each in priestly robes. Some wore the white tunic and head scarf of Obatala—the patron deity of the village—some the yellow of Oshun. Iya Shango, the slender woman in her mid-thirties who ran The Horseman, donned the bright red of her namesake—often a male deity but sometimes also taken by women of strong personality. A Shango

Iya Shanla, left; Iya Ghandi, center; Chief Elesin, right, in Elegba outfittings.

Boys drumming during egungun ceremony, Oyotunji. Week of Yemonja festival. Egungun figure, hooded, at right.

Egungun visits the warriors' shrine.

woman was like an Oshun woman but more macho. Both were considered to be extraordinarily erotic.

One of the celebrants was strikingly different. Compared to the classic simplicity of the priests, this one dressed out like something from Mardi Gras: red and white flapped breech-skirt, each flap with a symbolic emblem, and a full-sleeved shirt of silver foil. The head was completely covered by a mask, also of silver foil, and topped by a sea-blue head scarf. It looked like a fat snowman with a blue head, but it was the egungun, the dancing figure of the dead. According to tradition, no one was to know the identity, or even gender, of the person in the egungun costume, but the diminished population in the village made it merely a matter of counting heads to see who was absent, and from the size of the dancer you could tell it was a male.

The sun had come out between rain storms and the midday heat bore down. A few of the villagers had gone barefoot, and I started without shoes, too, but quickly hopped into them—the sandy white soil was blistering. The processional rounds of the altars that we followed for the next couple of hours was a microcosm of the spiritual journey a new initiate makes. Just as a yaguo receives the various gods that will guide and protect his or her life, so we broiled under the sun paying homage to them.

First, of course, was Elegba, as he is in every prayer, ritual, invocation or chant—or gathering of Baptists. Elesin was back among us, whirling and singing praises in Yoruba, lobbing candy at the thatch-covered shrine next to the oil barrel drum. Next to the cone-shaped laterite head on the low wooden plank serving as altar were beer cans, gum wrappers, chicken feathers, dried blood and a goat's head. To some of my cohorts, it seemed completely non-holy, but that was probably the point.

The Warriors were next, and now Yemonja took the lead, grinding her hips, opening her legs to the congas before Ogun and Ochosi, whose side by side temples spilled over with iron pots, chains, arrows, metal implements, even a toy rifle. She was smiling, doing everything she could to cajole these protectors, without whom no believer can survive long. Watching her, smelling her as she passed close in her dervish seduction, some hidden door in my mind opened. I began to perceive in some visceral way what I had intellectually sensed as the brilliance of the long initiation rites and of the voudou life itself.

Classic reincarnationists, voudous believe that when you die, you petition god, or Olorun, to return your soul to the living. Your major responsibility at that point is to learn what Ifa, the god of divination, has spun as your fate. To learn Ifa's plan, you must of course make contact with him. The only way to do that is through Elegba, who as gatekeeper is the only one who can admit you to the world ruled by the other orisha. But Elegba is also known as a master trickster and arbiter of chance—he offers as many pitfalls as possibilities.

Sacrifice, or ebo, is one of the most important methods of cutting your downside risk. Also important is the intervention of the egun—in particular your own ancestors—who are said to usher you through life according to the plans of Ifa. But even with sacrifice to placate Elegba and the help of your ancestors to align you with Ifa, you might not escape trouble.

Thus the Warriors. With their protection, you can move both through the spirit world and mortal life with assurance, especially in the vulnerable early period during which you seek your primary orisha: Obatala, Oshun, Shango, Yemonja, etc. and any secondary ones, especially in santeria initiations, where the "head" orisha is often supplemented by a half-dozen other santos.

When the process is complete, you possess not only a patron deity, but an infrastructure of spiritual links and armaments no less ritualized and active than those given an Arthurian knight. It isn't difficult to imagine the appeal of voudou to persons in difficult circumstances, from Bedford-Stuyvesant to Hialeah to Oakland to East New Orleans. Precisely that appeal poured through every plantation in the South and exploded in historic revolution in Haiti.

Voudou was the original Black Power.

I threw the change in my pockets to the Warriors as Ghandi came out of what had surely been a possession, gyrations slowed to a humble bowing and backing away from the shrine. She led us then back across the sandy lane to a pavilion of art deco yellow under huge droopy trees—the shrine of Oshun. Everything, all yellow. The cinder blocks and wooden beams of which it was constructed, the open wooden cabinet, filled with dolls, pots, fruits, flowers. The wicker chair in front. The porcelain cat, symbol of the Egyptian goddess Isis. All yellow. About the only things that weren't Oshun's favorite color were the surfaces of the two mirrors flanking the shrine, but the frames were.

I was seeing more and more of this, the voudou concept of reflection, linked opposites, pairings, duality. The Ibeji were perhaps the most dramatic representation, but in one way or

Shrine to Oshun at Oyotunji.

another the mirrors, the twins, the binary divination of Ifa, reincarnation, all led back to what seemed the simplest metaphor of all: the crossroads.

In voudou, not unlike Native American and Asian religions, the plane of existence is really a dual bisection—literally, a cross of horizontal and vertical axes. The horizontal delineates the living (above) from the dead (below). The vertical line separates the life cycle in the way of a clock, from re-birth at midnight, around clockwise and back to the midnight of the instant of death. In the classic Haitian vodun vêve (symbolic drawing), the crossroads icon is depicted as a cross surrounded by a circle. The cross interstices mark the inseparable dualities, and the circle indicates the movement of the time-space continuum. The crossroads are not only mirrors within voudou, but outward, to the rest of the world as well.

But I was noticing something else in Oshun's mirrors—cracks. I didn't know why until a few days later when, on a quiet afternoon, I heard pecking and walked down to the shrine. Her birds, the peacocks, were compelled by their own reflections to break the mirrors into shards. Blood tracks from their lacerated foot pads speckled the dirt. One of the villagers told me that keeping mirrors in stock was a real problem, as was protecting the birds from self-inflicted wounds, but what could anyone do? If Oshun, taking the form of the peacocks, wanted to shatter the illusion of her own image to see what lay behind, who would stop her?

The procession, meanwhile, had reached the shrine of its namesake. A blue and white wooden hut about the size of a snow-cone booth at the state fair, it contained, under lock and key, the secret worship pots, or superas. Liberally decorated with drawings of seahorses and other ocean life, the hut opened onto the village's largest ceremonial courtyard, a white sandy area big enough for a half-court basketball game, flanked on one side by a section of bleachers for spectators, such as there were.

Villagers in front of Yemonja shrine. They visit shrines of each of the deities during ceremonies.

On another side, opposite Yemonja's hut, rose a temple to her male counterpart, the ocean god Olokun. In front of that was an enclosed walkway lined with massive, hand-carved wooden statues. Much of the work had been done by the Oba himself, hewing out huge tree trunks, with attention in every aspect to Yoruba detail. How easy it was to see Oyotunji not just as a spiritual settlement, a living lesson-book, but as an ongoing work of performance art, an opus of such magnitude and scope of imagination to rival anything I had ever seen in a museum.

I walked over to the bleachers with some of the other guests and shielded my eyes with my hand enough to catch shimmering glimpses of Yemonja, mounted on Ghandi again, dancing and singing for herself, to herself, about herself. In a few days, at the closing ceremonies for the festival, I would be in the bleachers again, this time watching the Oba and three of his wives.

They had finished pouring a special mixture of cornflour and herbs on the sand for the spirits, thanking them for the

Village boys in front of a statue to the sea god Olokun. Iya Ghandi, as Yemonja, bare-breasted in front of statue.

week, and now, to celebrate, wanted to dance. They formed a line not unlike what kids in Philly might have called the "stroll" in the fifties, shaking their hips and bodies with so much exuberance it didn't seem possible they'd probably done the same dance hundreds or even thousands of times over the last two decades. Sometimes they danced in front of visitors, and sometimes just for themselves—it didn't really matter.

I had watched the king smile as he joined the line. A regal smile, a smile of accomplishment from a warrior-king who had surmounted impossible odds to turn what had been little more than a stupendous dream into the re-creation that spread around us. The myth made manifest. Who could look on this and not see the beauty?

In voudou, all life is of one weave—being, beauty and truth. The melding of beauty and truth is a community responsibility and celebration. Art is for society's sake. It is the expression of the divinity in all things, the very essence of voudou. "Do you know what the word for 'thinking' is in Yoruba?" the controversial New York voudou scholar John Mason once asked me. "It's synonymous with the word for art. To be artful is to be a thinker. The language itself is already geared to a certain view of what existence is."

—————

That evening I met Malaya for a drink at The Horseman. I had spotted her earlier in the afternoon while following the ceremonies but hadn't been able to talk to her much. She was a vision—tall, sinuous, her white cotton blouse and skirt glowing against deep black skin. A gold ring pierced one nostril, and I could see by the strands of pale blue and white beads around her neck that she had recently begun the process of initiation as a daughter of Oshun.

She had come to Oyotunji from Washington, D.C., with friends, partly from curiosity—though she'd heard of the village, she'd never seen it in person—and partly because she shared the Oyotunji idea of a religion in which American blacks would not be dominated by Cubans. Her own spiritual godfather was Cuban, but her African-American separatist feelings ran strong. She referred to her religion as "orisha worship," however, and not as voudou. I asked why.

"I just feel 'voodoo' has gotten a bad connotation," she said. "To me, it's like calling myself 'colored.'" I disagreed, but understood the objection.

Iya Orite, tending bar, brought over wine coolers and beer and joined us. Pretty soon we'd taken care of several rounds. I liked Orite (her name means "mother of the head throne"). She had a good head for business and seemed to function as a kind of de facto manager of village affairs. But you could tell she had a wild streak. She was a priestess of Obatala—known for organization—but had a "strong Oshun," a sort of African Scarlett O'Hara.

Orite had been in the village since 1974, when she decided to walk out of everything "normal" in her middle-class life and become a wife of the king. Malaya thought it romantic, but couldn't understand why the polygamy didn't matter. Orite said because they weren't living by Western rules. Adamant, though not defensive, she told us how the king and four of the wives had defended the practice on a May 1988 episode of "Oprah"— she later played it for me on her VCR.

In Yoruba society, the Oba and his wives had explained to the talk show audience, a man may marry as many wives as he can support; they may, in turn, marry and divorce successive husbands. A woman who is not taken by anyone else becomes the king's royal obligation, and he must marry her so that she will have standing and the possibility of land ownership in the community. Since women essentially acquire land through marriage—which they may then keep if the marriage ends in death or divorce—a woman without a husband is a woman without property or future.

This Yoruba custom obviously forces women to operate through male hierarchies; yet, as Orite pointed out, it also allows them a separate identity, not all that far from what Virginia Woolf called "a room of one's own," more accurately for the Yoruba a "roof" of one's own. I didn't know until sometime later how important this issue was for Iya Orite.

About nine, the king's wife said she had to get back to her house. Malaya and I stayed, talking and listening to King Sunny Adé on a jambox. It was getting late but I wasn't sleepy. Neither was Malaya. We decided to drive out to Hunting Island, about forty-five miles away, past Beaufort. But it was a good night to be out, windows down, sunroof open, breeze cutting the heat.

We got back to the village after midnight. I parked next to the gate in the clearing and as we left the car a figure carrying a rifle approached us, demanding to know who we were. It was Chief Elesin. He was a little aggressive, I thought, since he probably recognized my car, and certainly me as soon as he shone the flashlight our way. It was about then I realized his interest wasn't so much in possible intruders as with impressing Malaya. And with his dark crimson guard robes, rifle and booming voice he certainly commanded attention. The three of us sat in the patio and talked. I was unsure of the dynamic so concluded the best thing was to say goodnight.

She came to my room at 6:15 the next morning. She had slept in one of the guest chambers in the Afin. She was leaving early—her traveling companions had to return to Washington. I was awake from the morning drum call, but not by much. She was all in white, moving in the dawn toward my cot, full of Oshun. It occurred to me I might have misjudged the previous evening. "You have to stand up," she said. "You have to hug me." I did, wearing nothing but Jockeys, and she pressed herself close.

Then she left and I lay back on the cot, the sheets still damp from my night sweats, and slept till eight, when I heard fresh tourists gathering in the bazaar patio outside my hut for the day's activities. I had to get one of them to open my door—the wooden latch Malaya had thrown shut when she left couldn't be turned from the inside. The dozen or so fresh tourists were pretty surprised to see a sleep-rumpled white man come out, clad in striped towel and unlaced Nikes, bound for the showers. But I knew if they stuck around they'd see stranger sights than me.

# 15

## THE KING AND HIS COURT

AS FESTIVAL WEEK passed, and ceremonies became sporadic, I filled the days as best I could. Many hours I would sit in the shaded patio or walk among the shrines listening to villagers tell me how they had left their former lives and traveled to South Carolina and then decided to stay, to take up the way of the orisha. Elesin had been bumping around between colleges when he learned of Oyotunji in the mid-seventies and had poured virtually the whole of his adult life into it. Orite had studied theater in New York. Iya Shango had moved down from Buffalo, New York, and never looked back. Chief Alagba, the husband of Iya Ghandi, had once been in public relations.

Early on the morning the festival reached its final day, I spotted Iya Ghandi hurrying across the commons toward her house. I'd been after her to have a beer and tell me about palo mayombe. She said it would have to wait until tomorrow or the next day. I sighed, having been told that before. She shrugged and took off. After a few steps she paused and turned to look me over. She had to "present" Yemonja to the sea at Hunting Island that morning, she said. Maybe I could go with her, I said. "Good," she said. "We can also use your car."

The plan was for me to carry Chief Alagba and two of the drummer boys. That would give Ghandi room for herself and two girls in Iya Shango's little sedan, plus room in the trunk to store the most important of all the passengers, the pots consecrated to Yemonja. Each was filled with sea water from the previous year's festival and had to be replenished. It was very important not to spill anything. Having an extra car freed up enough space to secure the four tureens so they wouldn't shift around.

The weather was fine and clear as we drove Highway 21 through Beaufort's usual congestion and across the flat marshes leading to the coast. Chief Alagba, head of the Egungun Society, told me his ideas for promoting Oyotunji. Villagers had been in a number of movies, for example Alex Haley's *Roots*, and he said the Ogboni Society, the Council of Landowners which ran village affairs, wanted to create and market a video—thus the

Yemonja pot, center, on beach at Hunting Island, South Carolina.

chief's extensive taping of the Yemonja festival and the camera case riding on his lap.

He mentioned something I'd heard, that Iya Ghandi wanted to leave, but it seemed a painful subject. He loved her, and she him, but she wanted to go to Miami, or some other larger city, and there wasn't much he could do to stop her. It made me sad. No matter what your religion, losing your woman is hard.

When we arrived at the beach the sun was blazing. I regretted at once not having brought a hat, of a bathing suit, though at least I was in shorts. We parked alongside the cars of ordinary fun-seekers. Iya Ghandi began to carry the pots, one by one, down to the water's edge—balanced on her head. Each pot was covered by a "veil" of blue or white cotton cloth—what was inside was supposed to be secret. But on one trip, the wind blew the veil away. The pot, a crystal tureen the size of a punch bowl, was filled with milky-looking sea water, shells and parts of crab and fish.

I reached down to pick up the veil.

Chief Alagba refills sacred pot for Yemonja with sea water at conclusion of week-long ceremonies.

"No," she said quickly. "Don't touch that."

I drew back and apologized.

"It's okay," she said. "But you aren't initiated." She looked around for Alagba, and scolded him for not acting as quickly as had "a stranger." I exchanged a glance of sympathy with him, but there wasn't much I could do on his behalf.

We walked the boardwalk to the sandy white beach beyond the fringe of trees, some torn down by a recent hurricane. The tide was coming in and the area was filled with sunbathers. We didn't look like them. Iya Ghandi, clad in white blouse, loose white pantaloons and head scarf—as were Chief Alagba and Iya Shango—arranged the pots on the sand and waded into the sea, shaking a castanet and singing a Yoruba praise hymn.

Chief Alagba began taping. The children sat near the pots, watching. Iya Ghandi came back from the sea, barefoot and wet from the knees down. She knelt, took her obi from a bag and cast them on the sand. She said it was a good reading and smiled. At that moment, a pair of Marine jets boomed in from over the horizon and headed out over the Atlantic.

Ghandi and Alagba then carried each of the tureens into the waves, where they emptied the old water and replaced it with new. When they'd finished, they covered each of the pots again, said a prayer, and the ceremony was concluded.

The kids were in the water in a flash. Lacking a change of clothes, I hung back on the beach, but it was so hot I at least peeled off my shirt, the better to blister.

Alagba waved, and I turned to see Chief Elesin trooping down the boardwalk in black mesh tank top and shorts like a San Diego surfer, ice chest under arm and radio tuned to a funk station. As soon as he reached the sand he peeled off his clothes down to a leopard-pattern bikini brief. On his lean, muscled body, it looked good. He sprinted toward the water, then stopped abruptly, as if he'd forgotten something. He ran back toward the pots and fell forward on his hands, in what resembled a modified push-up, the position of respect to royalty or the orisha. He had forgotten to pay his respects to Yemonja. When he had done that, he sprang to his feet and cart-wheeled into the surf with one of the drummer boys.

"Elegba," Iya Ghandi sighed, as though at an irrepresible teen-ager.

I walked up the beach alone, watching all the sunbathers watching they knew not what.

The tide was coming in fast. I got back to the group just as Iya Ghandi had begun to move the pots to the edge of the dune line. "That's what they're after," she said of the incoming waves. I said maybe we should go—I had an appointment with the king and didn't want to be late. She said it was time to leave anyway.

Then she spotted something down the beach, walked off, and came back with a dead gafftop catfish. I'd noticed it earlier in a pile of seaweed. To me it was just decaying refuse. Not to her. "This means big money," she beamed, and plopped it into Yemonja's pot. It would be food for the orisha for the coming year, and would bring good luck.

We carried everything back to the cars and the kids showered off the sand and salt. On the way home the two boys and Chief Alagba fell asleep. I wished I could have, too, and I was on fire with sunburn, but I drove fast and made it back before three, just in time for my appointment.

But the Oba wasn't there. Instead, burly Chief Akin Tobi, who had played the egungun figure, came up to me, shyly, and asked if I would mind driving the twenty or so miles back into Beaufort. The royal station wagon had broken down and the Oba, Iya Orite, Miwa and her six-month-old baby were all waiting at Bradford Tire. Could I bring them home?

—≡—

The Oba and Iya Shanla went away for the weekend, in part to patch up some of the strains of husband and wives, and I went away, too. It was good to return, though, and I settled back into my hut and routine with perhaps undue ease. Something was seductive here; I could understand why people stayed, and why each time someone left, a piece of the community fabric was torn away. Maybe the Oba knew I knew that. I don't know why else he invited me to that week's meeting of the Ogboni Society. The council sessions weren't secret, but it was unusual for an outsider to be admitted. It was, of course, a good way for me to observe the nuts and bolts of village decision-making. But I knew there was something else the Oba really wanted me to see.

At twilight, a shirtless teenage boy escorted me to the meeting chamber inside the Afin. The fading light and the still, thick air gave the long hut at the far corner of the walled compound the aura of the timeless court of a fairy tale prince. As soon as I walked in I saw the Oba seated on a small, elevated dais along one wall. Despite the humidity and temperature well into the nineties, he was smoking his intricately carved bone pipe.

I took a seat in a folding chair at the far end of the room and watched as six members of the council finished their invocation dance before a shrine to the ancestors. It seemed to go on a long time, but when they had finished, and returned to their seats, the Oba put down his pipe, and, without speaking, began to throw his opele. He smiled. The reading was good; nonetheless, he called for precautionary ebo. Three roosters for Ogun and three hens for Oshun.

Iya Shanla, sitting near the king, excused herself momentarily to retrieve an electric fan from the royal quarters, which helped move the dense air around, but not a lot. None of the circulation reached me, anyway. Even sitting quietly, I was bathed in sweat and covered in mosquitoes from the unscreened windows and door.

As recording secretary, Shanla reviewed the previous week's minutes. They had discussed dedication of the new shower and bath house and the pros and cons of tourism. Then came administrative discussions. Despite the exotic ambiance, I began to wonder if my intuition about the invitation had been wrong—maybe this council meeting would be as routine as ones I'd covered as a reporter.

"New business" shifted the tone immediately. First was the matter of Iya Orite's land. The Oba wanted to give her title to a small plot for a house and small garden. As the king's wife, property was her due by tradition. She knew it and they knew it. On the other hand, the rivalry with Shanla made any gift to Orite appear as favoritism. Some of the other villagers may have been troubled by it, too, if the comments at yesterday's sharp-tongued gelede, an annual burlesque-style convening of the village "witches" to publicly air gossip and grievances, were an indication.

By protocol, Orite was required to petition the Ogboni council for approval of the grant—it was a limited monarchy; the king couldn't just do as he pleased. Orite had done her lobbying, though, and got a unanimous vote. The six council members—now seven with the late arrival of Chief Elesin, who had been giving a reading to a client from Hilton Head—sealed the pact with a capful each of Seagram's gin and bits of coconut from a small pass-around plate. Last to partake was Orite, who knelt before the Oba and pressed her head to the floor in obeisance.

Next the Oba asked the council to consider the request of a mother of a troubled thirty-two-year-old man, diagnosed schizophrenic. She wanted the village to take her son for the summer. Some of the members were against it, thinking the man's problem too much trouble. The Oba had a different view. "We know a lot of times people are dismissed as having behaviorial problems simply because they can't relate. Maybe this would be what he needs to snap him back together. We are all schizophrenic to the extent we are living in two opposing cultures. All Afro-Americans are."

To find the correct path, the Oba cast the opele, both for the village and for the man. Explicating the throw, he told the council, "Ifa has sent this man and we should not try to avoid it. Obatala and Esu (Elegba) say there will be a creative solution. Ideally, he should be initiated." Both wives were against the plan, for although the king would collect most of the fees for the man's initiation, it would surely be the wives who, in return for their shares, would have to deal with the daily caretaking. But eventually Orite sided with the king and the majority. Shanla didn't. And neither did Iya Ghandi.

In the moments after that, the room gradually fell silent. A few priests whispered to each other, or exchanged knowing looks. The king re-lit his pipe. From the quiet came a rustle of cotton. Ghandi stood up to speak, her right before the council. Everyone already knew what she wanted to say.

The Oba listened quietly, though he looked as sad as she did defensive. He didn't want to lose her, but it wasn't up to him. Nor any mortal. Ultimately, Ifa would reveal what Ghandi should do. That didn't make the possible departure of the village's only Yemonja priestess any less burdensome, or his heart any less sick about it. No wonder festival week had seemed to carry such odd vibes—it was the goddess's own curtain call.

Ghandi sat down, and the Oba leaned back in his chair, pipe in hand. He seemed to study every face. I knew this was why I was there. I wiped sweat from my eyes and dabbed drops of it off the pages of my notebook.

"We are living in a chaotic period," he began. "It is important to always keep in mind that in a period of creativity there are always chaotic situations that don't follow an idea or a plan, but are happening. We thought the arrival of Yoruba culture would eliminate all problems. We have learned that this is not necessarily the case." He paused to let the point sink in.

"We are like people in a lifeboat in a storm. We cannot control events. But we have to keep doing what we have to do. . . .

The pagans endured because they were prepared to accept confusion. That is the whole concept of Esu. If we are looking for an ideal situation, forget it. Hold what we have intact, continue to explore, advance. We have to remember we were sent here on a mission, and we must hold onto our moorings."

Toward the end, he was looking directly at Iya Ghandi, who sometimes returned his gaze, sometimes looked at the floor. No further action was taken. The king apparently felt it best to let the issue lay where it was. But everyone knew she would go. And within the year, she did, following a bitter intra-village quarrel. Exiled from Oyotunji, she disappeared from even its outermost networks, and, like so many people in the voudou world, spun away into another reality, to another fate of life and spirit. Iya Shanla eventually left, too.

# 16

## ADVICE AND CONSENT

A FEW DAYS LATER, I asked for my reading. As with Lorita, I'd been putting it off. The king agreed, pleased I'd finally come around, and set a time for that afternoon. I would follow a woman from Georgia who'd driven in especially. It all ran late, of course, but eventually one of the king's daughters came to lead me back to the Afin. The Oba was in Iya Orite's house—her own, now. From the outside the little two-bedroom looked like a trailer home that had taken root in stages; the interior was plain folks, too—paneled walls, sofas, big portraits of family on the walls, a few throw rugs, a TV.

Iya Orite was in the front room straightening book shelves and setting up an ironing board. Several village children had taken up spots near the kitchen in front of the TV, watching cartoons. Orite asked me to leave my shoes by the door—African custom. As I removed them, I saw the Oba in a wicker chair in the opposite corner. He greeted me with a big smile and motioned me over to one of two footstools separated by a straw mat he had laid out on the floor. We sat facing each other and without further small talk, as I was now a client, not an observer, he drew his opele, the babalawo's divining chain, from a small pouch at his waist.

I had been told to bring $30. The Oba said to fold the money three times into a square, say my name, then drop the money to the mat. Rapidly invoking the orisha in a ritual litany, he made his first "drop" of the opele, on top of the money.

He quickly scanned the chain, on whose links eight palm nuts are mounted in swivels, to count which nuts fell "up" and which "down." I couldn't believe how fast he read—like a computer. In a way, that's what he was. The Ifa system, which encompasses, in ascending order of authority, the obi, the cowries, the opele, and yet another called the ikin, is so logic-driven Microsoft could write software for it—literally. (And may yet— the Internet is now full of voudou and santeria web sites, including one for an Ifa society; many of the people mentioned in this book are now reachable via the Net). No matter how many times I pondered or observed the many forms of Ifa, the intellectual and philosophical backbone of voudou theology, I marveled at both its mathematical precision and its organic creativity.[1]

Regardless of the divining instrument used, each permutation is based, like digital technology or a coin flip, on an open-closed option. The coconut husks of the obi fall white side up or dark side up. The cowrie shells face up or down. The palm nuts of the opele show the smooth or rough surface. The job of the priest is to scan the throw and use the numerical "picture" to build a sequenced paradigm of fate, expressed as the odu, for each client.

That's why the Oba's rapid tallying, as he proceeded through the first, and most important throw, and on through a half-dozen more, each one diverging off the previous, tributaries of the generality of life to the specifics of mine, was so impressive. With the four obi husks, five basic combinations of odu are possible.

The sixteen cowries offer seventeen variations. The opele raises the mathematical possibilities to 256. (The *I Ching*, in comparison, has a base of 67.)

The geometrical leap of the opele's range occurs because the chain is actually a kind of super-processor for the oldest of the Ifa methods, the full casting of the eight palm nuts, the ikin. With the obi and cowries, a single throw can yield a full odu. The ikin requires that eight nuts be cast eight times to generate an odu. The process is considered to be the most traditional, and marginally more authoritative, but also far more time-consuming. Most priests have turned to the opele, ekuele in santeria, which can create an equivalent number-picture in just one "drop."

But ikin or opele, the babalawo, to whose use these methods are restricted, is required to be able to recognize each of the 256 potential patterns on sight, and know how each relates to the other and to the orisha pantheon. Each odu, in other words, is distinguished not only by a particular configuration, and formal name, but is also associated with certain traditional verses and parables. And each odu is considered to be a manifestation of a different orisha, or even a different personality trait within an orisha.[2]

To read an odu is to see an incredible range of thousands of options. It would be as though when you saw a country on a map you simultaneously made links with every book written about it, every leader of it, all the people in it and its entire history, and could merge all that knowledge in a single thought. An odu is an entire novel of existence and imagination, grasped in an instant. In that, it seems as Eastern as a Buddhist insight; the complexity often reminded me of *The Glass Bead Game,* Hesse's metaphoric bridge from Europe to Asia.

As he worked through my reading, the Oba was trying to peer through a tremendously complex prism. But that was not the cause of the odd look on his face. My "dominant" odu, determined on the first cast, was Iwori-osa, indicating the influence of Ifa and Oya. But with each subsequent, or refining cast, he had repeated the name of a different orisha—each time with increasing tone of puzzlement. What was happening—though I did not know it at the time—was that I was not being divined in the way we had all expected.

As I watched the Oba's brow furrow, I knew what had been behind my reluctance to show up for a reading all week. This is how it had gone in Atlanta, too.

I asked the Oba if there were a problem.

Balancing the chain in one hand, focusing somewhere in the distance momentarily, then looking back at me, he said he'd been trying to determine which was my African spirit guide—the mystery everyone in the village had been waiting to solve. He had thought the answer would be fairly straightforward—Obatala. But Obatala wasn't answering.

Iya Orite, who had been observing from her ironing board, came over to kibbitz. "See if it's Elegba," she said. The Oba cast the chain. The chain said no. The Oba and Orite looked at each other. Nobody'd really gone beyond those possiblities for me. Orite had some more ideas. Oshun? The king threw the opele. No. Shango? Same answer. Orite walked away, smiling with a kind of puzzled curiosity. Suddenly she turned. "Ask about Ochosi."

The Oba threw the opele again. This time, instead of shaking his head, he looked up at me. It seemed a very long moment. He grinned and wrote something down in his client book. That was it: Ochosi. The hunter. One of the Warriors. That was who I was.

I felt a slight smile turn the edge of my mouth. I was surprised, too, also having figured myself, perhaps from power of suggestion, for an Obatala. Now I wasn't.

I waited for the king to finish inscribing his notes. In fact, he told me later, he had seen Ochosi on the second throw, in a configuration known as Irete Tura, which indicated the presence of both Ochosi, in the dominant position, and Elegba, on a secondary level. But the weakness or ambiguity of the successive throws hadn't really convinced him Ochosi was for me. He'd made the additional casts, even waiting for Iya Orite to be the one to pose the definitive yes-no question, to be sure.

Had this been Africa, and had I been a real initiate, he would at this point have begun to recite the appropriate verses from my dominant odu. Then he would have told me the apataki which fit the odu and verse. After that, he would have helped me relate the meaning of the verses and the parable to my life. In America, where most clients have no acquaintance with the odu, or with verses, or with parables, priests generally summarize. "Well, the reading looks good, but you need to be more careful with your money, or take better care of your wife," etc.

For me, the Oba also had to explain the nature of my new spirit, about whom I knew little. Ochosi, he said, lives and works alone. My only companions were Ogun and Osanyin, the reclusive wizard of herbs and medicines, who, like Ochosi, lived deep in the forest. Ochosi is syncretized with St. Norbert, the Catholic saint who is sometimes depicted in forest garb with a dog. No wonder, it occurred to me, Robin Hood was one of the great heroes of my boyhood.

I was an important spirit, the Oba explained—one who went forth to bring back sustenance for the people. Yet I did not wish to live among them. As Ochosi, I was a networker. I linked people together through sharing the information from my solitary travels. The Oba said it would be good for me to work in or around a "structured environment," by which I think he meant a job, but that I also must be free to move, search. I would never have a long relationship with a woman, because I would be too solitary. I was a spirit who went between the world of men and of nature, and preferred the latter.

It didn't sound like fun. Edward Abbey would make a good Ochosi, living alone in his rock canyons in Utah, but was that really me? Alas, the more I pondered it, the more it seemed true. I really was a hunter—a writer, a searcher for knowledge. I gathered information and brought it back to the community of the literate. Still, I was perplexed by the unexpected shift of my spiritual identity.

Previous indications that I might be Obatala hadn't been guesswork—Baba Tunde had called it thus in Atlanta. The king explained that such a conflict over one's orisha identity was possible, but when that happens, the higher level of Ifa rules. In my case, the opele of the Oba outranked the cowries of Baba Tunde. The Oba himself had initially thought he was Shango, only to be read as Obatala, and then, later, had become a priest of Ifa. Iya Orite said she, too, had gone through a kind of orisha crisis in the course of initiation to Obatala—three orisha had been "in a battle" for her "head."

There were further complexities. The Oba said my reading also revealed a strong Obatala presence after all, appearing in his "stern" personality. Oya was in there as a supplement, too, making me "stubborn, headstrong." I also had a "cultural" Oshun, who drew Obatala's tendency toward intellect and organization into artistic spheres. And there was a "cultural" Elegba—from the second odu, the one which had revealed the presence of Ochosi. Further, each of these secondary orisha, in each aspect, had to be particularized to me, or I to them. Were I to pursue further steps towards initiation, I would have to incorporate their "personalities" into my own. Oya, for example, doesn't like intoxicating drink—I do, but can't tolerate much. Because of Ochosi, I would favor the green of the forest in my clothing. I do, though maybe because I'm part Irish.

As the king explained all this to me, I felt my spirit brighten, as if I had finally discovered my true identity—and liked it.

But the critical part of the reading remained. Because it is binary, Ifa is a philosophy of pairs—good and evil, fortune and misfortune. In every reading, good news is tempered with bad. There is always a downside risk. In voudou the bad news is called osobo—a warning. In order to secure the positive things that have been foreseen—or reduce the negative consequences of a bad reading, such as mine in Atlanta—the osobo must be mitigated. In voudou, mitigation comes through sacrifice.

The king said my warning "speaks to travel, to the streets and highways." The orisha with jurisdiction in those areas were Elegba and Ogun. If I wanted to ward off possible harm—harm that might jeopardize the realization of the other, dominant forces in my reading, I should make ebo.

I looked across at the Oba. He was leaving it up to me.

"Okay," I said. "What would we have to do?"

He cast the opele. To appease the hunger of the gods and persuade them not to interfere with my fate, but to help me, I should sacrifice three young roosters. It would cost $150.

"We'll do it tomorrow," he said, and glanced toward his wife, as though confirming a dental appointment. "Iya Orite will tell you what all you need to do."

I stood to go. As I was putting my shoes back on, Miwa, who had come in a few minutes earlier, walked over to her father to beg for a reading. She was trying to decide whether to move to Atlanta to take a job. The king said he didn't really have time, but, as everyone in the room knew, time wasn't the issue. Neither he nor Orite wanted to face the loss of their daughter to the big city, and a life that would draw her ever away from Oyotunji.

But Miwa, like her mother, was persistent. The king gave in, and Miwa took her place on the stool I had just vacated. The king threw. Orite moved closer. The Oba scanned the chain and looked at Orite, who also saw the message. "I hate to tell you this," the king said, "but I have to be honest. The odu says you will prosper." In that moment he was not a king, nor a babalawo. He was a father who knew his daughter had the blessings of fate to leave a home which would feel her absence in thousands of ways for thousands of days.

—==—

The next morning I got up and waited for the roosters to arrive. It had been a busy week and village supplies were temporarily exhausted. Iya Orite had called the local farmer who brought in new livestock once or twice a week to request a special delivery. He was supposed to arrive by nine or ten in the morning, and we could go ahead. The king had to leave the village for the day, so if the roosters weren't there in time, she, as priestess of Obatala, would make the ebo. We would use the royal Elegba and Ogun altar in the small yard adjacent to her house.

Noon came and went. So did the king. No farmer, no roosters, no ebo. I couldn't believe it. How could it be so hard to find chickens in the middle of Southern farm country? I resigned myself to a day of waiting—not that it really mattered when I fed the orisha, or when I left the village, or when I got to the next place down the road. I didn't even wear a watch anymore. During the lull, I walked down to the dirt and grass-covered parking area outside the sentry gate and watched Chief Alagba trying to replace a universal joint under his old white station wagon. He lay in the dirt for hours, up to his elbows in grease, and never complained. He told me he'd been driving back from Beaufort when the joint started going out, and he had gotten all the way back to the village, just under the shade tree where it now sat all jacked up, before it completely clunked out. "God was with me or I wouldn't have made it this far," he said. I said it looked like god was with him and against him, all things considered.

By mid-afternoon the chicken farmer still hadn't come. Tired, cranky and hot, I slumped deep into a chair outside The Horseman. To my surprise Iya Ghandi came up and said she'd take me to get the roosters I needed. If we left now we could be back in an hour or so. We took off at once, and after stopping at the gas station/mini-mart in Sheldon for a loaf of bread, vegetables and peppermints for her kids—funny how my car always fit her needs—we made good time on Highway 21. A few miles past Beaufort, Ghandi pointed out a plain looking ranch style house on the left side of the highway. I turned into the driveway and parked amid the tire ruts. I could see now what had been secluded by trees from the road: a kind of suburban livestock zoo. In the field behind the house, a trampled down area of old farm equipment, lumber and storage sheds, a fenced pen held both free-range stock and dozens of wire pens and crates filled with slaughter animals of all descriptions. I saw mostly chickens—hundreds, perhaps—but also pigeons, guinea fowl, peacocks, geese, turkeys, pigs and goats.

Back among the pens a forty-ish white woman—petite, blonde, tough and sassy—scattered feed. She greeted Iya Ghandi familiarly and introduced herself to me. When I marveled at the extent of the enterprise, she smiled proudly. Gray's Hill was a respected supplier of live poultry and livestock to numerous local butchers and retail stores. Villagers were regular clients, either in times of special needs or when the farmer who usually supplied them was late. I said that was pretty much our case. The woman looked at me quizzically at first, maybe because I was white. Then, suddenly, she got it. She knew why I was there. So what did we need today? Three roosters, said Iya Ghandi. No problem, said the woman.

She picked up her catching pole, a kind of broomstick handle with a net on the end. Roosters and pullets scurried so plentifully at our feet that it was no chore for her to trap one, two, three, just like that, scooping them up as though they were land-locked butterflies. I wondered, briefly, if fate also dictated which of the many young roosters were the ones that would be caught, or if it was just another exercise in survival of the quickest? Not that any of the chickens in this commercial lot faced the prospect of a long life. As the woman netted each bird, she gave it to me to hold. Then she put the catching pole aside and picked up some lengths of barn twine, with which she bound each bird's legs as I tried to keep the flapping and squawking to a minimum. "If you think this is rough, just wait," she said to the last one, cinching the knot above its claws.

I paid $22.50 for all three. The price was high—dead and packaged in the store, poultry wouldn't fetch a third that much—but I suppose the idea was that they weren't dead and packaged. Iya Ghandi warned me to put newspaper on the floor on the passenger side, where she would hold them, and we also covered their heads to keep them calm. Across the highway, three utility company linemen were watching us closely. As we drove off I could see them wisecrack to each other.

Back at the village, I walked down to Iya Orite's house and told her I'd been to Gray's. She was glad, and maybe a little surprised, that Ghandi had helped me. She said to give her an hour to prepare.

I went back to my hut to wait. I had plenty to do. I hadn't packed to leave—not really sure if I'd be staying another day or not, depending on whether the ebo got delayed. I threw my clothes into my flight bag, drained the melted ice and spilled orange juice from the Igloo cooler, pulled my striped towel off the nail in the wall, and stashed everything in the trunk of my GTI.

Then I looked for Chief Elesin, who had promised to make me an Ochosi figure. The king had recommended that I "feed" it with the blood of the roosters during my ebo. But I couldn't find Elesin. I did see the long-lost farmer, an elderly black man in straw hat and overalls, finally chug up in an old pickup carrying a few crates of chickens. Even though I'd finally supplied my own (the price deducted from the fee), Iya Orite gladly purchased what the farmer delivered. She'd have plenty of use for them.

----

[1] Background on Ifa divination from the patient explanations of Oba Oseijeman Adefumni I of Oyotunji, and Chief A. J. Ajamu of Miami, as well as to two of William L. Bascom's authoritative accounts, *Ifa Divination: Gods and Men in West Africa*, 1969, Indiana University Press, Bloomington, and *Sixteen Cowries: Yoruba Divination, Africa to the New World*, 1980, Indiana University Press, Bloomington. I have also drawn from conversations with Dr. Afolabi A. Epega of the Bronx, and his book *Ifa: The Ancient Wisdom*, 1987, Imole Oluwa Institute, New York.

[2] The odu known as Irete Fu, for example, would look like this:

    II      I
    I       I
    II      II
    I       I

Deciphering the odu means unlocking the sequence of the casting. Though it appears complicated, the procedure is relatively simple once you grasp the basic rules. The first is to read everything backwards. To read the odu Irete Fu, start with the top figure in the *right* column, then move horizontally across the top figure in the *left* column, and so on down for each row.

Each of the eight marks in the columns is an indication of how many nuts were left behind, or with the opele, how many were face up or down. The methodology derives from the older ikin method. When the babalawo throws the eight nuts onto a sacred mat, he can only use his left hand to scoop them up. But he can't hold them all (or so tradition dictates) in his fist, and either one or two are left behind. Three or more disqualifies the throw.

After each throw, the babalawo indicates in the dirt, or these days on paper, whether one or two nuts remained. He does this eight times, marking the results in two columns of four rows each. But reversed.

Thus, a double mark (II) indicates a single nut, while a single mark (I) indicates two remaining nuts. That means—reading the top row, right to left—that on his first throw, the babalawo left two nuts behind, then one on his second. And so on.

# 17

## SACRIFICE

THE ISSUE OF sacrifice has been one of the most difficult for those wishing to approach or understand voudou, but to the true believer, it is the essence of the religion. From the point of view of the voudou priest, ebo is a necessary fulfillment of Ifa divination. It is the way in which humans seek direct intervention—or direct nonintervention—in their particular fates. Sacrifice placates Elegba—or any of the other orisha, or the ancestors, who may affect our lives. Sacrifice is a way of honoring the gods while seeking their assistance. It is karma's hedge against chaos.

Ebo is at once a bribe, a tithe, a token of fealty and a eucharist. To seek divination and then fail to pay the gods their due—ebo—would be to welsh on the deal, and to risk either losing a good fate or falling into a bad one. Sacrifice is among the holiest of obligations of the voudou worshiper. Omission of sacrifice could be one of his or her most dangerous failures. The voudou gods are not Christian angels. They are angry, brave, jealous, vengeful, generous—very human in emotional response, as were the gods of the Greeks or Romans. They take offense and they reward devotion.

Without sacrifice, divination is meaningless—you have not lived up to your part of the bargain. A worshiper simply can't have one without the other. "The purpose of divination is to learn the hidden factor," Dr. Afolabi Epega, a Nigerian chemist and babalawo I met in the Bronx, once told me. "Then you know how to plan to omit future problems. Sacrifices will help you forestall the bad. The foreknowledge of it also will make you get more cautious. With the necessary precautions, maybe things would be different. If you made the proper sacrifice, then maybe you could avoid it. You see, faith can be multiplied. That's why we practice this."

The apataki are saturated with cautionary tales of misfortune for those who fail to perform ebo and thus offend the dieties. In Greek mythology, self-pride resulted in hubris, punishment by the gods. I'm not sure the orisha are that concerned with self-pride. But they are notoriously tough on disrespect. The ancient parable of the fall of Corn, narrated for me by Chief A. S. Ajamu, formerly of the village, is a classic caution against failure to pay one's dues:

> Corn—yabado in Yoruba—wanted to come to the earth. Of course, before going to the earth you go to get divination to find out what it's going to be like, to find out if there's anything you need to do before you come there. So Corn, like anyone else, went and got divination from a babalawo named Peta. The babalawo told him that he was to sacrifice to Esu before he went. But Corn felt like his destiny was based on what he wanted to come to the earth for, and he didn't see any sense in making a sacrifice, so he rushed on. He was eager to get to earth.
>
> After he got there, people were amazed by his colors—gold colors, beautiful. They were so

amazed by his colors that they began to plant the seed in the ground and they were further amazed when it began to grow, how pretty it was.

They planted it very close together. The old people used to tell us to put a whole lot of seeds together. Why? Because the minute they pop up and the seed bursts open and the first little green shoot comes up there's a bird that loves to come down the row and just 'Chit, chit, chit, chit.' Watching their pattern, you usually find out that they miss every other one so you can still have corn. So you plant some for the birds, and some for yourself.

So Corn noticed that that happened, and that wasn't so bad, and so he went ahead and people were amazed at how pretty it was as it grew with its silk on it, and they found all different kinds of uses for every part of it. Eventually, of course, they began to grind it. That was kind of rough. Then they began to cook it. Then they began to scrape it off the cob and do all kinds of things with it and—Corn began to see then why he should have made sacrifice.

"But the final straw was that when people couldn't think of anything else to do with it, they began to pop it. So of course when they put the heat to it, that was the last straw, and we are told that even today that when people go to pop corn you hear Corn screaming out the name of the babalawo, 'Peta, peta, peta, peta.' That's what he's saying, because Corn remembers his divination in heaven.

Perhaps my knowledge of the consequences of shirking back from the gods, once invoked, was what convinced me, even more than curiosity, that I could not refuse to participate in ebo, either here or in Atlanta. Since I had undertaken an intellectual bargain, so to speak, to ascribe to divination by asking to learn its ways, I could not back out later. I couldn't say I was interested in having my fortune read but not in giving something back to the keepers of fortune. Refusing ebo would be bad faith. And so, step by step, I bound myself to the logic of my oath.

—==—

Outside the world of voudou, however, sacrifice is still largely perceived as evil and satanic—the work of madmen, not holy men. There always seem to be examples of some psychopath dismembering someone or something and calling it a sacrificial rite. Any strange cult killings are usually seen as fringe evidence that voudou is evil because voudou, too, uses sacrifice.

The discovery of a bloody drug cult operating in 1989 near Matamoros, Mexico, for example, spurred a widespread backlash against voudou. The leader, Adolfo de Jesus Constanzo, was a Cuban-American who had grown up in Miami and knew enough about santeria and palo to concoct his own coked-up versions. Apparently, his idea was that human sacrifice would protect his gang from getting caught. He stretched palo's use of a human bone in the nganga to the idea that you had to keep killing fresh victims to keep the pot working. That the theory bore as much relation to voudou or palo as Jonestown to Christianity was not only lost on Constanzo's gang of morons, but on most people who read about the gruesome killings or saw clips about them on TV.

That story was in the news much of the summer I was on the road, and those in the religion everywhere I went were intrigued by the investigation. But there was a marked difference between their reactions and those of nonvoudous. Among voudous, Matamoros coverage was a matter of information, not reproach. Nonvoudous, on the other hand, kept trying to draw me out, the supposition being that deep, deep down, weren't the killings in Matamoros, like the fictitious ones in movies such as *Angel Heart* or *True Believers,* what voudou was really about?

*Wasn't voudou really about human sacrifice?*

Yes and no. In Yoruba tradition, human sacrifice—as opposed to that of animals and fowl—is a matter of historical evolution. For many centuries, voudous in Africa sacrificed humans to their gods, as did many religions, including Christianity, if you consider Jesus to have been sacrificed on the cross. But the practice, which had been almost exclusively limited to sacrifice of criminals and prisoners of war—to state executions, in other words— stopped in the seventeenth and eighteenth centuries, at least partly through pressure from European colonial governors who thought capital punishment should be reserved for themselves.

Yoruba legend accounts for the cessation in a different way. The story is that a famous Yoruba king was confronted with a demand from Ifa to sacrifice not criminals, but his own daughter—as Abraham had been asked to sacrifice his son to prove his faith. The king anguished. He did not want to anger the gods, but he loved his daughter dearly. He consulted Ifa again, and from the reading concluded that perhaps he could substitute a warm-blooded mammal for his beloved child. It was worth a chance. The god accepted the offering and the piety of the king, and from that time, it has been considered acceptable in orisha voudou to offer mammals, not humans, as the highest type of blood sacrifice.

It is important to note, however, that the shift in attitude was about the kind of ebo, not the concept itself. Anyone considering following the path of the orisha must accept that. The Oba made that plain to me one afternoon in a singularly astringent analysis.

"I didn't have a problem with Matamoros," the Oba had shrugged, lighting his pipe as we sat alone in the village bazaar. "Human sacrifice is a part of every culture. Americans still sacrifice humans when they execute somebody. They execute them not because they broke the laws of god or the cosmos, they broke the laws of America, laid down by some people who said this or that or the other. They bring in a preacher or a priest, then they get a ceremony going. And the priest reads some verses out of his Bible and he makes prayers, and then they execute the man."

He brushed away a mosquito. "That's really a ceremonial sacrifice. And this is essentially the same thing and the same reason that they did it in Africa. These were criminals who had been condemned to capital punishment. They held them, and once a year they'd execute them all at the same time. They also sacrificed prisoners of war, at an annual ceremony when they had to send people to the king's ancestors to be his bodyguards.

"But only a king could order a capital punishment, a capital sacrifice. And that was my argument with the people in Matamoros. They were not kings. So that was a criminal act, what they did. If a king had ordered it, or a government, then it's legal."

He looked at me to make sure I was following the point.

"Only the government has the right to kill people. The average individual cannot kill, but the government does or the governor does in the name of the people of the state—the same way it was in Africa. The king did it in the name of the government, of the people of the nation, for the welfare of the nation. That was the concept."

The Oba had obviously considered the question for so long, and in such detail, that he talked about human sacrifice as dispassionately as a scientist analyzing a laboratory theorem. I tried not to let my face show that I found the discussion unsettling, that in some way I was suspending the idea that we were talking about killing people. But he saw my thoughts. Re-lighting his pipe, he tried to account for my lack of serenity.

"The idea of death in Africa is not the same thanatophobia that Westerners have," he said. "Remember, Western ideas of death have come mainly from Judaism, which is mainly: once you dead, you done. Christianity tried to alter that a little bit by adopting the ancient Egyptian idea of resurrection, but you still never returned. In the African system, if you killed a person, after twenty years or so they're back again, and so death is never as final in the African mind as it is here. That's why Africans for the most part don't have a big thing about dying. They know they're going to come back anyway."

I accepted that—the sociology and mythology of it. But there was still another aspect: the bottom line. All philosophical issues aside, did sacrifice really work? Could a serious person believe it? Dr. Epega, author of *Ifa: The Ancient Wisdom*, was a very serious person, and he believed sacrifice could affect fate. The late Lydia Cabrera, the respected Cuban scholar whose path-breaking study of palo mayombe, *El Monte*, is considered the definitive reference on the Kongo practice, believed in the powers of sacrifice. All manner of serious people believed so.

I just didn't know if I did—truly.

In addition to honoring or placating the orisha, blood sacrifice is considered to have the real-life property of matter-energy-matter transformation. That's how it's supposed to work. You pray, something happens. Mind and spirit become manifest in matter. I have never been comfortable with this idea. It seems like alchemy, or, at best, unverifiable mythology—snake stories. But mind-matter conversion is central to voudou, and perhaps to all religion.

In Christianity, in Islam, in Judaism, in Buddhism, we seek to transfer power from God to ourselves (or our purposes) through focusing energies on thought-waves—better known as prayers. We believe—belief being the key principle—that our prayers will be relayed to God, who will transform them into the desired action or material effect. It is common in all these religions to supplement the prayer with candles, statues or texts as focal objects of concentration.

Voudou's use of charms, shrines and so on are no different, but to that is added what the other religions have largely abandoned, except symbolically: the necessity of living focal objects. In that sense voudou is truly pagan, which is to say nonChristian. But does that render the system rationally invalid? If scientific philosophy can accomodate Christian Creationism, for example, is there some reason it can't accommodate the feeding of the gods?

Not to the Oba of Oyotunji, and he was a serious person, too. "Actually what we're doing is activating fire energy," he said of the voudou version of transubstantiation. "You don't have to use animals. You can use plants. But blood is much more active and energetic. Any physicist can explain that to you— blood is a much more dynamic energy than, say, sap.

"When we do ebo, during the ceremony we sing, 'May this blood change into money.' What we're doing is asking that this blood which we're sacrificing activate and change so that it brings money to this person. The reason we smear the blood all over them is to activate their fire energies.

"But you've already got the energy in you," he said. "You're born with all the energies of the cosmos. The day you took your first breath you got it in you, to greater or lesser degrees. If it's weak in one area you can do things to make it stronger. One thing is you might take a piece of iron and hang it around your neck like a chain or put it around your leg."

I remembered the piece of chain I carried in my pocket, bought from a voudou priest here three years ago. He had said it would give me strength, and suggested I wear it on my ankle.

But he never told me exactly why, and I had found it more convenient to keep in my pocket. I showed it to the Oba.

"That's good," he said, examining it professionally, "but you can get even more strength from that piece of iron if you go to a priest every week and let him put blood on the iron. The blood activates the metal and brings out the iron energy that is already in you. That blood is what is going to strengthen you and that is why you keep going back to the priest. Same way you keep going back and forth to a doctor when you use up your pills— you go and get some more."

"Voudou is physics," the Oba smiled. "That's what it really is. Because you're working with energies. A priest is working with energies. He's saying that everything has got energy in it. Your fingernail and your hair has got energy. And they see a voudou priest making a little ball with these things and grinding them up into a powder." The Oba's hands spread upward and his voice rose in mock horror. "Wooooo!" he exclaimed. "That's evil, because they can't understand it."

His voice dropped back to a normal, even a serious pitch. "But the point is the man is working with *physics*. Scientists have now discovered that every single follicle of your hair has got your DNA in it. And you can find a criminal by getting one hair. And you can break it down and it's got a DNA, an energy, unique to that individual. If you wanted to clone somebody, you could get the DNA from his fingernail or his hair, and that's physics."

He chuckled and got up to leave. "To the Yoruba that's old hat. They also know that everything you touch, you leave your energy on it. Humans have a terrible electrical force. There are plants like that—if you touch them they will close up and die. But the Africans discovered that first. They discovered the human aura."

Esu/Elegba altar, inside the royal compound, Oyotunji village.

Esu/Elegba altar. Feathers, palm oil, blood, honey and other elements denote recent sacrifices. Pumpkin is for Oshun; old sewing machine and other iron pieces are for Ogun.

Iya Orite emerged from her house to greet me for my ebo. She looked beautiful. Her hair was freshly powdered, well set off from the glowing skin of her bare shoulders. As she walked toward me, she tucked her white wrap-around dress, or lapa, in at the top, as the women were always doing to keep the garment up. She seemed almost business-like, though, as she picked a chair from the side of the house and carried it to the middle of the unshaded yard so that it faced directly onto the Esu (Elegba) shrine. Constructed from knee-high concrete blocks stacked against the outer wall of the Afin where it abutted the forest, the altar was arrayed on two levels. The top was mostly for an iron bin filled with machetes, railroad spikes and other metals. The lower step was cluttered with pots, bowls, and ordinary daily items: rolling pins, mousetraps, gourds, pumpkins, coconut bits, candles. A rusted sewing machine sat to one side.

Two red, carved wooden pillars the size of tree trunks framed the sacrificial stage and behind them stylized drawings of the deities in swirls of red and yellow, blue and black, covered the wall. A placard said, "Oyotunji Esu." Below it lay a smattering of feathers and what looked like entrails and gore. Some of it was, but most of the orange and yellow ooze was just palm oil and honey.

Orite told me to sit in the chair. As I did, she went to the altar for a red plastic cup of water. The three roosters sat low in their wire cage to the side. Dipping her fingers in the cup, she sprinkled herself, the altar and the roosters. She opened the door of the cage and carefully snared all three by their legs, then brought them to me to hold. Almost at once, she took them back. She told me to stand, step forward with my eyes closed and extend my palms.

I did, but opened my eyes when I felt the warm bodies being rubbed all over me. Orite chanted in Yoruba until the cleaning was finished, then passed the roosters for me to hold again. I took them as she had, my left hand around their rough yellowish legs, my right hand atop their feathery smooth backs. They barely stirred.

She told me to give her one.

Taking it, she approached the altar again. She turned to me and told me to hold my throat. "No, just a little," she laughed. I loosened my grip until I was just pinching my larynx above the adam's apple. She bent over the altar, holding the rooster, praying. I heard Esu's name, and then my own. Without further ado, she plucked enough feathers from the throat for the skin to show, then took a paring knife from the altar and decapitated the bird in one swift, unapologetic motion. The head dropped to the ground. The body shook in an involuntary spasm of escaping life.

She held the carcass upside down by the legs and allowed blood to drip over the Esu statue. I heard the names of more deities being recited. I was still holding my throat and clutching the legs of the two living birds.

She brought the kill to me and told me to sit. She held the wound directly in front of my face.

"Taste the power of the blood."

She didn't say how, but I couldn't see any other way. I touched my tongue to the severed neck muscle. That seemed to be the way. It was warm, salty, though not unpleasant. It was just blood.

Next, she took my right hand and drew a line of blood along the index finger. She marked a small cross on my palm line. Then she bent low and touched the bird's neck to my right shoe. Remembering Atlanta, I asked if I should remove it. She shook her head. "You're not going to be working barefoot are you?"

The second bird was for Ogun. I tasted the blood but she did not mark me with it.

The third rooster was Ochosi's. I pinched my throat again, and this time, in addition to dripping blood over the rest of the altar, she also let some fall on four coconut husks I hadn't previously noticed. Again, she brought the carcass to me so I could taste the sticky-sweet fire-energy.

She annointed my forehead, touching her fingers to the neck's protruding stub, painting a spot just above my eyebrows. She laid the body of the final bird next to the altar, alongside the other two, and poured honey and palm oil over everything. Some of the honey went on my forehead, next to the blood, and over the blood on my right hand. I tasted the mix with my left forefinger.

Now that they had been properly seasoned, and therefore likely to be more powerful and accurate, it was time to consult the obi. Iya Orite cast the husks several times, without comment. When finished, she picked up a half-pint bottle of dark rum, filled her mouth with it, and spewed it over the fresh feathers, blood and emoluments. Three times she did this. Then, taking another mouthful, she bent over slightly to spray a mist onto my feet. She handed me the bottle and told me to drink a good mouthful. I did.

Back at the altar, Orite picked up the obi again and made several more casts. She said she was trying to determine Esu's message. As usual, I was a tough read. But on the last throw she stood up and smiled. It was favorable. Esu said I was moving in the right direction, that things would work out. She said there also had been a message from Ogun. It said not to rush, to expect things to be slow at first. Ochosi's input was the same as Esu's; he also might bring me money.

I should get an Ochosi figure, Iya Orite said, and bring it to her for feeding sometime later. I said I'd tried to get one from Chief Elesin but he hadn't delivered it. She shrugged, as if that were expected, and said I could find plenty of Ochosis in Miami. I could send it to her and she could feed it for me even though I wasn't present. They did that for many clients.

As we talked, I was aware of the sun beating down from above, of standing in a patch of yard inside an African renaissance village in one of the most virulent Southern slave states, splotched with blood from a ritual no one in my family, none of my friends, and few, perhaps, of you, will ever perceive as other than satanic, or, at best, cruel. But I felt as though I had been baptized.

Orite picked up the rooster bodies and told me to pluck feathers from each, then scatter the tufts over the altar for each of the three orisha. When I had finished, she wiped my head, hands and feet with feathers. I finally swallowed the blood that had been on my tongue. Then I knelt and repeated a Yoruba chant she recited for me.

We rose. As I looked down at the altar, I became aware of rap music. It may have been playing the whole time—twenty minutes, perhaps—but I hadn't heard it. I looked off toward the royal enclave. Two teenagers, one of them a trouble-prone boy from Philadelphia seconded to the village by his mother for discipline, were listening to the radio while repairing a roof.

I thought we were finished, but then Iya Orite picked up the obi and threw them once more. The husks landed ejife, very favorable. She said, "Okay, you have to take the ebo to the railroad tracks." I followed her to a clearing behind her house where we found a metal bucket to hold the heads and bodies. She pointed out a path leading into the woods and said to follow it and dump the remains between the rails.

The narrow trail through the underbrush was well-trodden, strewn here and there with parts of goats and chickens. I came to the cinder shoulders and climbed up an embankment. Along the open track bed, I saw none of the bones, entrails or feathers that littered the forest path. I guessed that rail crews or natural scavengers had kept the right-of-way tidy. Quickly, as though I might be seen, I dumped my ebo as instructed. The birds fell out in a triangle shape, which I considered a sign of good luck. I looked both ways and went back.

Iya Orite was at the shrine, lighting a candle for me. I paid the fee and told her goodbye. I wanted to get out on the road right away. She wished me luck and asked me to send her a couple of gallons of palm oil if I came across any in Miami—she was running low and it wasn't easy to find locally. I said I would, though I never did get around to it. "Aláfia," she called, as I walked in the hot dirt toward the Afin gate.

I checked my hut a last time. No one was around to say goodbye to so I got in my car and drove out the lane, through the verdant tunnel, past the still hard-to-read sign, the caverns measureless to man, and turned east on Highway 21 toward the interstate. I figured to get to northern Florida by evening with a hard push, which was exactly what I wanted. A line of cars had bunched up near the entry ramp. As I got closer, I could see there'd been a big wreck moments before, and smoke was coming up from a truck in the ditch. But I had made ebo. Again. I would be safe, driving so fast.

# 18

## EXILES AND APOSTLES

FLORIDA STRETCHED DOWN to Miami like an endless carny strip. I kept thinking I was going the wrong way—it was all NASA and Gannett media empire and *National Enquirer* and fuzz-busting Canadian Toyotas down the I-95 zipper. To the west lay the interior of the state—mostly swampy nothing; the east was the ocean, the beach, the resort outposts of Yankees and other people who still thought Florida was paradise. Miami lay at the very bottom—a huge metropolis of too many nationalities to count and, geopolitics being what they were, heavily bent toward the right-wing death squad side of the political morass. But that was where I was headed.

This sideshow state had produced the first American writer to take the path I was on, the journey through the spiritual kingdom of U. S. voudou. In 1929, at age twenty-eight, Zora Neale Hurston of Eatonville, Florida, returned to the South with a B.A. from Barnard and contacts with Langston Hughes and others in the Harlem Renaissance to initiate the studies that would earn her reputation as a pioneer folklorist of rural Southern black culture. Her most original work explored the voudou legacy.

*Mules and Men*, 1935, collected oral accounts of hoodoo (as distinct from orisha voudou) in Florida, Alabama and New Orleans, gained by a two-year research trip through the South and parts of the Caribbean. *Tell My Horse*, 1938, recorded the West Indian experience.

Hurston took the Africanized religion of the Southern blacks seriously enough to do what no one had previously: record its many tales and participate in its rituals. In *Mules and Men*, for example, she recounted having lain naked all night in New Orleans to receive the spirit. She drank the blood of sacrifice, was cleansed by hoodoo men, sampled herbs and oils, lit ritual candles. Later, she boiled a black cat to make a mojo of its bone:

> When he screamed, I was told to curse him. He screamed three times, the last time weak and resigned. The lid was clamped down the fire kept vigorously alive. At midnight the lid was lifted. Here was the moment! The bones of the cat must be passed through my mouth until one tasted bitter . . .
>
> . . . Maybe I went off in a trance. Great beast-like creatures thundered up to the circle from all sides. Indescribable noises, sights, feelings. Death was at hand! Seemed unavoidable! I don't know. Many times I have thought and felt, but I always have to say the same thing. I don't know. I don't know.[1]

Hurston was a pioneer; and, I hoped, a kindred spirit. She knew she was onto something vast, important, and yet so diffused in the American South that trying to grasp it was like trying to hold a handful of sand. Even today I feel in her writing her chill, her doubt, her sense of awe, her despair. To enter the spirit world of voudou is to know, in some terrible place in your writer's heart, that no matter how many times you taste the blood, feel the spark of a spirit, that you can never make the myth as manifest as does the reality of the act.

When I got to Fort Pierce, the beachside resort town where Hurston, fifty-nine and broken, died in a welfare home in 1960, nothing indicated her burial site. It was a pleasant enough town— palm tree avenues, a lazy pace, populated these days by a mix of snowbirds, tourists, and commercial-minded Anglos intent on putting up as many housing and shopping tracts as possible. I went to the town library, where a staffer helped me trace the Garden of Heavenly Rest, a county-funded cemetery in the poor, mostly black and hispanic side of town. On the way there I passed Sarah's Memorial Chapel, where Hurston's body had been prepared for pauper's burial. The avenues seethed with hoods in late model cars and no visible means of support.

At the northern limit of North 17th Street, about a mile in from the shoreline, I came to a crushed shell road leading to an open field full of high weeds and flat gravemarkers, except for one in the center, flanked by two evergreen shrubs. In 1973, the writer Alice Walker had come across much the same sight. Appalled, she contracted for a headstone that would at least proclaim the nature of the soul lying beneath. She wrote the epitaph herself: "Zora Neale Hurston. A Genius of the South. 1901–1960. Novelist, Folklorist, Anthropologist."

Others had been here, too. Squatting next to the grave, I counted about two dozen pennies, and one game token from a Howard Johnson's at Lake Buena Vista. I knew what they meant. I knelt a few minutes in silent thought, facing, as did the length of the grave, the Atlantic ocean. I had three dimes and placed them next to the other coins, as I had done at Marie Laveau's vault. That night, sitting on the beach, quite alone, I decided to hang back from Miami a little longer. I wanted to visit Chief Owolawo.

Grave of Zora Neale Hurston, Fort Pierce, Florida. Headstone donated by the writer Alice Walker.

———

Owolawo lived outside Gainesville, in the moss-draped back country of Alachua County. In there, Florida wasn't beaches and tourists, but trees, moss, mosquitoes and snakes in jungle-like density that would reclaim anything you didn't hack back, plow under or build over. He'd been taken by surprise when I called. I had learned about him, and gotten his number from Iya Orite, his spiritual goddaughter, but I hadn't been sure if I'd have the time to stop by. Thus I appeared as a complete stranger, an intruder at a pay phone. He almost refused to let me come out. I think what persuaded him was the idea of having his story preserved. And so it is: a year after I saw him, Chief Owolawo died of cancer. He was buried at Oyotunji following a full voudou ritual.

He lived in a ramshackle shingle and wood house saved from a look of dismal rural poverty by the addition of an African-

The late Chief Owolawo, priest of Obatala, outside his home near Gainesville, Florida.

style open veranda at one end. It looked almost like a trader's outpost in the deep bush. A mailbox out front displayed a stylized rendition, in bright red, of an elegantly simple African rooster.

I pulled up slowly along the lazy dirt lane and parked next to several old cars. Owolawo came down from the porch wearing a loose white African smock, light trousers and striped purple fela. He was so thin he seemed little more than a crooked-tooth smile and a wispy goatee. "He looks like Bill the Cat," his friend the Oba had joked, referring to a frazzled feline comic book hipster.

But I saw another cultural referent. Were he white, Owolawo, at fifty, might've been an old hippie, or some New England pilgrim from a southern Walden Pond. But he was a priest of Obatala and one of the fifteen original founders of Oyotunji. This was one of the reasons I'd come to see him. His fellow founders were

Stylized rooster on sign at driveway leading to Owolawo's property.

now scattered across the country like apostles. Many had returned to the big cities, but Owolawo had gone "country."

A commercial artist by trade, Owolawo had found his calling in the early sixties, when a friend told him about the new Shango temple Serge King was running on 116th Street in Harlem. When Serge went to South Carolina, Owolawo soon followed, and when Serge became the priest, Efuntola, Owolawo became his first godchild.

He stayed more than a decade in the village, building houses, felling trees, enduring the insects and hot summers and cold winters without water or electricity. But when he reached the age of forty-two, a year of change according to the voudou cycle of life, Owolawo felt he had to move on. Northern Florida seemed a good place. In Gainesville, Owolawo and his wife, also an artist, put together a living doing odd jobs and, increasingly, taking in clients. The stalwart priest of Obatala merged back into the ranks of hoodoo. He was known locally as a "root doctor." He didn't mind the association. "They might not be technicians or technocrats of African culture," he said of the local, untutored healers, "but they have the essence. They're a viable and vital link to Africa." He came to think of his role in the rural woods as that of "a missionary, not an oddity."

As evening approached, two young men and a woman drove up. They introduced themselves and went into the house, where Owolawo's wife was preparing dinner. Around us, children bounded up and down the steps of the veranda. I could imagine Owolawo among them in the long southern evenings, sitting in the wicker chair, smoking his pipe. He'd never return to the big city.

"I got my just desserts," he said. "I have enjoyed many pleasures people still are searching for. I see things—like, everybody is never sure about the future, okay—but I'm pleased because I'm doing what I like to do." His thoughts seemed to drift, and after a silence he said something that reminded me of Uncle Clem back in Ruston. A nonsequitur, reaching right up to the stars. "Right from the start it was like the feeling of a great religious project. It perpetuated and propelled us." He was talking about the village. In his heart, he had never left.

—————

Others in the voudou renaissance were not so serene, and as I left Gainesville for the road south to Miami, I knew I was truly leaving the blanket of all-encompassing spirituality that still stretched down from Oyotunji. In Miami, santeria was the game, and Cubans controlled it. Sectarian disputes had become as intense as they had at the time Serge King took his band of volunteers to the South.

It had gotten fractious back in New York again, too. Clashes between African Americans and Cubans had become the stuff of newspaper polemics and even scholarly debate—to become even more intense in the coming decade. And that was just part of it. I decided that my map of American voudou now had to connect the major poles of a battle which, within the voudou world, was not unlike the one in Christianity which led to the Reformation. In this case the Cuban santeros were the Church and the African-American orisha voudou advocates were the Protestants.

My journey would move to a new phase: conflict. And then, from conflict, to resolution. That would be the voudou way. In some ways the struggle was politics more than spirituality, but in the end, the arguments and divisiveness struck me as healthy, dynamic. No longer in hiding, voudou was alive and growing. In generating its own quarrels, it was flexing its new muscles.

And no one flexed his muscles more than John Mason.

In the world of voudou, Mason was considered to be point man in the struggle to separate the African-American renais-

Scholar John Mason and his son, Ade, at their home in Bedford-Stuyvesant.

sance from Cuban dominance. A forty-one-year-old priest of Obatala, he had been initiated in New York in the early 1970s, and had many connections to former villagers, including Owolawo. But while most of them had forsaken New York for the rural South, Mason had staked out his turf in the city.

Setting up in Bedford-Stuyvesant, he not only practiced the religion, but studied it voraciously, becoming a self-taught scholar. Books such as *Black Gods—Orisa Studies in the New World; Onje Fun Orisa [Food for the Gods]* and *Four New World Yoruba Rituals*, published through his own company, the Yoruba Theological Archministry, earned him a reputation as an expert on Yoruba culture, but it was his harsh attacks on santeria that brought him notoriety.

I vowed to seek Mason out at my first opportunity. No less than Hurston, he was an intellectual pioneer in the investigation and defense of voudou as a part of African-American culture. I was not to meet him in person until a cold autumn weekend later in the year, but in my mind I see him as another stop that summer on the road out of Oyotunji, Fort Pierce, and Gainesville, a road that really led all around America, to all the cities and towns in which the new apostles of voudou had set up outposts.

Mason's was a four-story, semi-detached brownstone nine blocks from the subway stop at Kingston and Troop. I had called him while on a brief trip to New York and asked for a meeting. He agreed despite what I sensed was pique that a white man was writing a book about voudou. I took the "A" train out because Manhattan cabbies refused to drive into Bed-Stuy. Not a great start to the visit, and I was feeling a little anxious anyway going to a part of town I'd mostly heard bad about. Or maybe I was just on edge because Mason had been so gruff on the phone. His voice practically had a "come if you dare" tone, and people who'd heard him lecture said he could get right in your face.

When I climbed the stoop to his house and knocked on the door, I half expected to have my head ripped off. A bowling ball of a man, not tall but heavy and solid, with one milky eye behind his reading glasses, he was all "Yo" and confrontation, sweatshirt, sneakers and torn pants. But it occurred to me it might be a posture. Mason's home was not that of a raging bull; rather, of a sensitive intellectual and family man.

He and his wife had undertaken a huge refurbishing task. Bed-Stuy brownstones are incomparable buys if you have the nerve to live there and patience to remodel. He showed me all four floors, including a stop in his cluttered office where, surrounded by ceiling-high shelves filled with hard-to-find books on Yoruba culture, he labored long hours at his computer. I liked the place instantly. It didn't make any difference what color we were—all writers make dens, and no one but another writer can quite appreciate the complexity amid the chaos of a well-dug burrow. But what he seemed most proud of was the pond in his back yard, where gentle lilies floated in the heart of the big, bad city as though they were in an eddy of the river Niger.

We talked at length about the religion, interrupted frequently by his two small children, whom he babysat while his wife worked. But almost at once we got into the battleground. I had mentioned visiting the African Studies department at the University of Florida at Gainesville and hearing about an aggressive speech he had delivered at a conference on orisha worship. I told him the academics were still talking about his vociferous objections to santeria's validity for African Americans, and the relationship of the religion to Christianity. He asked what they'd said. I smiled. "Well, 'separatist' was the nicest thing they called you."

His rebuttal was so loud my hand shot out to turn down the volume on the Sony recorder.

"I'm not a separatist!" he roared, plunging the cigar he had been inhaling into an ash tray next to his chair. "It has nothing to do with separatism. It has to do with calling spade a spade. That's exactly it, because what are you going to call me?"

He was taking a blunt shortcut, but Mason isn't known for obliqueness. He had moved the conversation directly to the heart of his antagonism to santeria, what he considered to be its control by white Cubans.

"Santeria! Where does that name come from? All of a sudden it's strange that we have this attempt to put a wedge between or in the midst of this African—they always say this—'African-derived' religion. That's bullshit. It's an African religion maintained by and promulgated by, pushed forward by Africans."

He leaned forward. "There ain't no 'African component' of santeria"—referring to a phrase frequently used by both popular and academic writers in analyzing the development of the Cuban form of voudou. "Now, see, this is my point. A term like 'African component' does not apply at this stage of the game. . . . There ain't no Catholicism in santeria."

I laughed, thinking he'd made a joke about "no Catholicism," and was waiting for the follow-up. But his deadpan expression told me he wasn't being ironic. He really meant it. So I laughed again, only this time with perhaps an edge of contempt. I didn't like being baited.

"What do you mean there's no Catholicism in santeria?" I said. "It's filled with Catholicism."

"I hate to tell you this"—his deep voice full of sarcasm—"Forget that Catholic shit. That's bullshit. That's all modern bullshit. This, this is New World bullshit—"

"It's santeria. Santeria was developed in the New World—"

"No—" His son, Ade, squirmed away to play in the kitchen.

"I'm saying what some people call santeria is—"

"I don't give a damn what 'some people' say—"

"Well, go look in a botanica."

"You know what a botanica is?"

"Well, what are you going to say that it is?"

We went on, getting nowhere.

Mason picked up his cigar again. Ade returned to the room and hugged his daddy's leg. Mason returned to his point, but without the temper.

"Here's the thing," he said, gently rubbing his son's head. "Voudou culture is now being redefined as white culture. What gets me is when we have Cubans who are ignorant of their own history, their own culture, saying 'Santeria is not an African religion, it is a Cuban religion.' It's as though some fucking Spaniard from the peninsula came up with this idea. What is this about santeria having an 'African component,' or 'Moorish overtones'?" Looking at santeria that way is racism that's even practiced by blacks against blacks."

He exhaled a cloud of smoke. "What I'm talking about is this: I'm talking about knowledge. I'm talking about knowledge as a thing that will free us from prejudice and stupidity. That's all we're talking about—knowledge. My job is to be more knowledgeable."

About 10 P.M., far longer than I had expected or intended to stay, I thought it might be time for me to be getting back to Manhattan, but I promised to take up Mason's invitation to show up the next day to see him do his "job"—to make other people knowledgeable, too. Each Saturday, he taught a class on orisha voudou at the Caribbean Cultural Center on 58th Street, Midtown.

Maybe a quarter of a million people in the city, Mason figured, had some involvement with voudou. Cuban, Puerto Rican, Brazilian, Haitian, Nigerian—many countries were represented in the Big Apple. I believed him. You could see signs of voudou's presence all over the place in the Bronx, Brooklyn and Queens—botanicas, bimbés in private homes and immigrant social clubs, the occasional string of warrior beads on the neck of a passer-by.

On the whole, though, those who did not bring voudou with them, who sought to learn about it in New York, had the same kinds of problems they would in New Orleans, Chicago or Oakland. You couldn't just find out about it in the same way you could inquire about becoming a Baptist or Jew or Muslim. So Mason truly was a teacher. But a teacher of voudou in America had to be especially committed; likewise his students. If you signed up for a class, you didn't just get a certificate. You might well be embarking on a path to fundamentally change your life. But each seminar Mason delivered, each student he inculcated, was another vessel of knowledge in a world of ignorance. You could almost see Mason as a missionary of his faith. But missionaries, to Mason, had been the bad guys in history.

---

[1] Zora Neale Hurston, *Mules and Men*, 1935, J. B. Lippincott, Philadelphia, p. 229.

# 19

## SANTERIA

THE FLASH IS everywhere in Miami. The city is now, to voudou, what New Orleans was a century earlier—the landfall of the Caribbean, the great demographic crossroads of the North American spirits: European, African and Native American. The difference from New Orleans, however, is that in contemporary Miami, the flash is above ground. You can find the spirits in almost every mix imaginable in almost every neighborhood you visit, from Little Haiti to Little Havana, from tenements in Hialeah to wealthy homes in Boca Raton. Botanicas flourish— some, boldly advertising as pet shops, openly sell livestock everybody knows is intended for sacrifice. A storefront santeria church had recently opened to the public. Caribbean music hops with orisha names night and day on the radio. Police officers and health workers are given cultural sensitivity briefings. The other difference is that, with the exception of Little Haiti, voudou in Miami is santeria. It is Cuban. Fueled in part by the Marielito exodus from Cuba in the early 1980s, the number of santeria followers in the city has grown to more than 65,000.

Coming in from the north, I ducked off I-95 as it cut down through Miami's northeast quadrant, then took an exit toward Hialeah, the staunchly Cuban enclave—a city within the city—near the famous racetrack and the airport. I had a few contacts—entrepreneurs, priests, scholars, but mostly it was spontaneity otra vez.

I crossed through the grim blocks of Liberty City, where black Americans had rioted for days after a cop shooting. The streets were narrow and filled with downscale retail storefronts—stereos, hair salons, Afro boutiques, like busy subway corners in the Bronx or in Chicago. And they seemed totally segregated—no white faces. And grim: boarded up businesses, unemployed men hanging out. Near one modest office building, a group of young Nation of Islam ministers in their dark suits and red bow ties passed out literature and pasted up posters about an upcoming rally.

I picked up Northwest 60th, just above Dr. Martin Luther King Boulevard, and proceeded on to Hialeah. Soon, the terrain shifted and I was in a lower-middle-class Hispanic neighborhood, where house-proud immigrants had made the best of the structures at hand. Cinder-block bungalows were afire with pink or blue pastels, yards freshly mowed, wrought iron patio furniture and plaster statues of the Virgin and the saints populating porches and yards. I slowed down and cruised with the windows open, turning up my radio when I chanced on an FM station playing Pinetop Perkins's version of the Willie Dixon classic, "I'm Your Hootchie Kootchie Man":

> . . . Got a black cat bone
> got the mojo, too
> got High John the Conquerer
> gon' mess with you.

The rain which had peppered the morning came back. I flicked on the wipers and poked along, just letting the feeling wash over me with the music: raw Delta hoodoo. In a way the blues seemed incongrous on Caribbean streets. I should've been listening to meringue or salsa, maybe. But it felt right.

A half-block ahead, a trio of black Cuban boys ran out into the curbless street. I slowed to avoid them, but they stopped at the edge of the pavement to hop into a broad, ankle-deep puddle. The one in red top and black jams, the colors of Elegba, laughed and flailed his arms.

I drew past as the other two joined in, and I could still see them at it in my rear view mirror, dancing in the rain, for no reason, with boundless energy. I remembered Robert Farris Thompson's way of seeing the flash—the "flash of the spirit," the unmistakable mark of the orisha—in the folk art and manners of the black South. I knew I was looking at the same thing. Joy to no purpose, save to the fun of it all, the complete pointless eternity of the impulse to rejoice where heaven and earth meet, in a pool of rainwater.

—==—

With some difficulty, I had set up an early morning appointment at the Church of the Lukumí Babalu Aye, a bright yellow and blue peacock of a building, formerly the sales office of a used car lot, at the edge of the Hialeah business district. Whatever I had expected had not included a TV remote truck and a dazzling Cubana reporter—slender, curvy, sculpted face, black hair down to her shoulder blades—standing on the curb with a cordless microphone. A photographer and soundman trailed behind, laden with equipment.

I set my handbrake, cracked my windows and got out of the car. Across the asphalt, a group of working-class men watched from the counter of a sidewalk espresso bar. TV crews and gringos going into the santeria church—who knew what was going on in that place now?

More than they probably knew. Since the first day it opened, the santeria chapel The Associated Press described as "the first known church in the usually secretive sect" had been under close scrutiny and municipal seige. The most intent assault came through the city of Hialeah's ban on the use of animals in sacrifices. In a celebrated battle that would not be over for six years, the Cuban-American founder of the church, Ernesto Pichardo, filed suit in federal court against the city, saying the ban violated his First Amendment rights. Three years later, the U. S. Supreme Court would agree to hear the case after two lower courts had ruled against Pichardo. In 1993, a landmark majority opinion written by Justice Anthony Kennedy sustained sacrifice as a form of religious expression.

Unfortunately, financial pressures, in part from the litigation, forced the church to close before the final ruling. But it later reopened, just a few blocks from its original location—symbolically, or at least dramatically—within a stone's throw of its city hall adversaries. Pichardo, who said the long court fight cost him "money and some hair," gained some credibility from the victory in the essentially hostile Catholic Cuban community around him and even among the media. When the Pope visited Cuba in 1997, Pichardo was one of the people CNN interviewed for background on santeria as practiced in that country.

When I was there, however, Pichardo was still in the thick of the battle with Hialeah and his case still pending its first court hearing. Occasionally, the battle got noticed in the Spanish and English papers, and sometimes on TV. I guessed that was what drew the crew that morning. I was piqued, though—when I had called Ernesto he hadn't mentioned anything about television.

But my qualms were unnecessary. As soon as I walked into the church, Ernesto offered me a paper cup of buche his mother had prepared, and said the reporter had just called, but only wanted a quick interview on an aspect of the lawsuit in the news that week. There would be plenty of time to show me around afterwards. Considering the local exposure she could give him, I felt more than well accommodated.

I'm not sure about the reporter. As I trailed her and the crew through the interior of the church sanctuary, I noticed her face pale, as if attempting not to look shocked. The room, about the size of a volleyball court, was filled wall to wall with santeria shrines. One of the largest, to Ernesto's patron, Shango, occupied an entire corner. Red drapes hung from the ceiling to form a backdrop to an altar filled with shakerees, cowrie shells and animal skins. To one side was a large statue of St. Barbara, the Christian saint whose colors of red and white and frequent depiction carrying a battle axe led her to be syncretized with Shango. Pichardo briefly explained to the reporter what the shrines meant—Yemonja, Elegba, and so on—but she seemed

Church of the Lukumí Babalu Aye, in its original location in Hialeah, Miami. Church has since moved a few blocks down the street, next to City Hall.

most unnerved by his off-hand reference to a room in the back used for sacrifices. Then he pointed to the dumpsters in the fenced parking lot in back. That's where the carcasses were thrown away—one of the big issues in the lawsuit.

I gauged her for an upper-class Cuban, about as likely to be involved in santeria as in a Marxist study group. That was another thing that got Pichardo into trouble. He was upper-class, too—his family had run a lucrative fruit export-import business. In the eyes of the staunchly Catholic and conservative Cuban community in Hialeah where he grew up, people with patrician backgrounds shouldn't be mixed up in black cults.

Pichardo and the reporter returned to the front of the church for the interview, and although I tried to eavesdrop on her questions—in Spanish—I couldn't hear much. After she had finished, they all left quickly. The soundman mentioned to me they were on a tight deadline.

Ernesto Pichardo's mother, a small but intense woman in her sixties, brought in a fresh thermos of coffee, then went to sit on the far side of the room with her other son, Ricardo. Ernesto beckoned me to join him at a wooden desk in front of a plate glass window looking out onto the street. He was happy to talk about his religion, he said—it was the center of his life and that of his entire family. He and his brother were priests and so was his mother, given to Yemonja in 1971, the same year of Ernesto's own conversion to santeria. In subsequent years he had continued to study and obtained the rank of italero, the priest who gives a santeria initiate the itá.

Talking rapidly between sips of buche, Ernesto explained that although the church had been in operation only the last two years, the actual incorporation had taken place almost two decades earlier, in 1974. His mother, he said, had been contacted by the spirit of a former Cuban slave. The spirit had said that the family had been drawn into santeria purposefully, that it was their mission to expand the influence of the religion among the people. It was their mission to set up a temple. The spirit said they should dedicate it to Babalu Aye.

I don't know why I hadn't made the connection earlier—Babalu Aye was syncretized with St. Lazarus. It was St. Lazarus who had appeared to Lorita Mitchell in a dream. In Miami, I was duplicating the same route I had made in New Orleans. It seemed altogether symbolic and ironic that the orisha had become manifest in the language of Lorita Mitchell, an African American, in its Christian guise—St. Lazarus. In the language of Mrs. Pichardo, a white Cuban, the same spirit had emerged in its African name—Babalu Aye.

From the first, Pichardo continued, he had sought to build support and acceptance for his church by trying to educate those who knew nothing, or nothing good, about santeria. He persuaded Miami colleges and universities to allow him to present classes or seminars, he set up a local radio talk show, he even obtained a grant for cultural study from the Florida Endowment for the Humanities. The objective throughout was to actually go public, because it was the only way for santeria to be taken seriously—the same reasoning that had led Serge King to South Carolina. "Everyone felt that unless we institutionalized," Pichardo said, "we would still be considered occult and barbaric. So we found a way. . . . Of course what's interesting is that at first the community's complaint was, 'So if you're so legit why don't you have a church?' And then two years ago we turn around and say okay, here's the church, and now they"—by which he meant not only the conservative Cubans but also some santeria factions who, probably to retain power, preferred to keep the religion's older, secretive affectations—"say, 'No, we don't want this.'"

His unlined face, almost too smooth, too pretty for a thirty-four-year-old, wrinkled with slits of anger. "What I scream and I'll continue to scream is that I refuse for our young generations to continue with this two-faced society. It's like, I don't know,

Reverend Ernesto Pichardo of the Church of the Lukumí Babalu Aye, whose suit to allow animal sacrifice in religious services was upheld by the U. S. Supreme Court in 1993.

you're in psychological slavery. It's like jumping back 400 years. It's like you do not have a social right to come out and say, 'This is my religion.'"

That he was white, not black, mattered not at all to him. The name of Pichardo's church—Lukumí—derives from the Yoruba word olokumi, which means "my friend." In Cuba, slaves who came from the Yoruba lands were known as lukumí. Cubans who adhere more to the African than the Catholic content still refer to santeria as lukumí (sometimes lucumí). Which was another reason the Pichardos were in trouble. They were not only trying to run a santeria church, but one which specifically emphasized the Africanness, not the syncretism. As it turned out, there just weren't many friends of the lukumí in Hialeah.

"Even Communism today publicly allows these practices," Ernesto said. "I mean today when you go to Cuba you can practice santeria openly." He tapped the paper cup on his desk. "Openly! You go to the neighborhood committee, they give you a license, a permit and a permanent document. It classifies you as a religious person. There's no food in Cuba, you know, but there are animals for sacrifices. Everyone's supposed to go to a government center and buy them there. And so here we are: Communist Cuba doesn't have a problem with this, but America, the role model of the world, says, 'No way.' That doesn't make sense."

By "America," he meant the Cuban community in America, and that was what ate at him. "Why do we have to sit here today in America and not admit publicly that these African traditions which intoxicate us so much are part of our make-up," he said, his voice rising, "that this"—he waved one arm towards the orisha shrines in the sanctuary—"is part of being Cuban? Why can we not simply accept ourselves as we are? Why do we have to try to mirror what we're not to the Americans?"

Pichardo explained how his attorney, deposing a man from the Humane Society, was trying to get him to explain the difference between sacrifice and euthanasia. "So my attorney asked the guy, 'If I had a pet goat on my farm and I take it to you and ask you to put it to sleep and then incinerate it, would you do that as part of your service?' The humane society guy says, 'yes.'

"And then my lawyer says, 'Okay, if I would take the same goat—but dead—bring it to you and say that I was a santero and I had just sacrificed it in a ritual and I would like you to incinerate it, would you do it?' The guy says 'no'. And the guy was asked why not, and he says, 'Because that's illegal. I would call the police right then and there because the animal was sacrificed.'"

Pichardo pressed one hand to his forehead. One time, he said, he had called the Hialeah waste department to ask if they would pick up chicken carcasses. They wouldn't. Pichardo argued with them, pointing out that the city picked up waste from all kinds of restaurants—lobster claws, chicken bones, pork ribs—why not a carcass from the church's dumpster? "But they kept saying no. They wouldn't pick up any carcasses from our waste basket." He smiled almost imperceptibly. "So they can pick up chicken bones over down the street at Kentucky, but can't pick up chicken bones over here."

Ricardo, who had been talking quietly with his mother, came over to remind his brother of "a pending appointment." They spoke in low, rapid Spanish for a moment, then Ernesto stood, stretched and stared across the street at a grocery where, he noted, you could buy freshly killed beef, fish or chicken. "It's not about the life of the animals," he said. Justice Kennedy would say, later: "Legislators may not devise mechanisms, overt or disguised, designed to persecute or oppress a religion or its practices."

———

One of the people I had most wanted to see in Miami came from a time before Pichardo, before the Oba, before Ava Kay Jones, before any of them were possible, so to speak. Lydia

Cabrera had grown up in a time when everything they represented was prohibido. Born to an upper-class white creole family in colonial Cuba, she was sent to university in Paris in the 1930s. Her life changed. Studying what were then called "primitive cultures," she realized she had been living in the midst of one.

On returning to Cuba, she asked questions of Tula, her family's longtime Kongolese servant. Tula and her friends took the young mistress into their confidence, and began telling her not only about what life had been like in the Kongo, but what the religion had been like, too. From their stories, Cabrera constructed *El Monte*, published in 1954. Later works, such as *Reglas de Congo: Palo Mayombe*, 1979, augmented what are considered not only authoritative scholarship, but handbooks of the practices and beliefs of palo mayombe.

I found her—a few years before her death—in a well-heeled, gated suburban condo village in southwest Miami. As I walked up to her door, I prepared myself to find a faltering old lady, as I had been told by an intermediary to expect. Nothing could have been more incorrect. Even as I was ushered inside by one of Cabrera's friends, I could sense a wonderful vitality in the house. Well-lighted, cool, full of plants, oil paintings, and artifacts, it felt like a nervy and even outrageous Havana salon, a Cuban moveable feast in which grace, intellect, curiosity and passion were as thick in the air as the scent of flowers.

Cabrera received me in a sunny room just past the foyer. Petite, fine-boned, she sat straight as a pin in a French provincial chair. From a portrait on the wall, I could see she had once been blonde and had doubtless broken some hearts. Now close to ninety and blind, she evoked the same lithe, offhandedly patrician air of the young woman in the painting, who dared delve where only demons were said to live. She shook my hand firmly.

I told her I had come because I had many questions about palo and very few reliable answers. I had heard palo was evil, that it was benign, that it was a study of herbs and plants, that it was the province of the dead, that it was unpredictable and destructive. I didn't know what was true.

She said it all was. Palo was practiced by Africans in Cuba for the same reasons it was practiced by Africans in Africa, she said—it offered a way of dealing with the problems of the world, some of which entail confrontation with evil. Palo prepares its practitioners for that struggle. A weapon, it is "both good and bad." But the most important, and difficult, thing to understand about it, she said, is that it works. She herself had seen the inexplicable happen, had seen people physically transformed— "things that can't be simulated"—by the spirit of the prenda.

She paused, having said the Cuban word for the magical pot of the palo priest. More than anything else, the black kettle is considered the symbol of evildoing in the religion. Through a prenda, a palero (or mayombero) controls the spirits of the dead. Cabrera was quite aware of the implications; I, at the time, was not. I had seen prendas filled with all manner of things, but mostly with herbs, sticks, insects, reptiles, soil and assorted talismans, from items of jewelry or clothing to scissors or nails. But what really makes the pot active are bones. In many parts of America, the bones of animals—cats or dogs, usually—are used, but in strict Kongolese tradition, the bone is supposed to be human. In Matamoros, Constanzo's pots had been full of tibia, femurs and skulls.

Small wonder palo has the worst of all reputations in the voudou-connected religions, even among sympathizers. But I knew there was more to it. Why would Cabrera have spent so much time documenting its nuances? Why were so many voudou priests cross-training themselves in the Kongo rituals? She thought about it a moment, and chose her words sparingly. "I have been very surprised to see people you never thought would be in it," she said. "But why are they doing it?" I pressed. She thought again. "Faith." Then she smiled. "It's also a good way to do business."

—=—

After our conversation, I went back to my hotel near the airport. The lobby was filled, as usual, with flight crews and international travelers. I often wondered how I looked, heading past the sunken fern bar toward the elevator, clutching my recorder, camera and sheafs of notes. It didn't always look like I'd come from tea. Sometimes I looked like I'd come from places you'd have nightmares about, if you were so disposed.

As soon as I opened the door to my room I could see the message light blinking on the telephone. I dialed right away—a palero I'd been trying to reach for days. This time he answered. In my crude but effective college Spanish I asked if I could come see him, but in the middle of the conversation he hung up. It was like trying to meet hoodoo men in Mississippi.

I scratched his name from my contact list. I'd been through several failed attempts to meet local paleros and was losing interest. Damn all this cabalistic shit. I'd tried to assure everyone I wasn't out to steal secrets. I really didn't want to know them and thought it unethical to divulge them. And that was beside the point. In fact, I had a starkly personal reason for spending more time chasing paleros than I really needed to, even, in truth, for seeking out Cabrera's insights. I wanted to know why I hadn't become a palero myself.

Lorita Mitchell had tried to talk me into it in New Orleans. I came close. The fee was reasonable—about $400, and the rites wouldn't have taken a fraction of the time required for voudou. Undertaking the intitiation would have been a way to learn a lot about the use of herbs—palo was a socio-medicinal system as well as a theology. And maybe I would have learned the source of its psychological power. But I had said no. In the end, I didn't want a prenda. I didn't want to believe what was in it.

Understand: Palo is what it is. It is about the power of the dead over the living. Whatever other propensities it has start and stop there. No heaven, no hell, no nirvana, no trail of spiritual breadcrumbs led from palo back to anything I could connect to. Voudou, Christianity, Islam—all essentially formulate a cosmic order based on higher beings. Palo is different. It looks not to the heavens but to the earth and to the dead inside the earth. If you cannot accept that—look right into it without fear— you are either wasting your time or commiting a dangerous psychological and spiritual act.

Even Migene Gonzalez-Wippler, the santeria popularizer, viewed palo as essentially malevolent:

> There are two branches of Palo Mayombe, one that is "good" and one that is "bad." The "good" branch is called "Christian" Mayombe and the "bad" is called "Jewish" or "unbaptized" Mayombe. This differentiation is made by the paleros because the "Christian" cauldron in which their secrets are kept is sprinkled with holy water and the "Jewish" one is not. To the practitioners of Palo who, like the santeros, are steeped in Catholic tradition, anyone or anything that is not baptized is evil and does not belong to God.[1]

However bizarre, anti-Semitic, and perhaps not incidentally Inquisitional in inspiration, such characterizations are more the rule than the exception. Yet I did feel alien from palo in a way I did not feel from voudou at all. Gonzalez-Wippler had not made me feel that way, nor Lorita Mitchell, nor, now, Cabrera. The person who had finally made me understand why I feared palo initiation, and would never undergo it, was Iya Ghandi. She was the person who made me believe that as much as I wanted to avoid the mistaken ideas about palo and try to see in it the power for good, or for protection, I also had to accept the other part of the equation. It was also bad. I had suppressed the idea, but now, in Miami, after hearing Cabrera tell me the same, the foreboding of evil with which Iya Ghandi had once shocked me was back, wanting to be dealt with.

———

I had been sitting in a hard wooden booth with Ghandi in The Horseman waiting out one of the daily Carolinian rainstorms. She was telling me about having been to the Kongo, and, trying to impress her, I mentioned Lorita's offer of initiation. I paid with a long silence and the kind of glare that could silence even the Oba.

"No *way* you can get a real palo initiation in this country," she said, as if it had taken that long even to find words for her contempt. "Anybody tells you you can is taking your money. I wouldn't do it, and I know all the secrets. You can find someone else, but it would take a long time, and you still wouldn't have the full power, and it might cost you at least $2,000."

I laughed off her surprising vehemence. I'd heard palo intiation was fairly simple and told her so. In New Orleans, I said, you could be initiated in a matter of days, although you had to pass at least one night in a cemetery. Now it was Ghandi's turn to laugh, if that's what it was. In the Kongo, she said, you are required, among other things, to sleep seven nights under a ceiba (African teakwood) tree, bury your clothes on three Fridays over a twenty-one-day period, take herbal baths, and at the conclusion make a circle of gunpowder, which is ignited to seal the pact with the prenda spirit. My idea of a quickie rite in New Orleans was worse than a waste of time. "These are dangerous things," she scowled. "You could be killed out there by some entity you don't even know exists."

I smiled and picked at the label on my beer bottle. I told her I didn't see how palo could be that dangerous. Palo didn't have nearly as many gods as did voudou, and voudou was considered to be more powerful than palo anyway. As for the prenda spirit, I said, how could it be any different than the spirits of the dead of orisha voudou? Actually, I said, I thought palo sounded more like low-level sorcery, and not as advanced as voudou.

"Really, palo is just a way of worshiping the dead," I concluded.

"Right. Worshiping one entity—the one spirit in that pot."

I understood completely. You worshiped a spirit trapped in a pot and summoned it to do your bidding. It was like rubbing Aladdin's lamp to reach the genie.

Then I caught myself. Did I just hear her right? The *one* spirit in that pot?

"Wait," I said, like a clever student about to trip up a professor on a technicality. "You don't mean just *one* spirit confined to the pot—you can use the pot to call any spirit you choose—"

I stopped in mid-sentence. A deep and private chuckle spread across her smooth black face. "No," she said, shaking her head. "It could be the spirit you want, but it doesn't have to be. I can tell you—in my case, it's not." The grin on her face spread wider.

My stomach fluttered a little, the way it does when my body has just figured out something it will take a while for my brain to accept. It had been my understanding that the pot was simply a focal point for summoning whoever you needed. I knew the ability to call up the dead was activated by a bone, but I had thought *any* old bone would do, animal or human. I thought the bone of palo, like the eucharist of Christianity, was symbolic in its power.

"Any bone can work," she continued, the professor who has once again caught the clever student in the trap, "but the spirit in the pot is the spirit of *that* bone.

"When I was in the Kongo they take you to the cemetery yourself and they go through different rituals for a certain amount of days and you dig up your own bone. You know who's buried there. And that's your spirit. And you make a pact with the spirit that he will work for you. . . . It will do whatever you say. Whether it's good or bad. It operates by your command. It can be very dangerous in some cases. Let's say for some reason it turns out you don't really know everything about the dead person and get somebody bad, like a mass murderer. In cases like that, the spirit can turn against you.

"The problem in the U. S. is that you have to go to medical schools, or places where they sell things to the doctors or medical students. You buy a tibia and keep your receipts so it is legal when the cops come. But if you go to the place of medical supplies and you buy a bone, then you are using the spirit of *that* bone. That's when you really might be taking a chance. You have no idea what kind of person that was. That's more of a case when you could get the mass murderer or something."

I looked at her with what I assumed was blank amazement.

"I find a lot of people in this country with animals in pots," Ghandi said, her tone now sharp and bold. "That is not a genuine prenda or palo. But since it's against the law in this country to go into a cemetery and disturb a grave they use substitution of a dog or whatever." She looked at me with a shrug of contempt. "That's what they're using in New Orleans, a black dog. But you know, I've been trying to figure that out. How are you going to send a dog to do the work? We say dogs have souls, but that's hearsay."

In her own home were four palo pots, she continued. One was her own, but the other three had belonged to her late parents. She cared for them and worshipped them along with her voudou pots (superas), though they are not allowed in the same room, because the spirits might intermingle.

"Right, those are the nganga," I said, using what I had believed to be the Kongolese word for the Cuban prenda. Ghandi shook her head. A nganga was more accurately a burlap bag. I said I hadn't heard of that. She said I hadn't heard of a lot. For example, had I heard of the ndoke? I hadn't. It was like an nganga, she said, but hung from a tree. The ndoke was what you used for "especially dangerous spirits."

I said it sounded like they all might be dangerous if you couldn't have any say about the spirit inside, if you were bound to the spirit of a bone which, by her own admission, might be that of a psychopath. I told her maybe that's what had happened in Matamoros. Maybe palo was a lot scarier than I had thought.

"I told you to keep away," she said. "Look, it's not really the prenda that controls things. The prenda didn't make those drug people kill all those other people. The prenda pot just sits there. It does not bother you if you don't bother it."

I nodded, thinking I understood, that the pot was really passive after all. I could accept that a little better. But that wasn't her point.

"But when you make a command, then it can bother you. Do you understand?"

I felt my jaw tightening.

"You have to know how to control that thing so that it doesn't control you. 'Cause if you don't have any control over it, it *will* control you. I've seen it happen to me, to where the spirit in the pot was almost controlling me. I had to say, no, enough is enough. I say to the spirit, 'Look, either you do it my way or I have to go and they'll have to dismantle you and send you back where you came from and that'll be the end of that.'" She looked off, as if recalling some dark moment in her life.

"You have to be really balanced to deal with it. My problem is I've been into so many things that sometimes I don't know who is doing what. Sometimes I can treat people in a hurtful way and later I think about it and say, 'Man, I'm sorry, I shouldn't have done that.' And later on I wonder if it was really me or if that was my orisha or if that was my prenda, or this or that. So

I don't worry about it anymore. It actually almost drove me crazy."

I could see in her eyes why villagers gave her wide berth.

"Getting a prenda pot, it's just like getting a gun. When somebody gets a gun, they say, 'I don't want to kill somebody,' and you say, 'Why you got the gun?' They say, 'To protect myself.' And I say, 'How you gonna protect yourself with the gun?' 'I shoot somebody,' they say. I say, 'You shooting somebody? You shooting somebody to kill them.'"

A tourist came into The Horseman, saw us talking, and started to walk up, but Iya Ghandi's sharp glance deterred him. She didn't like to be interrupted. "Whenever you buy a gun you have intentions to kill. When you get a prenda pot you have intentions of doing bad. . . . Like I said, it's a Kongo religion. They developed this for protection, and to attack.

"When people say to me, 'Why you got a prenda?' I say, 'To keep people like you off of me.' They say, 'You gonna do negative ju-ju?' Yes, I am, if it becomes necessary to save life or limb I will do whatever it takes to protect me. Because there's nothing wrong with a gun. It's the person who has the gun in his hands."

—=—

Driving up 1-A on Miami Beach late at night, listening to "Something in the Air Tonight" by Genesis. Strange name for a band, and kind of right to the point of what was in the air in my own mind. What of all this was real? My visit to Cabrera had touched off memories of Iya Ghandi and I couldn't shake a surly reaction to the way she had gotten to me in Oyotunji that day. Was she really a woman with powers to be feared?

I zipped under the palm trees, ran the yellow lights, followed the dark asphalt, catching glimpses of cruise ships moored in Biscayne Bay. I drove without purpose, up the length of the tourist highway and back down, and nothing cleared my head. To believe Ghandi and her palo pot and the spirit in it could bring harm meant I believed in the dark side. Accepting faith had been one thing. It was not so hard to see the gods. Had I been a fool not to see devils among the gods?

But good and evil were part of the same spiritual cloth, were they not? Maybe it wasn't the potential of palo to wreak hell that had made me question my new feelings of spirituality; maybe I was bringing the whole thing up for review. I didn't know, but I was sure having a dark night of the soul, and god, what a town to have it in.

Surely, either good or evil spirits could only have power if you believed they did. And if you accepted one, you had to accept the other. It wasn't that I was afraid of evil. I was confronting the idea of power: the gods not as forms of worship, but as weapons. Surely that was the operative element in everything I had been seeing in the past months, hoodoo to palo. Power.

Was that not the entire point of the lot of them—the orisha, the saints, Jesus, Mohammad, Buddha, Shiva, Wahkentanken— the lot of them? What did the Spiritual Church hymn beseech of Jesus? "POW-er! POW-er! POW-er!" Did his power not rest on voluntary illusion, on fear, on self-deception, the same as Iya Ghandi's palo pot? Was not the secret of the religious impulse that we manifest the gods and then we fear our manifestations, mistake them for having their own lives? Believing in spirits is a simple externalization of our powers. We kneel, pray and sacrifice—but ultimately, only to ourselves. There is no grand audience. The play is us, and the play is the thing. Was this not all there was?

If not, what was there?

I'd wanted to know that more than anything from Lydia Cabrera. She had thought about the consequences of what she had seen. As I had taken her leave that afternoon, I asked her. "Is there a human soul?" She sat quietly a moment, smiling slightly. Slowly she turned her body towards my voice. "I can't give you an answer for that. We are surrounded by mystery."

---

[1] Migene Gonzalez-Wippler, *Santeria: The Religion*, 1989, Harmony Books, New York, p. 238.

# 20

## URBAN HERBS AND LITTLE HAITI

EACH MORNING IN Miami I ate a big Cuban breakfast of eggs, bacon, black beans, potatoes, hot bread and café cubana. I liked to sit on the round stools at the freshly wiped counters of the small diners that pervaded Little Havana and watch the men at their tables reading the sports pages, mother and children coming up to the take-out windows for egg and bacon tacos and fresh juices. You could get lost in aromas of roasting meat for the lunch trade, simmering kettles of rice, wafts of sweet plantains frying on the grill.

I had been in South Florida about a week and was developing a taste for Cuba that didn't stop at my palate. It had gotten into my ears and down to my feet and would have made it to my groin if I'd had the chance; not that Frances ever called back. The music, the clothes, the way the people moved, looked and talked—it was very infectious. But ultimately it was Caribbean. There's a fair trade in revisionist academia which argues a hegemonic Caribbean influence in the slave and post-slavery culture of the U. S. That influence is obvious and was often heroic. Yet the African-American experience in this country was, especially before the twentieth century, profoundly and deliberately isolated from the Caribbean—except near port cities such as Miami, New Orleans, Charleston. The development of voudou thus took markedly different turns in the American South compared to Cuba, or Haiti or Brazil, with their much larger, denser African populations. The purpose of my journey was to see what had happened *here*. This was the unstudied terrain. This was where voudou's mark had been most tenuously held; it was also where the efforts to re-forge the links were most noticeable, for being most consciously retrieved. I did not want to lose sight of that. I needed to get back to black America. I wanted to see not only santeria in Miami, but orisha voudou. And I could; I had been in touch with Chief A. S. Ajamu.

I was to meet him at 2 P.M. at his house on the northeast flank of the city, up Biscayne Boulevard about where it gives way to the eastern edge of a continually expanding Little Haiti. A forty-nine-year-old Chicagoan who had once studied to be a Catholic priest, then became one for Obatala, Ajamu had lived in Oyotunji in the early seventies, striking out for Miami in the eighties.

It was lonely going at first. Cliquish santeros considered him an outsider. But over the years Ajamu made inroads, and now was known not only among the Cubans, but among the Haitians, with whom he felt the most spiritual kinship. His business had thrived, and at the time I called him, he was on the eve of an extended trip to Nigeria, from which he would return as a babalawo, the only such African-American priest in the city.

He greeted me at the door smoking a cigar, wearing a green caftan and a bright red fela (a cap). His hair was dreadlocked, which he said was in honor of the orisha Shalako. His concrete block bungalow was large and airy, in the style of the city. Half the house served as living quarters for him and his wife, a priestess of Shango, but two huge rooms on the other side—enclosed patios with louvered breeze windows—were devoted to business. The front room was a kind of cottage boutique, filled with racks of African-style clothing, jewelry and sundries. Folding tables next to the racks were spread thickly with literature about African culture, and with business cards touting Ajamu's other, perhaps more active, enterprise—the Divine Guidance Psychic Clinic, described as "Professional Practioners of African Science, Staffed by Traditional African Priests."

The boutique room led into an even larger, L-shaped space at the rear of the home. There, Ajamu or his wife conducted client readings at a long wooden table. Beyond that was another room lined with paintings of the orisha and altars to them—and also, touchingly, an oil painting of Ajamu's close friend and godfather, Owolawo. It was a ceremonial chamber. Bimbés, festivals, sacrificial rites—anything that could not be conducted in the back yard or in the open could be performed inside. It was the completely equipped home of an active voudou priest.

After showing me around, he said that "of course" I knew that before we could talk further he would have to read me. How else would he know if he could trust me? I couldn't disagree. We sat at one end of the reading table and he cast the cowries into a wicker tray. I felt like I was being given a polygraph, and, so to speak, I was. But I passed.

So did he. During the reading, I asked if the shells would tell me who was my African spirit. Despite all the possible orisha Ajamu might have suggested, and the long odds of it being Ochosi, that was exactly who he named. Only then did I reveal that was also who the Oba had divined. Ajamu puffed out a big cloud of cigar smoke, the way a poker player might who has just pulled in the jackpot but you don't know if he had a royal flush or a great bluff. True, he might've called Oyotunji before I arrived to find out, but even if he had done so, he would've been bound by the cowries. To have lied would have been to have effectively renounced everything he stood for. I believed him.

Our mutual suspicions allayed, he told me how we'd spend the afternoon. An herbalist with a national reputation, he had just gotten an urgent call from clients in New York who were preparing a yaguo for initiation to Ogun. They needed twenty-one special offerings, but the necessary plants couldn't be found in Brooklyn. Semi-tropical Miami was a different story. If you knew where to look. Ajamu did.

Not that it was convenient. The plants grew all over the place, in trees and ditches and roadside brush and abandoned lots, sometimes in easy reach and sometimes not. Amaju had done this before and had a route, but it had been a while since he'd had an order this comprehensive. If I drove and dealt with the traffic it would be easier for him to concentrate on remembering the secret spots. If I helped it would also give him extra time to get ready to go to Nigeria and anyway, he laughed, it wasn't everyday I'd get a chance to make an herb run with a voudou priest.

I'll drive, I said.

Our first stop was a closed-up nightclub off Biscayne Boulevard. Ajamu needed atipola—broad, flat leaves from a tree which happened to grow in a corner of the deserted parking lot. Atipola was sacred to all the orisha, but especially to Obatala and Elegba, and, therefore, a good way to start the collection. I parked in a shady spot. Ajamu went over to slice off his samples while I took a beach towel from my trunk and spread it over the back seat to hold what promised to be a sizeable pile of flora. The towel would be blessed, Ajamu said, from contact with sacred herbs, just like the machete he used for the pruning.

Before we left, Ajamu noticed a medium-sized tree growing in a grassy easement. He hurried over and pulled down a clump of greenish berries. "Sea grapes," he called out, "for Yemonja and Olokun." He praised them, brought them back to the car and, as with the atipola, bundled them with white string before carefully arranging them on the towel. I was ready to drive away, but Ajamu told me to wait yet again. He walked back to the sea grape trees, withdrew a few coins from his pouch, and pitched them to the ground. "You always give back," he said. "You never take something from the earth without returning something."

We cruised for several blocks as Ajamu tried to recall the mental map of his urban street garden. He worried that Miami was becoming like Brooklyn—denuded of the required plants. Already, he said, there were "modifications," substitution of close biological matches for African plants not available in the U. S. Some of the ritual procedures were being revised, too, for example the one that said no herbs should be picked that grow outside the sound of drums. Around the South Bronx, let alone Biscayne and 54th, that would be difficult, unless you counted boom boxes. But other strictures could be maintained. Herbs for initiation still could only be picked during daylight, and only by a priest with ashé (the power), so he could say the correct prayers "and put vibrations into it."

In a vacant lot in a blue-collar black residential area we found peonia, a multi-leaf green vine with bright red berries. Ajamu cut a few eight- to twelve-inch strips with his machete. Although intended for Obatala and Elegba, peonia also helps the initiate overcome spiritual indecisiveness. Like most of the other leaves and herbs, these would principally be ground up and boiled into special teas—exactly the procedure used by Lionel Brown's grandmother in Lafayette. This time he also said a prayer to Osanyin, the deity of medicines and companion to my own spirit, Ochosi. A one-eyed, one-legged man of the woods, Osanyin is frequently represented by a doll, or as a ventriloquist, and is sometimes said to be the spirit in talking birds. More than any other orisha, Osanyin may be the model for the Southern hoodoo healer and root doctor.

We drove in ever-widening city blocks in the northeast part of the city, going as far west as Liberty City, and then south toward Little Haiti. I wasn't always sure we were following whatever map was in his head. As we wound into one neighbor-hood—I'd lost my bearings by this point—of fifties-era ranch style houses fallen into disrepair, with blocked-up cars clutter-ing the driveways, I had the distinct feeling of being lost. It looked creepy, filled with cul-de-sacs and maze-like streets flanked by moss-covered trees. The residents, hard-looking Anglos, were what some Southerners call white trash. The vibes seemed about as unvoudou as I could imagine.

But Ajamu said to keep going, he knew there was this place . . . and then he saw it. I stopped next to a half-filled drainage ditch leading toward a dense clump of cane and brush twice a grown man's height. Ajamu got out, jumped the ditch, then dis-appeared for a moment in the underbrush. "Ashé," I heard him call out over the sounds of a machete's chop. He came out with the leaves of a small vine he didn't identify, and put them on the pile atop the towel. He was sweating but smiling, not so much because of getting the plant, but from remembering where it was.

He went back into the grove, and I could hear an exclama-tion of delight. He had spotted an avocado tree, from which he took the leaves, not the fruit, and near that picked the plant called elephant ear. Locked and loaded, we drove on to other neighborhoods—black, white, Cuban, middle-class, poor—stop-ping for "Wandering Jew," for the jaguey, for castor bean, and, across the alley from a convenience store in a starkly poor His-panic neighborhood, for cuttings of the needle-like peregun, a favorite of Ogun.

Then we were at the western edge of Little Haiti. Before we reached the main strip of brightly decorated businesses, restau-rants, clubs, churches and botanicas along Second Avenue, we pulled into a street of hard-luck houses near a crosstown over-pass. Ajamu directed me to a driveway just past a two-room shotgun shack where four or five men in T-shirts, sunglasses and pork pie hats sat on a sagging porch. I wasn't sure if Ajamu was any happier to be there than I was. In his dashiki and fela he didn't look all that less strange than a blanc in white dress shirt, black jeans and Ray Bans. But we needed an alamo tree, or ficus, for Shango. This was where it grew. I slouched in the car, trying to look nonchalant, as though I did this sort of thing all the time, while Ajamu got out to pluck a few leaves. As we drove away I saw the men on the porch all laughing.

On the whole, Ajamu said, he preferred Haitians to Cubans. Haitian vodun tends to be less syncretized than does Cuban santeria, and Haitians also tend to be black. I asked if living in Miami had not tempered his views, brought him closer to the Cubans. He had told me of many friends among the Cubans— Pichardo, for example. Friendliness was not the issue, he said, nor was respect. He respected the santeros and their adherence to African ways. But that was the sticking point. Deep down, Ajamu believed the African ways had been completely usurped. And it was time to change that.

"We don't have any reason to go through the santeria mystery anymore because it's not relevant," he said, echoing John Mason's sentiments. "Why are we trying to recapture our experience by going through the Caribbean? The only link that we have through anything African is directly straight across the water to Africa. We're not Cuban. We're *not Cuban*."

I hadn't heard him raise his voice before, and it was disconcerting, especially in a small car while he held a machete in his lap. Not a great time to play devil's advocate, but I felt I had to. "But you know the Cubans say African-Americans owe something to Cuba for saving the secrets of voudou, especially Ifa. They kept them alive in Cuba and they just disappeared up here—"

An uncharacteristic frown was my punctuation. "Look," he said, "it's like if you lose your tape recorder. What difference does it make if you don't remember where you put it? Turn there."

I did. "So let's say you get a case of amnesia and you don't even remember where you put your tape recorder and I hold onto it for you for twenty years," he continued. "When you come back for it, where are we going to get with this argument if you say, 'May I have my tape recorder?' And I say, 'But I held onto it for twenty years.' And you say, 'But it's still mine, it belongs to me.' And I say, 'Well, forget that, I held onto it for twenty years. And I even had something added to it. Look I put speakers on it, and I even got you a new cord and I changed the knobs on it.' But you say, 'That's nice, how much do I owe you for all that? It's still mine!'"

He thumped the dashboard. "I say: Leave the African American alone! If these people (Cuban santeros) were really honorable, they would not touch African Americans. If an African American came their way they would send them to an African American. That's the way an African would look at it. So that's a conflict. Oh—there, that's it. Stop."

We had found the "tree of life," what santeros call siempre vive, for Obatala and also a good herb for stomach and head aches. It grew near an expensive, sprawling but boarded-up corner house that had belonged to a building contractor who was actually a drug king pin who got busted. An iron fence and concrete posts circled the deserted property, Ozymandias-like. Since nobody was home, we were free to take what we wanted from the limbs hanging over the fence line.

The next stop was several miles away, at a church. We were back in good spirits again, concentrating on herbs and street signs, not Cubans and syncretism. The mango tree Ajamu needed grew in the lot behind what was now a small African Methodist Episcopal chapel. As I pulled to the side of the road, Ajamu wondered aloud if it would be okay to take a few leaves. It was a church, a holy place, and he wanted to be extra careful about having permission. But nobody was there to ask. I said I figured

Chief A. S. Ajamu, gathering herbs, Miami.

they wouldn't miss a couple of leaves. The lowest limbs were seven or eight feet high off the ground and Ajamu had to leap up several times to snatch his catch, but he did.

We found frescora, "a choice little herb" of multiple uses growing in the well-manicured plot surrounding the main entrance sign to the Miami-Dade County College north campus. Ajamu was a little nervous poaching on official property, even though he left the usual return offering of coins. I told him about the time in college I'd stolen the sign to the library and hidden it in nearby hedges for a few weeks, only to return it, somewhat piqued, because no one had been smart enough to find it. He didn't think it was a good analogy. We weren't doing pranks.

One of the leaves we hadn't been able to find grew in abundance on a hill near a country club golf course. But as we pulled up, Ajamu saw a new chain link fence. What had once been an easy stroll was now prohibited territory. He got out and walked up anyway, touching his fingers to the chain almost as if he wanted to see if it were a mirage. It was one of the few moments I ever saw anything like wistfulness in a priest. Even outside the fence, things had gone wrong. People had started using the area to dump garbage. Ajamu walked away from the all-too-real barrier and trod through the litter, looking in vain for vanished herbs. Fenced out and trashed. All he asked was access to what most people would consider weeds, but the world grew too fast here, too. No one respected the earth; no one had time for the needs of the gods.

We made two more stops but we were getting tired after three hours in the afternoon heat. Ajamu said he'd get the others later. We also had to stop by the photo shop before it closed to pick up his passport pictures. I smiled in a private fantasy. We were characters in some strange buddy movie, a road picture about two guys of different backgrounds thrown together to find the meaning of life in gathering plants from the streets of America. Peter Fonda and Ice-T. Taking Ajamu to get his pictures wasn't really an errand, it was just a thing to do with your pal.

We had to wait a few minutes while the short, paunchy, Cubano owner in guayabera and gray slacks concluded a shouting match over the phone. He told us it was his mistress—these young girls just want to party and have their own way. His daughter, a curvy woman of twenty-five in red spandex tube top and black pleated skirt, was running the cash register. She laughed at dad's plaint. Ajamu and I looked at each other, and we both laughed, too. The old guy was okay; he was still interested in life. His daughter was okay; she had a sense of humor. Miami was okay, too.

---

In Little Haiti, which roughly straddles its main drag, 54th Street, east of I-95 on over to Biscayne Boulevard, I got a sense that the wheel of life had turned so far down it had nowhere to go but back up. The community was in terrible shape. Drug

gangs, AIDS, linguistic isolation, unemployment and crime—
everything that was bad in Miami seemed to be doubly so in
Little Haiti. It wasn't a place you'd live unless you had to. But
there was something in the people's spirit that jumped out at
you.

I wondered if the bad rap on Little Haiti was yet another
projection of racism. What ever else Little Haiti was, it was black.
Maybe any part of town with that many black people who didn't
speak much English and were very, very unlike African Americans, just seemed like it had to be bad news. What black section
in any city in the United States didn't have that kind of reputation? I remembered my own anxiety about walking through
Bedford-Stuyvesant. John Mason did it every day; just a couple
of times set my nerves on edge. It wasn't that you couldn't get
hurt there, and I'm not a Pollyanna, but half my fear was based
on images propagated by white media and white society.

So as I drove through the dozen or so blocks of downtrodden
housing, baseline businesses like tire stores, small grocers, fix-it
shops, churches—and, of course, botanicas—that formed the core
of the Haitian quarter, I tried to look for what held the place
together instead of what tried to tear it apart. What I saw was
that life was hard, but people went to church, sent their children to school, hung out their laundry to dry, took whatever
jobs they could find, tried to make a life in America even if it
meant starting on the lowest rung any immigrant population in
this country has ever had to face. I saw in that tremendous courage and vitality.

But even the kindest view of Little Haiti had to come to terms
with one of the major reasons the community even existed: life
back home. If people in Little Haiti seemed determined to buck
the bad odds of Miami's mean streets, they were even more
determined to escape the horrors of the mother country.

Many times I had heard the plight of Haiti summoned as an
argument against the power of voudou. The poorest country in

the Western hemisphere, maybe in the world, Haiti had changed from an azure paradise with plenty of land for the people to an overpopulated and de-forested hell hole. The governments had gotten corrupt and stayed that way, usually with American help, ever since the revolution against the French coming up on two centuries ago. Haiti was a dangerous place to travel to and a dangerous place to live—even voting could get your head chopped off. Even growing up meant negotiating a gauntlet of disease, malnutrition and despair.

I had noticed a tendency on the part of western journalists to try to explain Haiti's staggering problems by dragging in half-baked references to voudou culture, as though a mysterious curse lay upon the land. And it was a great angle—it always had been. Why explain Haiti in terms of U. S. foreign and economic policy, of support for dictators just to keep out communists, and of the czar-like class suppression in the country when it could all be subsumed in the rubric of a fatal occult preoccupation? Maybe Haiti deserves its fate, the theory seems to say, since its people worship black gods. Maybe the black gods are fakes anyway. After all, what have those gods done?

There are plenty of responses to such voudou-baiting. One that occurs to me involves a simple turning of the mirror of religious accountabilty towards ourselves. If Haiti's gods have failed to deliver, what of our own? Does the presence of millions of homeless, of severe inner city racism, extermination of the farm belt economy, rampant militarism, bankrupt social services, creation of the instruments of world doom, funding of biosphere destruction (you think Haiti burns its resources!), and a virtual breakdown in national morality indicate the presence of grace from the white gods of the United States?

But that is a political response. The issue of the relation of voudou to the trauma of contemporary Haiti might be better understood through the lens of voudou itself. To priests of voudou, the country wasn't in trouble because of the failure of the loa—the Haitian term for the orisha—but for exactly the opposite reason. Haiti had lost its way because the loa had been abandoned.

In structure, such a critique is similar to that made by religious figures in many countries in crisis. Fundamentalist Christian preachers in America blame our social ills on a turning away from God; Muslims and Jews hear similar castigations from their mullahs and rabbis. It makes perfect sense to me that a voudou priest would view Haiti's plight the same way, as the result of what Catholics would call apostasy. The Oba of Oyotunji had expressed the voudou position on Haiti as well as anyone:

"Number one," he had told me one afternoon when the subject of Haitian poverty had come up, "the Haitian people got away from their culture. They wanted to be French. But after the country had been liberated by Toussaint L'Ouverture and Jean Jacques Dessalines, you had this king (Henri Christophe) who decided he wanted to be French. He wanted to wipe out the voudou. That brought in two different cultures which are almost diametrically opposed—Western culture and African culture. The result is a people half of whom want to be French and half of whom want to be African. It confuses the magic.

"Let me explain it this way. Haiti is like in a laboratory where a scientist has all his stuff. He can heal people, he can make animals die and come back to life. But even with all that power he's got in the laboratory, some fool can come in and wreck it all, just turn it into chaos.

"And you would say, how could that happen? These men are scientists. Well, what about Challenger? How could it blow up with all the geniuses that put it together? Every wire, every thing—how could it blow up? What happened? We're paying millions of dollars every year and we've got scientific genius that can split atoms. How is it that Challenger could blow up? People were dumbfounded.

"But even the most intricate experiment requires that by its nature the combination of energies are all working in harmony. If in Haiti, those energies are confused, it isn't going to work, no more than Challenger will work."

If the Oba's analysis was correct, the path to restoration of Haiti, and therefore of Little Haiti, lay in increased attention to the gods. But from what I could see of life on the street, and of hints of life behind closed doors, the loa were receiving plenty of care, and if you believed the loa were present even in the many storefront protestant churches—as the orisha were present in the black churches of New Orleans—the spirits were a singularly binding force throughout the community.

You couldn't drive a block on 54th without running into a church or botanica, or places that seemed combinations of both. One of my favorites was the St. Jean & Immaculée Botanic Store. The bright, hand-drawn mural on the front, depicting a lamb and a young St. Jean Baptiste (John the Baptist as St. John the Infant) perfectly represented a fusion of the two faiths that have been Haiti's legacy since slavery. The store's owner, Immaculée Calitixé, a voudou m'ambo, said the image had appeared to her in a dream. She named her storefront for St. Jean just as Lorita Mitchell had named hers for St. Lazarus and Ernesto Pichardo had named his for Babalu Aye.

If St. Jean was the prettiest, Botanica D'Haiti Macaya Boumba was perhaps the busiest on the street. Hand-painted lettering on the coral and yellow front of the store promised a lively inventory: "Religious articles, oil, ensense all kind, perfums, statuettes, variety items, bath. American Specializing in West Indian Produces." It wasn't a botanica, it was a botanica supermarket. Nor was it limited to voudou products. Catholic and Protestant needs, from Bibles to candlestick holders, full stock. Or if you didn't need things of the spirit, you could get bargains in loose-fitting Caribbean shirts, dresses, umbrellas, clocks, cassettes and LPs. Or anything.

(left) St. Lazarus, among other religious statues and supplies, in a Miami botanica.

(below) St. Jean & Immaculée Botanic Store, Little Haiti, Miami.

Botanica D'Haiti Macaya Boumba, Little Haiti, Miami.

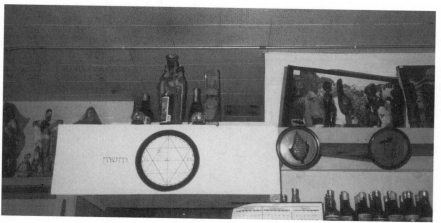

Inside Botanica D'Haiti.

Inside Botanica Eleggua in Miami. Christian and Santeria items are inter-
mingled on shelves, as is the practice in most botanicas.

As I walked in, three older men walked out, tucking their porkpie hats against the sun's glint, engrossed in a passionate conversation in Creole. At the cash register was Jacques, the owner, ringing up a sale. I introduced myself and found him quite willing to talk about voudou, but he said the person I really needed to see was his wife, Yvonne. She was a m'ambo—as he was a houngan—and it was really her store, but she'd gone to Haiti for the week and wouldn't be back before Friday. I told him I'd have to miss her. He said that was too bad and I agreed.

I stayed another ten minutes or so, decided nothing was going to happen for me, and left a card with my hotel phone number, in case Yvonne got into town early. I walked back into the midday heat and turned west in the direction of the overpass, but I didn't get far. Language barriers or no, word traveled fast in Little Haiti.

A street hustler in a white sports car zipped into an open meter space, jumped out, and, asked if I wanted to buy some voudou magazines. I looked him over: cheap reflecto shades, floral pattern rayon shirt open at the second button, lime slacks and faux alligator loafers. How about a tape of a voudou ceremony in New York? Some cassettes?

Yeah, buddy. I hadn't gotten twenty yards down the sidewalk, ignoring his increasingly sarcastic offers—taunts, more like—when I got called aside again. This time it was a muscular young man I remembered seeing in the botanica. Now, he was standing near the corner of a building at the edge of a small parking lot for some rundown apartments. "Hey," he hissed. He motioned for me to come over. For some reason I did. Sensing my wariness, he extended his hand quickly and introduced himself. Elvis. From Antigua. He didn't want to bother me, he said, only to make sure I understood that Jacques and Yvonne were "for real." He thought maybe I hadn't thought so, since I hadn't stayed.

Why he was interested in making the case for the two priests didn't really become clear to me until, as we were talking, I realized they were just a conversational gambit. What Elvis really wanted to find out was who I was. He assumed—as had Yolanda, the prostitute in Ruston—that because of my inquiries, I might "know more than I let on." And in case I did, he had a continuing problem I maybe could help with. At any event, telling me his story was a small risk on his part, the kind you take when gambling on faith.

A few months back, Elvis began, he'd been having a bad time with his girlfriend, who was really mad at him. He didn't know what to do about it, so he went to his houngan. Jacques gave him some advice—don't call the girl for awhile. He also gave him a potion. Elvis was to slip it into something she drank. Then she wouldn't be angry anymore.

"Did it work?"

"That was the problem," he smiled shyly. "It did."

She stopped being mad, but he began to have second thoughts. As he put it, "I didn't want to see somebody who'd call the police on me."

I realized some critical details were missing from this story. "*What* police? What happened?"

He looked at the ground. "Oh it, was an argument."

The sun was so hot I was getting dizzy, but I knew Elvis wanted me to hear him out. The short version was that even though she wasn't mad at him anymore, the girlfriend had already filed charges based on the "argument." He would have to go to court. So Elvis went back to Jacques, who gave him two sticks to rub in his hands and told him to recite two secret words outside the courthouse. He did, and his girlfriend didn't show up for the hearing. The charges were dismissed. "It really does work," he concluded. "That's why I tell you this."

All that left Elvis without a girlfriend, but Jacques gave him the means to get a new one. Put stone fragments from a comet—

for sale in the botanica—in your refrigerator overnight and then drop one in front of the house of the girl you wanted. She'd call you immediately. Elvis hadn't done it yet but intended to.

I told Elvis I didn't know about that. What good would it do to get a girl by trickery? Sure, he said, no question about that, but don't forget she might be under the influence of someone else. You might have to get some tricks just to even the odds.

"There is good magic," he said, then he touched my arm and lowered his voice. "But always remember the truth is that they can make things to hurt people, too, to kill them." He looked into my eyes, almost pleading.

That easily, I suppose, I could have become a spiritual adviser. But I think what Elvis needed was a decent therapist. The appeal of voudou priests, or priests of any religion, however, is that not everyone believes in therapy, but everyone does believe in magic.

—=—

Sunday morning I wanted to go to church, and I knew just where. Storefront ministries had sprouted amid the fix-it shops, beauty parlors and other bootstrap businesses all over Little Haiti. I didn't have any stock riding on any particular Christian sect, but I had a theory that a Protestant service in a working class Haitian environment would be a lot like a Spiritual Church service in New Orleans. There was only one way to find out. A little after eleven, I found a vacant seat in a back pew at the Independent Church of God, a small charismatic denomination temporarily housed on the lower floor of a white, two-story office building about halfway between the botanicas of St. Jean Baptiste and Jacques and Yvonne.

The sanctuary was large enough to hold several hundred people, and as I walked in, I could see that it did. As in the Spiritual churches, the women wore white lace head coverings, often complemented by lace shawls draped across their shoulders. The men were dressed mostly in dark suits, though the inside temperature was in the nineties. The walls were bare, almost spartan. I couldn't see any icons, not even a cross. The only adornments seemed to be a few framed photos of church leaders.

Two ushers, surprised to see a white man, were almost solicitous in finding me a seat, which wasn't easy considering the crowd. A half-dozen working-class men already in place in one of the rear pews slid over to give me room. I sat, nodding a silent greeting to the balding man in the light brown suit to my right. The usher, seeing I had no Bible, found one and gave it to me. It was in French. So were the services, delivered in Creole by the thin, hard-looking, sixty-year-old pastor. In his dark suit and white tie, he looked like a stereotype of the successful houngan, and perhaps in another setting he might have been, running a voudou hounfor (worship area) instead of a fundamentalist Christian mission.

I couldn't understand the words of the sermon, but from the audience response and the cadences of the minister's speech, I could pretty much guess the thematic structure, which in my experience is that of most Sunday preachings, black or white, give or take a few liturgical variants. Put the fear of God into the congregation—the best preachers do the best fear—and then show the straying flock the way back to salvation.

I heard Haiti mentioned a few times, and some reference to police.

"Amen," they would respond. "C'est vrai."

I tried to sing the closing hymn, mostly because the man next to me shared his song book, but I couldn't put much into it. My mind was elsewhere. Change a couple of items of apparel and the rows of Haitians standing in front of me, singing to Jesus, I could've been on a Georgia plantation in the eighteenth century. No wonder the Black Codes directed most of their fury at religious expression. The makers of those laws had seen in voudou not the simplistic superstitions they mocked in anti-black propaganda, but the powerful socio-politico-martial force it actually represented—in a land where the ratio of blacks to whites, in some states, was as high as 1:1. In the islands of the Caribbean, it was often on the order of 9:1.

I was seeing in Little Haiti what I had been seeing not only in the Spiritual Churches of New Orleans, but throughout African America: the substitution of belief. It was too far gone now, too far assimilated. The substitution was "positioned" over the centuries, to use a modern advertising term, not as repression, or brainwashing, but as conversion, as the saving of pagan African souls. Among some secular thinkers, the mergers and mutations are seen as evidence of a qualitatively new "Atlantic" culture, fresh-forged from the hell of the diaspora. Yet I could not look upon these souls and consider them saved, let alone as phoenixes. Observing what had happened here would always be, for me, the glimpsing of stolen fervor.

But what to do about it? If the pioneers at Oyotunji were right, African Americans, at least spiritually, had to re-group. To regain an identity, as Malcolm X argued, one must first separate and locate it. I remember getting into huge arguments in college, decades ago, over this strategic controversy which has, in one form or another, always divided white and black Americans—across racial lines—in cultural, legal and religious matters. Now, as then, I sided with Malcolm X, and with James Baldwin, who exiled himself to Paris, and doubtless that led me to the way I interpreted the voudou renaissance at the end of the twentieth century. I as a white man who had nothing to offer to this discussion but the interjection of my own body and consciousness as long-overdue witness.

Chief Ajamu had said to me: "Every religion has to have a story line, right? It has to have a mythology. So where is that going to come from? It comes from a select group of people. The whole story line is around the history of a particular ethnic group of people, a particular race of people. There's no such thing as a 'world' religion. If Christianity is a world religion, then Christianity should be the history of the world, but it isn't, is it? It is the history of one ethnic group of people, and their disputes and wars with people of color."

# 21

## ORISHA ANEW

FOR MONTHS I had followed the spirit, drifting with it from Texas into New Orleans, tracking its peaks and depths across the South like lines on a Richter scale chart. I had jumped up into Brooklyn and back down to Miami. And now I would jump again.

A call had gone out across the voudou network: history was going to be made in Atlanta. For the first time ever, American blacks would conduct, in the symbolic capital of both the Old and the New South, a full orisha voudou initiation in the traditional manner. Not santeria, not hoodoo, not some ersatz mix.

Initiations were not uncommon in the U. S., but mostly they were taking place in the urban ports—New York and Miami— or at Oyotunji. To conduct one in Atlanta was evidence the renaissance had moved openly into the heartland. But there was something even more special about the event: the initiate was from New Orleans. With one stroke, the two most important cities of the old slave belt were united in what was once unthinkable—perpetuating the vo-du in America. And it was almost too perfect that the woman chosen to forge the link was the dancer Ava Kay Jones, and that the site of her initiation—to the goddess Oya—was the home of Baba Kunle and Baba Tunde, the two priests who had given me my first taste of sacrificial blood.

I arrived for the final ceremony, known as Throne Day. Ava had been cloistered for a week of traditional Yoruba preparation rituals—prayers, dances, teaching of secrets—presided over by Baba Kunle, her spiritual godfather. She also had received her orisha pots and itá. Now she approached the conclusion, a kind of "coming out" gala in which the intitiate emerges from her ring of priests as though from a river of baptism, and greets her friends with a bimbé. Guests, participants and relatives from New York, Oyotunji, Miami, LA, and around the South had been filtering in for days. I had been told a number of important babalawos would be present, and sure enough as I made my way toward the patio there was Dr. Epega in a festive dashiki. We couldn't talk long—he was still helping with the rituals.

A gathering of babalawos at the initiation ceremony in Atlanta: Oba, left; Dr. Epega, center; Baba Kunle, right.

Divining tray, center, and instruments in Dr. Epega's home. Opele chain to right.

I wandered around, struck by the difference in ambiance from the rain-soaked evening on which I had first seen that yard, slogged through its puddles, passed the night of the summer solstice with fresh blood on my forehead. Hearing noises from the basement, I peeked into the downstairs kitchen, where a half-dozen women were cutting up chickens and goats that had been sacrificed during the night. I gave them a cheesecake I had brought as a gift.

Back outside I ran into, almost literally, Baba Tunde, sweating and en route to the house, but spiffy in white T-shirt, trousers, and head scarf. He looked tired from the previous evening, during which Ava had been fully consecrated. He greeted me with such a big smile I think he must have been a little amazed I'd really shown up. I knew he didn't have time to chat, but I quickly told him how the Oba had read me as an Ochosi instead of Obatala. Tunde seemed surprised. Then he said that sometimes Ochosi "hid behind" Obatala.

Ebo Shrine in back yard of priests' home in Atlanta. Iron pots for Ogun; small conical heads with cowrie shell eyes denote Elegba.

Someone called out from an upstairs window and he excused himself. I picked up a can of pop and walked over to the tree shading the sacrificial shrine where I had first made ebo. It had been fed recently and was thick with palm oil and feathers. I counted at least three Ogun pots and as many Elegba heads. I also saw a conch shell, probably for Yemonja, and a tripod of iron poles from which was hung a piece of cloth, possibly from a dress or dashiki. I wasn't sure of their purpose, though they were, like all the other evidence of sacrifice, connected to the initiation.

I wanted to see Ava but wouldn't be able to do so before dusk, when she would greet us all publicly, marking the beginning of her year-long apprenticeship, finally becoming a full priestess, an iyalorisha—translated literally as mother of the orisha. In keeping with the reversal of meaning common in voudou, however, the term also connotes the idea of bride and child. Ava would simultaneously be the mother of Oya and the child.

I waited out the twilight chatting with some of the other guests, trying to ignore the mosquitoes. Had a stranger accidentally walked into the back yard, and seen the array of African apparel, he might have thought he'd intruded on a party from a Nigerian embassy. I had begun to wonder how we'd all get into the room upstairs to greet Ava, when I heard a murmur of voices. A clump of people standing next to me were looking in the direction of the gate at the side of the yard.

It was the Oba. He walked in like a bolt of charisma, truly king-like in his dark olive dashiki, yellow fela, and leather sandals. He was immediately swarmed, and began hugging everyone back, including two of his ex-wives. I hadn't realized how popular he was outside the village. He seemed magnificiently happy, and with good reason. In some respects, Ava's initiation was the fulfillment of all that he stood for.

As he made his way across the yard, the Oba stopped before a huge man of well over six feet and at least 250 lbs. They looked each other over, grinned, and the man dropped to his knees, placing three fingers on the ground. "How you doing, Serge?" he said, rising. Brad Simmons, drummer for the evening, knew the monarch from back in New York. They hadn't seen each other in a while, and deep down, to him, Serge was still Serge.

A woman in her early forties edged into the Oba's line of sight. She moved up quickly once he spotted her and they embraced a lot more warmly than protocol required. I had spoken with her earlier, and knew she knew the Oba, but this was electricity. I eavesdropped. She wouldn't stay long, I heard her say, because she had to get back to Miami. But there was something she wanted to show him. They found two empty chairs and she dug into her purse. While they talked, she passed him a Polaroid photo. I could see the expression of the king of American voudou soften almost to tears. "Twenty-six years old," I heard her say.

I walked off into the yard. I felt some mist in my own eyes. I was thinking about my own daughter, Jennifer, and for a while I was not at the bimbé, but on the road again. For Jenny's visit that summer, I had promised her something different, so instead of having her meet me in Austin, we began our visit in Miami. She would drive back through the South with me to Texas, a chance for her to see new territory, and for me to have welcome company. I hadn't really planned on taking her to Oyotunji, which was several hours out of the way, but as we were speeding along through northern Florida, I knew I had to. I wanted her to be read by the Oba.

We arrived at the tail end of a Shango festival, and the village was typically chaotic. To save time, and conserve some of his own energy, the Oba told us to come down to his own house in the Afin. He'd been dancing all day in the sun, and greeted us

Jennifer, the author's daughter, watching Shango festival at Oyotunji.

Shrine for Shango, Oyotunji village.

at his front door in nothing more than a pair of baggy shorts. I was happy that he was relaxed enough to be informal, and he was pleased that I would entrust him with the reading of my only child.

He led us into his living room, a small, stifling enclosure filled with wicker furniture. Apologizing for the heat, he turned on a box fan, which helped a little. Then he picked up the straw beach mat he used for readings and unrolled it on the floor. He sat down, cross-legged, at one end of the mat, and leaned forward. He motioned for Jenny to sit opposite. I gave her $30. At the Oba's instruction, she folded it triply.

He threw the opele rapidly, making the requisite prayers, pausing only to write down the sequence of the odu in his client record book. I lost count of the casts, but there seemed to have been a half dozen or so. He studied the results for several minutes. Then he looked up and smiled. "Oya."

I was as surprised as when he had said "Ochosi" to me. Oya was the wife of Shango, and though she was the lord of the winds and a fierce warrior, the mistress of changes, she also was the ruler of the dead, equated in Catholicism with the Virgin de la Candelaria and in Haiti with Ghede. This was a heavy spirit. Jenny was a ten-year-old redhead who still traveled with Chester, her stuffed dog, and had only recently given up on the Easter bunny.

Most of the next day, driving through Georgia and Alabama and the Florida panhandle, Jenny had gone over the reading again and again. Her main concern was that the Oba had said she would become a successful business woman. For years, Jenny had wanted to be a veterinarian (as my father had been). I told her what I told everyone else new to readings: to take that which she wanted. And anyway, between Ifa and Elegba, things could change. She could still be a vet. She decided that was okay.

She never talked about the reading much after that, though we did buy the recommended coconut shampoo, and she promised to eat more fruit, as the Oba had advised, correctly diagnosing an intestinal ailment she'd had for the last year. In the fall, she called me to say they had to do a research paper for fifth grade. She had chosen Martin Luther King, Jr.

—=—

A little before 7 P.M., Baba Tunde called for us all to come upstairs. As I had guessed, the room was tight quarters for thirty to forty people, about the size of a large, one-car garage. The musicians were squeezed against one wall, and had already started playing; Brad on congas, the other two rounding out the rhythm with shakeree, bells, and assorted smaller drums. Ava sat alone on a straw mat in the far corner, beneath two large crimson sheets hung as backing for her throne, a wicker chair. African masks, fresh palm fronds, orisha pots and rows of white candles were spread around her.

Ava Kay Jones during historic Oya initiation ceremony in Atlanta. She was the first African-American initiated by other African-Americans in an orisha voudou ceremony in the United States.

Ava and others dancing during bimbé at conclusion of Ava's initiation in Atlanta.

Baba Kunle, left, and Baba Tunde, during bimbé.

Baba Tunde, seated. Ava at right, in white, during final initiation ceremony.

Bare-breasted, she was adorned in the traditional affectations of Oya: a floor-length skirt trimmed with long strands of grass, a feather-covered leather crown from which hung strips of cowries, covering her face like a medieval war helmet. Her arms were coated with white longitudinal markings, almost serpentine, and white dots, the dots of ashé, covered her hands and bare feet. A palm fan lay to one side, as did Oya's black horsetail whisk and machete.

The drummers were good, and before long just about everyone was dancing, getting in the mood. I perched on a chair at the back of the room for a better view, and more air—it was a sweat bath. Eventually Baba Kunle, in a sparkling white Obatala robe highlighted with aqua embroidery, moved toward the throne. Formally launching the "presentation," he helped his goddaughter to her feet and invited her to dance for her visitors. She rose in a swirl of lithe grace and floated through the room, smiling at each face as it came into her gaze. When she passed mine, I could see she was pretty close to giving herself over to possession.

A half-hour later the Oba escorted Ava back to her seat and gestured to the musicians to stop playing. As senior priest he was to give a short speech of welcome. He greeted the guests in Yoruba, according to protocol, then repeated himself in English, and that might have been the end of it. But, like everyone else in the room, the king's heart was full. Something more needed saying. He looked out at us, cleared his throat. Feet shuffled, clothing rustled, a few people fanned themselves with their hands, but where there had been dancing and drumming now was an electric stillness.

"All across American now in every major city you are going to find that the gods of Africa have descended," he began. "They are sitting on their thrones and the people are coming to greet them and welcome them." He looked at Ava. "Gradually, we shall overcome—through these initiations, which so many of the people, of the voudou inside of the people, are seeking."

"Amen," came some voices. Then, many.

"Ashé! Ashé!"

"People of Atlanta," he proclaimed, throwing open his arms, "present yourselves to Oya!"

One by one, priests and guests complied. When my turn came, I did as the others, approaching Ava's throne, falling forward into a prone position. Then I eased my body full to the floor, face-down, and leaned onto my right elbow. I rose, sort of proud of myself. Baba Kunle was grinning so broadly I thought he would laugh. He greeted me African style, touching shoulders alternately.

When we had finished, a little after 10 P.M., Kunle escorted Ava away, and the drums started again. She soon came back, but now, as an iyawo, changed into a plain white gown, with a white coverlet draping her face, head, and shoulders. Simple, clean, pure.

Though she could not see because of the coverlet, everyone danced again in front of her. One of the priests picked up an aluminum cooking pot filled with water. He took it outside, emptied it and then brought it back, turning it upside down—a sign that the old vessel had been drained, that the life of the iyawo was now empty and ready to be filled with change.

It was pretty much over. The Oba interrupted the drumming a last time to officially close the ceremony with a long prayer in Yoruba, and guests began trickling outside. A few weren't ready to let go, though, and badgered Simmons into a brief encore. But he was spent, and in almost no time slipped out into the night. A woman who wanted to "really start the party" went to the basement for some record albums. Someone else was foraging for rum.

I went downstairs and stood in the door between the kitchen and the reception area, the spot that had been an indoor lake during the flooding last June, and I knew the spirits had taken me as far as they could. As far as I could let them.

It was that abrupt. It was time to go.

I wouldn't be able to see Ava again that night but I knew she'd understand. I walked outside. It felt good to breathe the freshness of the night. A few children, relatives of Ava who'd come all the way from Louisiana, were picking away at slivers of cake and frosting, looking around wide-eyed but not saying much.

I said my goodbyes and headed for the gate. The first time I'd passed through, I had no idea what lay within. Now I wondered what waited outside, in the "real" world, a world which, in many ways, was never going to be the same for me. I nodded to a thin, elderly man I'd seen but not talked to all night. He was dressed in white sport shirt and slacks, and carried a Bible.

# 22

## AMEN

I LIKE RITUAL because it is a form of art—a contrivance of human thought in the attempt to reach the eternal and unknowable. Ritual lets us believe in things we can see and do, because the gods are too remote. Christians reach God through symbols: the cross, the saints, and especially the human form of God, which they call Jesus. The voudou worshiper has the orisha, the ancestors, and altars and a thousand kinds of talismans, herbs and objects of magic, all of which exist to make contact with eternity.

I like ritual, but I do not believe in it. Ritual is bureaucracy; ritual is control; ritual is exclusion. Even as it attempts to make knowable the unknowable, ritual confines, in the same way that criticism and categorization confine art. An artist who studies criticism, form and categories must break and defy them in order to create something new. Otherwise art is photocopying. What is a religion that does not create something new? What is a religion that is not alive through the people, instead of just in the rules? It is what Nietzche said it was—dead.

But voudou is not dead. The longer I journeyed through its soul, the more I saw that it was a constant act of creation. For every rule and ritual I observed, there are dozens of variations—voudou is not the same in any two countries or cultures, and in that sense the idea of a new Atlantic culture that mingles what started in Africa and what altered itself here is true. In America, voudou is not even the same in any two cities. In the end, I could not say where voudou started or stopped, because, like Dambada Wedo, it doesn't.

In its vitality and regeneration—even in its passionate factional disputes—is the proof of its oft-challenged validity. People need voudou. They have done so under the most desperate conditions and despite the most prolonged persecution. They need it because it provides the same comforts, metaphors and insights as do all religions; it links the quick, the dead, the consciousness of both. And though I could not follow it further, it gave something to me as well. I was not a true believer, but I had seen the truth of belief. If I lack the certainty to say there are gods, I learned there is faith. Faith, transferred, is art. Art is creation. The preacher, the priest, the artist, the healer, the grave-digger, the two-headed man—we are all the same. Above all, I saw voudou in that way.

That fall, Lorita Mitchell called to tell me she had changed denominations within the Spiritual church, from the Metropolitan to the Israelite. She was to be re-ordained as a minister during the organization's upcoming annual convention—that weekend. And it wouldn't just be her, she said—her sons Gary and Andrew would also be ordained. I scrambled to get there, and by Saturday morning stood in front of the Israelite Universal Divine Spiritual Church of Christ at 3000 Frenchman, a stolid brick building on the corner of a working-class black neighborhood northeast of the Quarter. The business part of the weeklong convention was almost finished, and today was devoted to nonstop preaching, with different ministers following each other like acts in a gospel tent. Lorita was scheduled for noon, but things were running late.

Only a handful of people were on the porch, but as soon as I walked inside I could see where the others had gone. The aging patriarch of the denomination, Archbishop E. J. Johnson, was at the pulpit, passionately defending the efficacy of a cornerstone of Spiritual belief: prophecy. I found a seat amid the crowded pews. Prophecy was another name for Ifa.

"Five years ain't too long for a prophecy to come true," Johnson called out, his voice strong and full.

"Amen," answered the congregation.

"Ten years ain't too long."

"Amen."

"Twenty years ain't too long," he thundered. "I had people come up to me and say, 'What you prophesied *forty years* ago come to pass, and I don't know what they mean 'cause I already forgot.'"

"Amen."

I glanced around the huge sanctuary. Above on the balcony, a ceramic bust of Blackhawk; elsewhere, portraits of the saints, the black Virgin, a gallery of ornately framed portraits of elders. In the center of it all, a traditional likeness of Jesus.

I nodded to a few of Lorita's parishioners. Willie Mae and Alma, at whose sacrificial ceremony I had met Ricky Cortez, sat to one side. Nearby were Betty, the school teacher, and James, the security guard, to be ordained that evening as a missionary and deacon, respectively. Many of the faithful were from throughout the denomination's domain, the Midwest and South; their vestments designated rank like uniforms at a military ball. Mothers of the church—senior women but not ministers—in purple or white robes; other female members—usually referred to as "sisters"—in simple Sunday black or white dresses, shoulders draped with white shawls, heads covered with white lace caps or veils. The Bishops stood out in heavy velvet red robes. The Ministers, male or female, wore black, scarlet or indigo robes, depending on their level. Children were in clean white shirts and dark slacks or skirts, and the lay men in the audience wore their best double-breasted suits or fresh-pressed summer shirts and slacks. It could've been Little Haiti.

Archbishop Johnson wound down his sermon, and, as late-comers continued to trickle in, nodded to the organist. It was time for the show most had come to see. With a flourish of white cuffs and ringed fingers, the smiling, heavy-set musician in a blue suit threw up a wall-of-sound gospel riff that utterly domi-nated the room. Exactly on cue, Gary hit the stage. He was a concentration of power—solid black robes, white cap, face glow-ing, handsome as the night he'd led me around the French Mar-ket. Clapping with each step forward, his rich voice took easy command as the wall of sound became the old standard: "Jesus on the main line/Tell him what you want."

Soon even the Archbishop was clapping and swaying. We all were. The crescendo boiled up like water in a kettle, and just when it was about to scream with release, Lorita emerged, trailed by Anthony, one of the twins. In white to Gary's black, they joined hands to face the congregation.

It was truly a show. St. Lazarus Spiritual Church pumped up ten-fold in a sanctuary Lorita could have only dreamed of hav-ing as her own ministry. She fit like a glove. In the next hour, as the hymns and singing spread out across the chamber, mingling with the incense, she spanned—for herself and those who had seen her grow up, come of age and persevere—the distance from Mother Jorden, Bishop Francis, and all those who had come before to all who would come hence. "Hup!"—Archbishop Johnson, bent double at the waist, drawing his arms into his body to her preaching. "Hup!"—the energy of the Spirit leaping from him into her, her in his long-traveled shoes, her own now, bearing down on sinners, reaching out to saints.

"When we was poor we didn't have no bread to eat . . . but it didn't stop me from serving the Lord," she called out. "When I was a young girl I wanted to wear the short skirts . . . but my minister said no . . . the Lord have something in store . . . and it came to pass."

And now she knew of Jesus and the Holy Way and she was standing before many who would have once scorned her and hid their children from her gaze. "Put your hands together now," she commanded from the pulpit, guttural and growling in the place between sex and god Gerard Manley Hopkins could only imagine. "We going to pray."

I took the hand of a sister in white who reached back from the pew in front of me. I lowered my eyes and listened, but I still couldn't pray in a church. That would never change for me. And yet I always felt at home in Lorita's ministry. That would never change, either. Others would refine it; others would make the nationalist break from santeria; others would clarify the relationship to bedrock Afro-American Protestantism. But in the long run, voudou in America was going to be as it was in the life and practice of Lorita Mitchell.

When the praying was finished, we sang another hymn, and then it was time for the prophecies. So many people wanted readings they had to form three lines—one to Lorita, the others to her sons. Things just seemed to break loose. A dozen people whirled into trances. Several had to be helped away, calling out Jesus's name. Some sisters "cleaned" others, drawing out bad spirits. A young woman in purple jumped from the pews, bent double, thrust her arms out violently, and began hopping in a spasmodic dance—completely gone. A man grabbed her round the shoulders and guided her to a pew. She sat there a moment, sagging forward, head in hands. Then she snapped upright and was back in the aisle, and had to be helped to a seat again.

Lorita cleaned a man in a wheelchair, kneeling before him to bathe his badly swollen feet with holy water. One day he would walk again, she told him, but he must pray to Jesus for it. "I don't care what the doctors say," she scoffed, rising up. She, too, began to spin. She came right down off the dais into the aisle with all the other possessed souls. At one point she passed by me, less than a foot away, clenching the man's slippers in her hands. She didn't even see me. And I'm not sure who I was seeing. Her eyes were glassy, her cheeks puffed out. She was snorting, nostrils widely flared.

It went on for a half-hour. The collection plate made the rounds, and Lorita advised those who wanted their prophecies "to work fast" to come up to get the small white candles she'd brought. They should light them at home and read Psalms and pray. But there was a cost. "Sacrifice five dollars for your candle," she said, "because God will return it to you doublefold." She was asking them to make ebo.

While the people came forward, I thought back to what I'd seen a moment earlier. Lorita had stepped to the center of the dais, framed by the symbols of the Lord and the Spirits in rows of burning candles and statues behind her. To either side stood her two strong and handsome sons. They joined hands and raised their interlocked arms high, beaming in a triumvirate of power and exultation. The organist rolled out a lively "Come on, Spirit," and they stepped forward as smoothly as in a Motown revue. In my notebook, I drew a crude depiction of the scene and wrote under it a single word: Triumph.

# APPENDIX I

## VOUDOU IN THE MEDIA

A REPRESENTATIVE SAMPLE of voudou accounts in the nineteenth-century New Orleans press easily shows the establishment, repetition and reinforcement of the negative cultural stereotype that has stuck with the religion. The stories usually appeared about the time of St. John's Feast (June 24), a Catholic holiday also often said to have been used for voudou gatherings. In general the accounts involved a clandestine celebration in some swamp or backwood, about midnight, with wanton revelry, blood sacrifices, mumbo-jumbo singing and dancing, and were presided over by an eerie mammy or old man. The reporters were invariably white. Sensationalist and racist phrasings were commonplace, as was the creation of an atmosphere of murkiness and horror. It was as if the more bizarre and phantom-like the stories, the more likely was the audience—white, literate Orleanians—to believe them. I present here many of the accounts at length, not because of the sparkling nature of the reporting, but because each is a treasure chest of detail in the creation of what today we might call the "negative spin" on voudou mythology.

One of the most interesting accounts actually appeared later in the century, but is of special interest because it claims to present one of the earliest known stories of a voudou event. An unsigned piece (the author is possibly Zoe Posey, from whose collection of original newspaper manuscripts this is taken)[1] in the June 26, 1874 *New Orleans Daily Picayne*, it was presented along with news stories but it purports to the re-telling of an event from 1723, previously preserved only in oral form. It thus openly reflects what certainly must have been prevailing attitudes toward voudou—that it was witchcraft, sorcery, damnation—but also quite powerful in an evil way.

In the narrative, a French pioneer named Castillon, a decent man, falls from the state of grace after eating an apple from a tree of knowledge inhabited by an Eve-like spirit. He takes up the ways of Africans and Indians, and, no doubt as a consequence, becomes an evil man, a usurer, a conjurer, a murderer, destroyed at last as a victim to his own Faustian bargain. All amid dark and stormy nights, violence, mayhem, sex and the half-lit world of swashbuckling New Orleans, the northern tip of the Caribbean. It's a semiotician's dream, and no bad yarn either.

---

## THE HAMADRYAD

### A Wild Story of 1723.

### The Birth of Voudouism in Louisiana.

There is, on Bayou Road, an old house that has defied alike the hand of time and the humid, destructive breeze of our swamps, a breeze before which stone and iron melt away like ice. This building, a sturdy centenarian, has its story, like many a more aristocratic mansion, a story that was universally known and believed half a century ago, but which, like all the old ideas and glories of Louisiana, is fast being forgotten and unheard.

A century and a half ago there lived in the city of New Orleans an old Frenchman by [the] name [of] Jean Marie de Castillon. Jean, or "Babillard," as he was re-christened, was an ideal old Frenchman, vain, childish and garrulous, but the very best of company. His fund of anecdotes was inexhaustible; in these old Jean was always his own hero—victor on the field of battle, in the cabinet or in the drawing room.

Every morning and evening, Castillon would promenade through the marsh Place d'Armes or along the fish-smelling levee, ogling the fille de la casette or voluptuous sirens from St. Domingo. Yet, even these could not allure him; and he would wander from their temptations to the company's warehouses, where he was sure to capture some new listener, a wild, half savage voyageur from St. Genevieve, or a staid Alsacian from the German coast. Then he would pour forth his stories, until a plea of "business" rescued his unhappy prisoner.

Among the many "coinages of his brain," one never failed to bring down his audience; this was his claim to a Marquisate in the aristocratic province of Berni. Some of the army officers, dangerous pegrès drafted from the prisons of Paris, would jokingly respond to this claim, that old Castillon was more than noble, that he was royal, and bore upon his shoulders, like the kings of France, a blood-red fleur-de-lys, printed there in large characters by the hangman of Arles. At this rough camp joke, Castillon would twist his moustaches, contract his busy [sic] grey eyebrows, and drop his hand upon his sword hilt. He never drew the weapon; his courage was so well established by his [s]tories that this was deemed all that was necessary in such a chevalier Bayard.

With all his nobility and his chateaux (en Espagne), Jean was distressingly poor. He had a home—a rickety, uncertain cabin, provided by the Government—but his cupboard was as bare as that of Mrs. Hubbard, of Mother Goose fame. The neighbors never refused him a meal; for this Castillon always paid most liberally in stories and jokes. When, however, a famine came and the crops were burnt by the Indians or destroyed by the flood, old Castillon would take his pirogue, meander through the spider web of bayous and lakes that surrounded the city, in search of berries, wild fruit or anything edible he could pick up.

On October 18, 1723, when old Castillon was out on one of those predatory expeditions, occurred one of the greatest storms that ever swept the Gulf of Mexico. For five days and nights after this old Castillon was missing and given up for lost. "The storm," "Indians," "Alligators," "Carried off by the Devil," were the exclamations of his acquaintances, ready to build a two-volume romance on even less foundation than this very natural disappearance.

Just as these stories were growing stale and cold, old Castillon appeared. He had set out a stout, hearty, jovial old gentleman; he returned dirty, haggard, reduced in size and with a strange saturnine scowl upon his usually beaming face. Not a word did he say to the friends who congregated around to greet him, but marched straight to his little hovel in the rue de Condé, pulled up the plank that served as a draw-bridge to his castle—for in those days every house in the city was on an island to itself—and lay hidden from view for a whole week. The only token of his existence was the flame and smoke that curled upwards from his mud chimney, and this flame told some that he was at work in his kitchen, others that the devil was paying him a friendly visit.

When, at the end of a week, Castillon left his hut, he was thinner, more yellow and emaciated than when he had entered it. Instead of promenading on the levee with his supply of yarns for sale, Castillon now frequented a grove of trees that grew just back of the city, about equi-distant from the city walls and the

Highlands of the Lepers. Old Marie, Queen of the Voudous, and Buechin, the Indian doctor, were consulted by the curious, but could only explain, what everybody knew, the Castillon was bewitched—voudoued.

The following is Castillon's own version of the story—so at least Mimi, a nymphe, swore was confided to her by the old man himself in a tender moment:

In his wanderings on the day of his disappearance Castillon came upon a strange outré grove of trees, known to the Indians as "The Fairies' Grove." Seeing some bright golden fruit that grew luxuriantly upon these trees, Castillon determined to lay in a winter supply of these Hesperian apples, if it should be proved that they were edible. It was not at all an easy task to climb these trees: they were tall, smooth and almost limbless. Thirty feet from the ground they burst into three branches of limbs, one growing centrally upward, well covered with long wiry leaves; the other two horizontally from the side, lithe, thin and almost leafless.

It was only after superhuman efforts that Castillon reached the fork of the tree. Seating himself there, he greedily devoured one of the fruit that had first attracted his attention. No sooner had he finished it than a strange feeling came over him, the earth seemed to spin around with frightful rapidity, the trees commenced playing leap-frog, and the very sun itself seemed "dancing as on an Easter day." So dizzy did he become, that unable any longer to hold on to the branch, he let go and fell head-foremost to the ground.

When Castillon awakened from this shock it was evening; the sun, red with the glow of the coming storm, was just sinking behind the horizon. Yet even a greater change had come over the trees whence he had fallen. Slowly the mighty branches softened into arms, the leaves melted into hair, whilst the scaly bark, dropping from the trunk, exposed to view a face of the most startling beauty. Castillon was almost paralyzed at this sight; he thought that the fall had disordered his brain, or that he was asleep. But no! Everything was distinct; and a pinch assured him that if his mind was asleep his legs certainly were wide enough awake.

Before Castillon had fully recovered from his fright, this newborn "daughter of a race divine" addressed him in soft, melodious music:

"Amidst the horses of heaven and the blooming realms of everlasting light," said she, "I once roamed free and happy. I was commissioned to guard this country, the Garden of Eden, but which now the hand of man has so scourged and ravaged. You know the story well; I did but leave Adam for a second, he could not resist temptation, he fell, gave up immortality for knowledge. He suffered for it, so do I. Within this tree, the tree of knowledge, am I forever confined, until I shall be rescued by a descendant of Adam. You have eaten of this fruit. To you, now the mysterious language of nature is revealed; the mists that cloud the past and the future are blown away. On you is imposed the task of rescuing us; do you consent?"

So sweet the accent, so fair the face that Castillon, whose blood old age had not yet cooled, forgetting alike fear and superstition, sprang from his mossy couch and swore by his life, his honor and his soul that he would rescue them.

After lying there, half stunned, for several days, protected by their Briarean arms from the storm, Castillon recovered sufficiently to come to the city. He daily resorted to these trees, and, seated in the branches of one of them, like a St. Simon Stylites, seemed to be ever meditating some great problem. His visits to the grove became daily more frequent, and finally he entirely deserted his little hut in the city, and built him an eyrie in the tallest of the trees; never after this did he set foot within the walls.

This, with the sudden change in Castillon's disposition, greatly excited all the gossips of the town. He, who had never had a golden portrait of his Majesty, Louis, le bien-aimé, suddenly became one of the richest persons in the colony. He was somewhat of a usurer, and never refused the young bloods of the city a loan for a dissipation or a carouse. His money never brought any good, it always corrupted the owner, whispered evil thoughts and wishes, and brought ruin and disgrace on the oldest families of Orleans, Canada and St. Domingo.

Castillon soon became regarded as a mighty wizard and magician. Thousands resorted to him to solve some love knot more intricate than that of Gordianus, to probe the future, or to get rid of a dangerous rival. In none of these tricks did he ever fail. His prophecies, clear and unequivocal unlike those of Delphi and Noswodamus [sic], are still current among the old Creoles and negroes. His miraculous power was always ascribed to his familiars, the trees.

No one doubted but that the grove was enchanted. In 1752, when the little city was consumed by fire, and the flame spread beyond the city walls far out into the swamp, this grove alone was spared, and in 1745, when Big Sun and his Choctaws came swarming down from the Natchez massacre, murdering the planters on the German and Tchoupitoulas coasts, scalping Capts. Beaufré and Vinette in the very sight of the city walls, this house alone escaped. Like the palace of Shedad in the paradise of Irem, it was invisible to all who meant it harm.

It was strange, also, that no naturalist could designate the genus to which those trees belonged, no hendecasyllabic Latin word ever found appropriate to describe them. It was also said that Castillon coined the golden fruit that this grove produced into brand new louis d'or. It was known for certain that he had a large sum of money hidden in his house, and the ex-convicts of the colony cast many a longing glance at this treasure, until one morning Pierre, le Chourineur, one of the most accomplished gueux of Paris, was found dead under one of the trees, with a broken neck, which he had got in attempting to climb into

Castillon's eyrie. After this, the burglars feared this grove more than the Hotel de Ville, and would make a long detour when on one of their cracking expeditions, to escape its evil eye.

Of course, with all this halo of romance around him, Castillon got a monopoly of the supernatural business of New Orleans. A certain essence of his, for one's enemies, which he distilled from the leaves of his trees was fully as popular and effective as aqua tofana.

Castillon was several times suspected and accused of poisoning, but nothing could ever be proved against him. *As for his fetiches and pretended magic, the Government was too sensible to interfere; they were part of the religious belief of the negroes, and did much to keep quiet a very dangerous class of the population.* [Italics added by author.]

What was the contract between Castillon and the trees, by which he gained this supernatural power, was ever the popular conundrum. It was supposed that he had agreed to sacrifice a certain number of lives before the nymphs could be freed from these trees. However that be, old Castillon certainly paid up his installments of human lives and human souls, rapidly enough.

On a March morning of 1778, occurred the greatest storm in the history of America. The city of Havana was almost totally destroyed, and it is calculated that two-thirds of the population of Martinique and Dominica were killed. The hurricane swept with unexampled fury around New Orleans and all along the bank of the river.

The next morning a part of soldiers who were sent out to rescue the overflowed farmers on the lake, passing by Castillon's house, discovered a man swinging by his neck from a branch of a tree. A close investigation showed it was Castillon himself fearfully mangled and torn, and hung like Absalom. Whether he died from suicide, or through an accident, or whether he was himself the victim of those spirit trees, they alone can tell. The picket on the city walls said that through the thunder and lightning of the storm he could distinctly hear the cracking and sobbing of the branches of those trees mingled with the curses and shrieks of old Castillon. Certain is it, that, ever after the trees were dumb and mute, and seemed to have lost all power of speech, and there are some who say that Castillon's life was the last demanded to set these spirits free.

Though silent, the subsequent history of this grove is interesting.

In 1776, for purposes of defense, a line was ordered by Lope Herrery, Military Intendante, to be drawn around the city and all the intervening trees cut down. Among the victims was Castillon's grove. Some recently arrived Galicians were put at work to fell this grove, but were compelled to desert from their work by a fever or epidemic that broke out amongst them. The fever spread through the city, where it continued with great mortality for several months. This disease, then styled vaguely "the plague," was unknown to Louisiana doctors, and only subsequently identified as yellow fever. It was traced clearly to the Galicians and ascribed to the fact of their working in the sun and in the swampy lands back of town before they were acclimated; but the popular opinion always remained that the trees had more to do with it than the swamps. . . .

. . . . Such is the plain, unadorned story as told and believed half a century ago. During the present century the trees have grown quiet and taciturn. True it is that on some stormy night when the wind is blowing, neighbors pretend to hear these trees sighing and groaning, to see them waiving their brisrean [sic] arms as if in prayer.

But whether sacred or not in fact, this grove is sacred in the eye of the law. By the will of Castillon, it is left with the condition that "if said legatee shall injure, deface or destroy a certain grove of trees, etc. the above mentioned and devised property shall pass to the corporation of the Church of St. Marie, for a daily mass to be sung for the soul of said Jean Marie de Castillon."

The property has not reverted, the trees still grow there, although the land is built up; through the roofs, the galleries, the kitchens of various houses, these trees still spring. The mightiest tree of all, that tradition assigns as Castillon's favorite mistress, stands immediately in the middle of a parlor.

They are all that remain of Castillon, for notwithstanding his alleged wealth nothing was found in his eyrie but a dozen or so bags of dry leaves, all that remained of his ducats and louis d'or.

—=—

It may be obvious that, despite its title, this story is really a Gothic romance. The lead characters are white, and voudou is not so much African as European sorcery, fully cloaked by Christian mythological symbolism. Voudou is contextualized within European versions of the occult, which allows the reader to at least take comfort in understanding how old Castillon went astray—he ate the apple, got greedy, ran away from his community into the savage wilds and took up with supernatural or foreign beings. He violated the norms and ended up paying with his life. (In a curious way, this departure from community/flirtation with evil/punishment and shunning is also part of the zombification ritual observed by Wade Davis in *The Serpent and the Rainbow*.) The idea, in most of the news accounts, that voudou cannot be in any way subsumed into European Christian culture and is beneath even contempt, had apparently not fully developed in 1723 (assuming that is an approximately credible date for the fable's origination). The Castillon myth does, however, advance the core of the anti-voudou message: that exposure to voudou came through the kind of Edenic temptation that resulted in the fall from grace from God; therefore voudou is not of God, and if it is not of God, it is of Satan.

The more "reportorial" news accounts of the period are also more directly related to voudou. A June 26, 1871 *Daily Pica-*

*yune* story got right to the point: "Voudou Nonsense," exclaimed the headline. "A Plain Unvarnished Account of the Lake Shore Revels—Full Particulars of the Hell Broth and the Orgies—A Played-out Hoax." If the Castillon fable presents voudou as fitting material for a tall tale, this piece (actually published a few years earlier) shows that as grist for the news mill and cheap thrills, voudou would bear the brunt of journalistic cynicism if it failed to live up to the bad image created for it.

In the piece, a reporter joins a crowd of white Orleanians in search of St. John's Eve voudou activities. The party journeys "through dismal, mouldy, darkened streets to the Pontchartrain Depot," a trip which "further awakened our imagination and brought out our ghost-seeing faculties." From the depot, the ghost-seeing reporter got over to Milneburg, on the north side of the lake [today a kind of upscale suburb], where he [or she, author unsigned] claimed to find about "four thousand or more fellow voudou hunters." But the "voudous are not to be found," he reports, and must have "taken to the swamp through fear of the police, who are out in force." The curious are about to leave, when:

> Suddenly there is a shout of "voudous" and the entire crowd, over a thousand strong, dashes down a side street (to) surround the house where the voudous are said to be. A low, murmuring sound, as if played on a dissipated and worn-out jew's harp rouses peoples' expectations to a point of frenzy. . . . Merchants of the greatest respectability cling to the balconies, lawyers crowd up half-suffocated to get a view of this theological dance. By dint of energy and perseverance, we reach the front rank. What do we behold? A stout greasy, fat, old negro woman, a smaller ditto, and a close-shaved boy of about twelve are dancing slamjig to

the above mentioned sickly jew's harp. It is hot, truly, and monotonous.

Presently, says the reporter, the crowd (now revised to be "2,500") breaks up unsatisfied. But a few hang around, and then hear that:

> miles down the coast on Hog Bayou, hundreds of them (voudous) are now in the very midst of their dance, have cast aside all their clothing and morality, and are so inflamed, so aroused by the dance that they gnash their teeth, foam at the mouth and tear and rend each other with their teeth.

But when the crowd gets to the second location, it's another blank. The mood turns surly. Liquor has already been flowing through the evening and now, long past midnight, everyone gets smashed and tries to get the train back to New Orleans. Many get stuck for the night among the mosquitos and humidity. "A voudou hoax," harrumphs the reporter:

> If it is one of the canons of the voudou church to propitiate their evil deity by crimes and wickedness, then truly is he propitiated tonight. . . .
>
> To sum up the matter, about 12,000 eminent, respectable and intelligent people were hoaxed to the lake to witness the drunken gambols of ruffians and women of the worst character . . . about a dozen carriages were smashed; a thousand persons got drunk, and about half that number were locked up in the jail, and finally, to relieve all this vice, crime and debauchery, there was not a funny incident or redeeming feature.

What is intriguing about the story is not the mass stupidity of the white people out looking for a summer night's lark and finding out they'd only conned themselves, but the size of the crowd (between 1,000 and 12,000, according to four different estimates, alas, in the same story) and the intensity of feeling. Just as the passage of certain kinds of morality laws is actually sociological evidence that the prohibited actions (drinking, dancing, fornicating, etc.) are popular enough to warrant ruling class reaction (the banning proves the activity), so the great frustration of the white crowd of voudou seekers at the absence of the perceived African cult orgy only shows how desperately they wanted to believe in its existence.

Not all the journalistic forays ended in cynicism and without promised result. St. John's Eve coverage in the *Picayune* of June 25, 1875 started off with a false alarm similar to that of the previous account. Curious onlookers traipsed to a bayou area along Lake Pontchartrain only to find nothing—but then to learn of the voudou ceremony actually being held in an even more swampy location. But this time the reporter and the onlookers arrived at a bayou house over the "black, sluggish waters" and found what was described as about twenty-five "colored men and women . . . engaged in some sort of dance." Some of the onlookers, on paying a small fee, were permitted to enter the house and watch:

> A large white sheet was laid in the middle of the floor, in the centre of which was a pyramid, some five feet in height, of some kind of candy. Around this, in four separate piles, were fruit and flowers, and at each corner of the sheet were four bottles containing perfumed water. Candles stuck in small glass candlesticks were placed at inter-

vals on the sheet. On the top of the pyramid mentioned was a small covered basket of palmetto, which was said to contain The Voudou.

At each corner of the sheet, and one of the sides were seated alternately a man and woman, while in a corner on a box was an immense "gombo" negro woman. . . . On each side of her were ten men, leaders of the ceremonies . . . the men and women seated around the sheet began a low, monotonous chant, clapping their hands and striking the floor alternately. This was kept up some half an hour, when three of the men and two of the women rose up and commenced to dance around the sheet. Suddenly, at a signal from the "boss woman," one of the men took up one of the bottles, and after sprinkling the four corners of the room and each one of the spectators, drank a portion of its contents. He was immediately seized with a sort of convulsion, laughed, screamed, foamed at the mouth, and leaped backwards and forwards on the floor like a demon. One of the women then took a candle and passed it over his body like a mesmerizer when he fell to the floor as if in a fit. He was lifted up, all shouting "la voudou, la voudou," and the spectators were informed that he was bewitched. The Queen then ordered him to go round and shake hands with everyone, which he did, rolling his eyes and shouting.

. . . the closed room was excessively warm and most of the spectators had reached the fainting point, when, with a piercing yell from the whole assembly, the Man Bewitched seized the small basket, and opening it, drew out a small garter snake which he passed around his neck and over his head, foaming at the mouth and leaping about—the others rising and dancing.

Another yell from the voudous louder than before, a grand shriek and at another signal the lights were put out, the snake's head was solemnly pulled off and thus ended the ceremony. The devil or fetish being supposed to have been in the snake, and being thus killed, he was got rid of and his worshipers were free.

It was daybreak, the sun was just rising, and cast its rays over the waters of the lake as the party broke up.

From some of the details in the piece—the use of candles, the notion of possession—it is likely that some sort of ceremony was in fact witnessed, although the pejorative phrases "eyes rolling," "like a demon," etc. indicate a spin to the interpretation, one which marks the reporter as largely ignorant of any content to the spectacle. The other pertinent aspect of this report is the admission that the ceremony was deliberately staged. What was shown was almost certainly a form of theater.

Many press accounts claimed contact with ceremonies—though, again, the similarity in the structure of the stories suggests that repetition of the established myth about secretive swamp orgies was as much a part of the reportage as was any kind of first-hand observation. "Outlandish Celebration of St. John's Eve," said the *Picayune* headline of June 23, 1896. "A Living Cat Eaten by the Voodoo King," the subheads continued, stacked atop each other. "Unparalled Scenes of Savagery in the Pontchartrain Swamps—Becoming Impassioned, the Fetich Worshipers Tear Off Their Clothes and Dance Naked."

In this story, a reporter seeks out a voudou celebration, encounters false leads and backwoods locations ("a secrecy which

has baffled even the most sagacious espionage of the police")
etc., until finally getting the tip that leads him to the "real" ceremony, and a chance to write what everyone is dying to read,
the myth validated in print. Here is a substantial portion of the
account:

> Inquiries were futile, and it seemed as if the search
> must result in failure, when the reporter met up
> with a well-known Creole physician, who proved
> a Golconda of information. . . .
>
> Shortly before 10 o'clock the physician and the
> reporter left the Esplanade cars at Bayou Bridge
> and procuring a skiff and a lantern proceeded well-
> armed and with padded boards down the placid
> waters of Bayou St. John toward the old Spanish
> Fort. About a half-mile below the Soldiers' Home
> a solitary fisherman's hut marks the spot where a
> narrow canal branches out abruptly from the side
> of the bayou and leads off toward the Lake through
> a gloomy and desolate swamp. . . .
>
> The night and the surroundings were well
> suited to the weirdest of dramas. High above the
> palmetto bushes a wan gibbous moon gleamed
> sullenly behind a veil of misty clouds, and reso-
> nantly through the thin forest of cypress trees came
> the sound of the Indian lake breaking among the
> rushes. A solemn and awful chorus of frogs punc-
> tuated by the occasional hoarse bellow of an alli-
> gator rose up from the marsh, and swarms of
> gigantic swamp mosquitoes buzzed incessantly
> . . . presently a skiff hurried by bearing an
> ancient negro crone, rowed by two stalwart
> mulattoes . . . at something before 11 o'clock forty
> negroes and mulattoes of both sexes and ages vary-

ing from twenty-five to the extreme of senility were gathered on a clearing beneath a gigantic cypress.

. . . A bedquilt was laid upon the ground, and upon this the crone, who appeared to be the Queen, took her seat. She was dresssed in a loose-fitting calico gown of gaudy pattern, with a red madras handkerchief arranged on her head. Her face was expressionless and her eyes gazed vacantly into the black shadows of the swamp.

. . . . The fire was heaped up ready for lighting, the packages were laid open, and then the party stood inactive as if waiting for something to happen. Suddenly a commotion was heard in the bushes, and presently the form of a huge negro, clad in a breechcloth strung with alligator teeth, with a necklace of bones round his neck and shells in his ears, burst upon the scene. He looked round him with fierce command, muttered some cabalistic words and then proceeded rapidly from one package to another, throwing them open. From one package he produced a tripod, which he placed over the fire, and to which he hung a cauldron. In this one of the other negroes poured a bucket of water from the canal, and then the King struck a match and lit the fire.

## HIDEOUS ORGIES

A circle of animal skulls and bones were then placed round the fire, and the King lifted a bottle to his mouth and took a long pull. The effect of the liquor seemed to be powerful and immediate, for in the light of the fire which was now blazing brightly the King reached for the soap box, and with one wrench of his muscular hands broke off the lid and produced a black cat, which for one moment he held clawing, scratching and mewing and then with a fierce twist broke its neck. Literally tearing the cat's head from its body, he sucked the blood from the mangled trunk and then threw both head and body quivering into the now boiling cauldron.

This seemed to be the signal for a species of go-as-you-please orgie, for the moment the body of the cat sunk to the bottom of the cauldron the entire party laid aside their reserve and began jumping this way and that, getting up steam for the grand dance round the fire. One got hold of a drum, another of the bell, and several others of what appeared to be the skeleton heads of oxen. Upon all of these the voodoos began beating at once, stopping every now and then to rush to one of the baskets and take long drafts from the bottles.

The old crone sat placidly in her place until some thoughtful member of the band passed her a bottle, when a number of good "swigs" seemed to put life into her and she presently leaped to her feet and joined the now thoroughly demoralized crew round the fire.

Moment by moment the enthusiasm of the voodoos increased. Here and there they danced with grotesque and obscene gestures, stooping and bending, dancing away from the fire, but always returning. . . .

The only intermission to the song and the dancing was when one or the other of the dancers would suddenly dart out of the circle to heap more wood upon the fire, and incidentally make an attack upon the intoxicants.

After probably a half-hour of the most indescribably grotesque dancing round the fire the voodoos had worked themselves up to such a frenzy that they began tearing off their clothes.

NAKED SAVAGES

One by one the garments were thrown away until finally, in the flickering light of the fire out there in the midst of the swamp, with the long Spanish moss dropping and swinging over their heads, nearly a half hundred impassioned black savages danced as naked as islanders to the beating of ox skulls and tom-toms, the weird crooning of hags, the sharp ejaculations of bucks and wenches, and the monotonous roar of a million swamp frogs.

At the height of the revel the king kicked out the fire, and in the light of the embers upset the cauldron upon the ground, and grasping the cat in his fingers, began thrusting the awful mess in his mouth, his followers, as well as they were able in the uncertain light, following his example. The voodoo dance was now nothing but the lewdest and most outrageous orgie, with license the spirit of the scene, and death by tumbling into the canal and getting drowned most imminent.

"Let us get out of this," said the physician . . . and the reporter readily assented.

Even in the twentieth century, the papers rarely changed their attitude, though the emphasis shifted away from the annual recitations of St. John's Eve debauchery in favor of voudou as the secret motive in blackside killings. "April Fool Day Slayer Blames Hoodoo for Deed," said an April 7, 1940 *Picayune* headline. "Friend Admits Mystery Killing. 'Hoodoo' Over Love Is Blamed," echoed another on the same date, both referring to a shooting involving a man said to have believed he had been "hoodooed" into marriage.

In 1915, a November 7 issue of the *New Orleans American* proclaimed, "The Voudous—Superstition Which is Passing." The subhead explained why that was a good thing: "Mystic Religious Rites Handed Down from Jungle Wilds—Many Ignorant Whites Took Part in the Horribly-Disgusting Orgies—Thousands, Two Decades Ago, Sought Advice of the Voudou King and Queen."

According to the article, "One seldom in these days hears of the voudous, unless perhaps he comes in contact with the lower element of the negro race, for ever (thanks to education) the better class of the colored population fight shy of those who make any pretext whatever of being connected with that religious band of fanatics." Even Marie Laveau, said the paper, is "a dangerous, wicked woman in the truest sense of the word." But those days were over, the paper concluded, because "through the vigilance of the police authorities, the voudous have practically been stamped out."

The passion for accuracy and religious pluralism did not remain peculiar to the Southern media. Northern papers and magazines knew sensationalism was good for sales as much as anyone else, and any news from the South which proved that part of the country was weird and primitive was especially welcome (an attitude that doesn't seem to have changed much over the years). An April 1886 issue of *Century Magazine* devoted many pages to creole culture, including a passage about voudou, which summarized the religion in this manner:

That worship was as dark and horrid as bestial-
ized savagery could make the adoration of ser-
pents. So revolting was it, and so morally hideous,
that even in the West Indian French possessions a
hundred years ago, with the slave-trade in full blast
and the West Indian planter and slave what they
were, the orgies of the Voodoos were prohibited.

This of course completely inverted the history of the Code
Noir and forced baptism of slaves, for a start. The remainder of
the piece was approximately as accurate. Its lone example of a
voudou ceremony described familiar scenery: a midnight orgy
in a darkened swamp along Lake Pontchartrain.

*Harper's Weekly* got on the voudou beat June 25, 1887 with
a long piece signed by Charles Dudley Warner. Much of the
article was taken up with a first-person account with an
unusual twist that may actually have been based on true observation—the scene was in a house in New Orleans. Warner's
knowledge of voudou was not much advanced on those of the
New Orleans newspaper reporters, however, though it may have
seemed so to an audience utterly unfamiliar with the religion of
the slaves it so recently had seemed so earnest to "free." According to Warner:

> . . . the barbaric rites of Voudooism originated
> with the Congo and Guinea negroes, were brought
> to San Domingo, and thence to Louisiana. In Hayti
> the sect is in full vigor, and its midnight orgies
> have reverted more and more to the barbaric origi-
> nal in the last twenty-five years. The wild dance
> and incantations are accompanied by sacrifice of
> animals and occasionally of infants, and with can-
> nibalism, and scenes of most indecent license. In
> its origin it is serpent worship. . . .

Some years ago Congo Square was the scene of the weird midnight rites of this sect, as unrestrained and barbarous as ever took place in the Congo country. All these semi-public performances have been suppressed, and all private assemblies for this worship are illegal, and broken up by the police when they are discovered.

Warner was able, he said, to find someone who knew of a voudou ceremony anyway, and he thus attended. The ceremony was sans sacrifice, though it did have dancing, invocation of the Apostles Creed, and singing and use of fruit-laden altars—all of which would have fit at a voudou ceremony, depending on what kind of ceremony it was. Warner could not conceal his consternation, however, at the discovery of a twenty-year-old female seated next to him:

> [Her] complexion and features gave evidence that she was white. Still, finding her in that company, and there as a participant in the Voudoo rites, I concluded that I must be mistaken, and that she must have colored blood in her veins. Assuming the privilege of an inquirer, I asked her questions about the coming performance, and in doing so carried the impression that she was kin to the colored race. But I was soon convinced, from her manner and her replies, that she was pure white. She was a pretty, modest girl, very reticent, well-bred, polite, and civil. . . . She told me, in the course of the conversation, the name of the street where she lived (in the American part of town), the private school at which she had been educated (one of the best in the city), and that she and her parents were Episcopalians. Whatever her trouble

was, mental or physical, she was evidently infatu-
ated with the notion that this Voudoo doctor could
conjure it away, and said that she thought he had
already been of service to her. . . . In coming to
this place she had gone a step beyond the young
ladies of her class who make a novena at St. Roch.

The ceremony proceeded. From the account it sounded very
like the kind of services I observed at Spiritual Churches in New
Orleans in the 1980s. Warner was clearly uncomfortable:

Toward the close of the seance, when the spells
were all woven and the flames had subsided, the
tall, good-natured negress motioned to me that it
was my turn to advance into the circle and kneel.
I excused myself. But the young [white] girl was
unable to resist longer. She went forward and
knelt, with a candle in her hand. The conjurer
was either touched by her youth and race, or he
had spent his force. He gently lifted her by one
hand, and gave her one turn around, and she came
back to her seat.

. . . . In the breakup I had no opportunity to
speak further to the interesting young white neo-
phyte; but as I saw her resuming her hat and cloak
in the adjoining room there was a strange excitement in her face, and in her eyes a light of triumph and faith. We came out by the back way,
and through an alley made our escape into the
sunny street and the air of the nineteenth century.

Interspersed over the years were stories not about ceremonies or crimes but the other thing that fascinated people about

voudou—its magical content. "Voudouism—Charms of Wonderful Efficacy Compounded of Snakes, Toads, Frogs, Cats Ears and Lizard Eyes," exclaimed the *Daily States* of August 26, 1881. The *States* also ran a piece October 15, 1899 under the headlines: "Sambo and Evil Spirits, Charms, Dreams and Birds of Ill-Omen—Satan's Winged Friends—The Rabbit's Foot a White Man's Charm—Coon's Eyes Rather in Favor—Birds That Are Feared, Hatched or Destroyed." The article recounts a number of alleged charms and spells, but first puts everything in context:

> Of superstitions about human beings the most notable is the belief in the voodoo, which is a charm cast upon a person or animal, and the voodoo doctor, who is the person able to cast the charm. Some voodoo charms are cast by incantations and some by the evil eye, some by merely wishing harm to the objects intended to be injured. It is noteworthy that no voodoo, or voodoo doctor, is credited with power to do good. The working of the charm is always inimical. The voodoo man can do harm to an enemy, but no benefit to his employer, save such indirect benefit as may accrue from the enemy's hurt. In all the wide range of negro superstition there is nothing which will be productive of beneficient results, save only a few love charms and dreams which tell the dreamer how he may find money. Otherwise it is all gloomy and hurtful.

This level of reporting is unequivocal in its contempt and hostility towards voudou, but it was not hate that really undercut the religion as a valid theology. Many religions have existed amid mere hate. The fate of voudou in the South, and then the rest of the country, however, was to be reduced to a sham, an outright con game that no person of intelligence or character, black or white, would truck with except out of a Kiplingesque bemusement. And then, of course, to draw back from, with— times being what they were—unflinching Victorian judgement. Even critics of the Jazz Age in the early twentieth century, as the Catholic writer Sir Richard R. Terry in *Voodooism in Music*, a 1934 polemic published under Vatican authority, were able to draw on this well of opprobrium:

> My personal object[ion] to jazz is not that of the newspaper correspondent. It is of a more serious nature. I see its danger as an instrument in the service of the strange and subversive cults that are furtively feeling their way into the Europe of today. If I single out Voodoo it is because I lived for some years amongst Negroes; not the sophisticated Negro of the United States, but the more primitive type of the West Indies. . . . Music of a certain type (and jazz is now approximating to that type) is such an important adjunct to certain degenerate cults (Voodooism is only one of them) . . . that it seems something of a duty to make a note of the direction in which the White races are drifting—all unconsciously. [pp.16–17]

The *Sunday States* of October 7, 1900, though, perhaps best rounds out yellow journalism's encounter with black spirituality. "Voudouing in the City—Vicious Practice Has Not Yet Died Out," warned the headline, this time augmented by a pencil drawing of two coffins, one opened to reveal a skeleton. The subheads continued: "Many Cases in Court—Queer Articles Used in Negro Witchery—Recent Case in Point—Coffin and Accessories Found on a Step." The piece went on to summarize as well as any other single document, the attitudes of the day:

> A gruesome practice, most prevalent in and almost entirely confined to the Crescent City and towns of Louisiana where the traditions of old time slavery among the negroes still prevail, is the art of "hoo-dooing," or more properly speaking, "voudouing," since the first is a corruption of the second expression.
>
> . . . . It is an historical fact that the natives of the dark continent are wont to practice such weird incantations to dispel evil spirits (much as did the aborigines of America, the North American Indians), and to bring ill fortune to their enemies, or to bring upon them pestilence, famine and misfortune in arms—even extermination.
>
> During slavery times the slave owners of the South experienced incalculable difficulty with their charges through the fear engendered by the "vou-dou" artists' subtle, and to the ignorant minds of the blacks, terrifying practices. The legends of the "vou-dou" have been passed down from generation to generation of the negro in this country, and naturally enough have found an easy lodging place in the minds of many of the more ignorant whites. It is by no means uncommon to hear of the arrest of white persons who are charged by others with attempting to "hoo-doo" them, though fortunately for the latter race, the practice is confined entirely to the grossly ignorant classes.
>
> . . . . All that is necessary to scare a negro half out of his wits is for another to mysteriously threaten to have him or her "hoo-dooed," then to

equally as mysteriously, during the dead of the night, place on his or her door steps a little red flannel sack containing a peach kernel, a piece of bone, a few goods feathers, a lizard's tail, the bill of a chicken, and a pinch of sulphur, or other similar articles, then sprinkle any old kind of dust about the sack, on the door step of the person to be "hoo-dooed." That nigger, when he or she wakes up in the morning and finds the "hoo-doo" has been at work on him or her, will take sick in nine cases out of ten, and remain under the doctor's care for weeks. . . .

There is no law prohibiting the practice of "vou-douism" in this state or city, but the police when complained to of persons practicing the dark art, "kungerin' de spurits," as the negroes term it, and when they are reasonably certain of the guilt of the person accused or suspected of the "hoo-dooing," generally

ARREST THE PRACTIONER OF WITCH-CRAFT and incarcerate him or her on the charge of malicious mischief and disturbing the peace. Recorders have frequently had to deal with this and . . . to pass upon the cases of alleged "hoo-dooing."

. . . . Lovers "hoo-doo" their rivals and the dusky damsels who may have jilted them; "hoo-doo" their creditors and those of their relatives who may have quarreled with them; "hoo-doo" their landlords, their wives and their children, and "hoo-doo" their sweethearts to make them return their love!

. . . . To fully appreciate the astonishing extent of the belief of the negroes in the efficacy of the black art, it is necessary to sit through a trial of an alleged "hoo-doo" in one of the recorder's courts. The witnesses will tell in most positive and graphic manner of the exact nature of the "hoo-dooing," just what the "hoo-doo" did and just what ingredients were used in the invokation [sic] of the evil spirits. It is easy to realize how implicitly they believe in the nonsense.

Especially noteworthy about the various popular press accounts of voudou is that although in some cases some portions are true—there was dancing, and singing, and sacrifice (though not human), and in some black communities of the South hexing is common, even today—all of these activities were seen by terrified, ignorant, and contemptuous white observers who didn't know what they were seeing. There was no context. It was as if the history of Christianity had been written for Roman dailies based on observing services in which the "blood of the Lamb" was offered even to little children. As if everything we know of Judaism came from bemused reporters of Islam, or vice versa.

What most of us, and our ancestors, know of voudou, is but the culmination of the white attack on African culture, a no-quarter, interwoven campaign of laws and ideology in which the oppressor interdicted the accepted version of the ancestral belief, perverted it, tokenized it, and drove it into obscurity and illegitimacy. A phony aura of evil was allowed to survive as nothing more than proof of the foolishness and depravity of the very people from whom the real thing had been hijacked.

---

[1] Zoe Posey material and other documents from that era are held in the Manuscripts Section, Howard-Tilton Memorial Library, Tulane University, New Orleans.

# APPENDIX II
## THE REVOLUTION DENIED

FROM ALMOST THE inception of the slave trade, kings, constitutions and legislatures codified the incubating negative ideologies about Africans into edicts and ordinances, creating a legal and rationalist framework. As early as 1493, only a year after Columbus made landfall in the West Indies, Pope Alexander II ordered Spanish explorers to convert pagans (Indians and, later, slaves) in the New World territories. In 1685, as the French moved into the Caribbean plunder zone, Louis XVI issued the infamous Code Noir (Black Code) requiring, among other things, Catholic baptism for all slaves (as well as expulsion of Jews). One of the most important applications of the Code Noir, however, was its adaptation by Louisiana's territorial governors, who implemented their own Code Noir in 1724, which yielded to the Black Code of the Louisiana Territories of 1806, sustained until the Civil War. The other Southern colonies (and then states) enacted Black Codes of their own to regulate ownership, maintenance and punishment of slaves, free blacks, creoles and mulattoes.

One of the most consistent targets of the Codes was the practice of religion, especially anything non-Christian, i.e., African, i.e., voudou. Each state, through the Codes, created for Africans a legalistic anti-matter of First Amendment rights which restricted or outlawed most kinds of public gatherings or public expression, especially, singing, dancing and drumming by slaves and/or free blacks. So severe were the statutes that even black worship of Christianity was typically restricted to the presence of a white overseer if not prohibited altogether as in a Georgia statute of 1792 (Charles Goodell, *The American Slave Code*, 1853, p. 327).

In South Carolina, an 1800 law prohibited slaves or free blacks to "meet and assemble for the purpose of mental instruction of religious worship, either before the rising of the sun or after the going down of the same" (George Eaton Simpson, *Black Religion in the New World*, 1978, p. 220).

An 1829 Georgia law forbade any black, free or slave, to teach another to read or write, the punishment being a fine and/or whipping. Whites who did the same faced a fine and jail term. It is telling that in 1747, just after slavery was introduced to the Georgia colony, a law was passed recommending religious instruction for slaves—yet before the century was over at least two sets of laws reversed that position (Blake Touchstone, "The Large Planter and the Religious Instruction of Slaves," unpublished M.A. Thesis, Tulane, 1970).

In Mississippi, black preachers needed permission from their owners to preach to other blacks, and in Alabama, five whites had to be present when a black preached; even white preachers had to be licensed to speak to black congregations (John Hope Franklin, *From Slavery to Freedom*, 1947, pp. 199–200).

New Orleans was a great port city, with the influences of three European powers, but it was not immune to racial fears any more than Savannah or Montgomery or Atlanta. City law prescribed punishment of up to a year in prison for whites who taught blacks to read or write, who were "author, printer or publisher of any written paper or papers" and who used "language with the intent to disturb the peace or security . . . in relation to the slaves of the people of this State" (Ordinances of 1834, p. 541, Louisiana Supreme Court Library collection).

An 1817 ordinance (like that of Mississippi) restricted the hours of worship by slaves to "between daybreak and sunset" and forbade slaves to gather in public "except when attending divine worship, within the churches or temples," and then only during daylight. Punishment was ten to thirty lashes. Article Six of that same ordinance prohibited gatherings for "dancing or other merriment" except on Sundays and then only in "such open or public places as may be appointed by the mayor."

That was the year Congo Square was designated for public dancing. The likelihood is not that the city fathers had suddenly decided to allow blacks to openly perform traditional worship ceremonies; rather it was that it would be easier to monitor such ceremonies—long gone underground—by putting them in a designated fishbowl. Of course, even at those ceremonies there was the possibility, to be punished by twenty lashes, of breaking Article Nine of the 1817 muncipal code which outlawed "whooping or hallooing anywhere in the city or the suburbs, or making any clamorous noise, or singing aloud any indecent song" (from Ordinances of 1817, p. 218, Louisiana Supreme Court Library collection).

In 1829, the city, responding to the successful slave revolt in Haiti as well as the unsuccessful ones that were subsequently ignited on continental shores, followed the lead of the state legislature by banning the importation of slaves "who have been accused of any conspiracy or insurrection" in any territory of the U.S. In 1830, ordinances prohibited the entry of any free persons of color (presumably from Haiti), and the same year, the fear of slave revolt was so strong that laws were passed to punish white agitators, too, who were widely suspected of being Jacobin radicals. Even Yankees had the willies: George Washington and Thomas Jefferson both had propounded schemes to gradually get rid of slaves by shipping them back to Africa, or to Haiti. In 1835, New Orleans suspended the slave trade altogether, something the U.S. Congress had ordered in 1807, effective in 1808.

Restrictions didn't even stop with the Civil War. A city ordinance of 1882—well into Reconstruction—prohibited the use of parks for "political meetings, religious gatherings" (Charter of 1882, p. 400) and further outlawed the staging of "dramatic" works without a permit and "disorderly conduct . . . at any public spectacle." This could be interpreted to block public voudou ceremonies, or most other gatherings of blacks, just as readily as had the more overtly stated Black Code laws.

It's small wonder the *New Orleans Bee* was editorializing as late as 1861 that "the black man in his own home is a barbarian and a beast. . . . When emancipated and removed from the crushing competition of a superior race he . . . descends step by step down to the original depths of his ignorant and savage instincts, and at length is debased to nearly the state which he is found in the wilds and jungles of Africa . . . the normal condition of the negro is servitude" (in Alfred N. Hunt, *Haiti's Influence on Antebellum America*, 1988, p. 142).

What one does wonder about that kind of sentiment, and the web of laws and social policies in which it became possible to think such things, is what all the fuss was about. If Africans were such savages, so prone to requiring tutelage, why was it necessary to enact four centuries of homicidal legalities to prevent them from saying whatever silly little things they had on their ape-like minds or praying to whatever far-fetched spirits they had brought with them from their homelands? Or was it that the Africans were quite human indeed? And that one of the things humans do in oppressive circumstances is make trouble. They revolt.

Even today, the climate of terror in which the ruling society of the South did its business is stupefyingly untold: Gabriel

Prosser, Denmark Vesey, Nat Turner, St. John the Baptist Parish, Louisiana—the bloody rebellions percolated with increasing frequency into the last days of the antebellum period. Every isolated plantation, every rural community, and even some of the big cities were sitting ducks.

We can only wonder what might have happened to the shape of America had the Asian and South American liberation struggles of the twentieth century come earlier, giving expertise as well as solidarity to the vast untapped slave guerilla armies of the American South? Haiti had been unnerving enough. Imagine: A massive African revolt instead of the Civil War. Why else did the South plunge into strategic folly? To protect cotton? To protect slavery? No. To stop the demographic nightmare. Further deterioration of apartheid would have made white feudal hegemony untenable. Had African slaves joined ranks with white workers, many of them the "white trash" descendants of the once thriving European indentured servant (i.e., slave) trade, Dixie might have become the paradigmatic revolutionary model for race/class alliance in the Western Hemisphere, if not the world.

A glance at population figures shows a major reason that the fear of revolt—and thus the outlawing of any means by which the slaves might learn to organize or communicate dissent—was so prevalent. On the eve of the Civil War, the 1860 census listed 3.9 million slaves in the South and 8.1 million whites, making slaves about thirty-three percent of the population. But in the major states, the proportion of blacks was significantly higher: fifty-five to fifty-seven percent in South Carolina and Mississippi; forty-seven percent in Louisiana; forty-five percent in Alabama; forty-four percent in Georgia; thirty-one percent in Virginia (Eugene D. Genovese, *From Rebellion to Revolution: Afro-American Slave Revolts in the Making of the Modern World*, 1979, and almanacs).

In New Orleans, a key port city, the figures were even more African-weighted. In 1791, the population of 4,446 reflected 1,900 whites, 1,800 slaves, and 750 free blacks (Hunt, p. 46, and almanacs). In antebellum decades this almost startling ratio lessened, though the total numbers of Africans, slave or free, grew much higher and would continue to climb. In 1860 the black population was about 25,000, among about 144,000 whites. By 1880, about 57,000 blacks lived in the city, among 158,000 whites (John Blassingame, *Black New Orleans 1860–1880,* 1973).

High as these numbers climbed, they were still dwarfed by the black majorities of eighty percent or more in St. Domingue (Haiti), Jamaica and other Caribbean islands, leading Genovese to conclude the numbers—taken with other factors—weren't high enough in the American South to sustain a widespread rebellion. "[I]n general, their position steadily deteriorated over time until revolt became virtually suicidal" (*From Rebellion to Revolution*, p. 49).

While I concur and even applaud most of Genovese's analysis of the revolutionary climate of American slavedom, I propose considering the population factor in a different way. Blacks may not have constituted a majority, but their numbers were certainly high enough to launch, support and even win a protracted guerilla war, as reference to the successful wars of liberation of the twentieth century surely attests. Neither Fidel nor Mao, for example, controlled a majority of their country's populations at the outset of resistance.

Further, the high black populations were so strictly segregated and alienated from the dominant white culture that a revolutionary movement would have had little trouble delineating the shape and nature of the struggle to its own people. The sharpness of that separation—as simple as black and white—would have turned the nation-within-a-nation predicament of the slaves to psychological advantage, not liability. Very much as in Haiti, blackness could have been used as a weapon of terror to destabilize and defeat the white population in the same way that blackness as a sign of inferiority had been used by whites to justify slavery and control the black population. Signs and signifiers, fully reversed, might have added that unquantifiable element that has so often—the American Revolution would be a good example—undone predictable outcomes and turned worlds upside down.

Of course, population wasn't the only factor, as Genovese stresses. The slaves in the U.S. were poorly armed, if at all. They were also relatively spread out, and tended to be deployed in units of a couple dozen or less, vastly different than the megasystems of the more labor-intensive Caribbean plantations, where slaves were sent into the sugar fields 100 or more at a time, where, by the way, they didn't last as long as they did in the South. As George Eaton Simpson observes, although only about five percent of the Atlantic slave trade's human cargo wound up in the United States, by 1950 the U.S. was home to one-third of Africans in the Americas; the Caribbean islands, which had imported forty percent of the slaves, contained only twenty percent of the New World's Africans. "In the highly capitalistic slavery of the U.S.," Simpson notes with a kind of numbing understatement, "slave owners generally used force optimally, not maximally" (Simpson, p. 282).

We could argue at length, and many historians have, over why more rebellions might have occurred and why this or that factor was favorable or unfavorable at a particular historical moment. I would like to foreground what is usually in the background: the role of voudou. An analogous clue is found in the effect of decentralized methods of production, an important effect of which, the isolation of slave units, was the material counterpart to an equally if not more crucial quarantine—that of communication and leadership. How the Southern economy produced cotton and other crops was probably an accident of agricultural expertise, climate and transportation. How it dealt with the ongoing possibility of revolt was quite deliberate.

Every movement needs two basic conditions: circumstances and leaders. These leaders electrify the atmosphere of circumstances and fork the lightning of change. The Bolshevik theorist George V. Plekhanov called this the role of the individual in history; a voudou priest would call it the agreement to heed the conditions and plans of Ifa. Spike Lee called it doing the right thing. In Russia, Lenin became the personification of the Circumstances. In China, it was Mao; in Poland, Lech Walensa; in Iran, the Ayatollah; in Germany, Hitler; in Egypt, Moses, and so on. Who claimed the will of the slaves in the American South? Nat Turner, Gabriel Prosser, Denmark Vesey? Too late, as Genovese says, too little, too far out-gunned.

As any ruling order knows, the first thing you do in stifling trouble is to stifle those who would lead the trouble. Those who would lead the trouble among African slaves were the same cultural figures who had led the societies from which the slaves had come. The priests. The war against revolt was the war against voudou, and the war against voudou meant the extermination of the African priesthood. That the priests continued in another form may only have spelled the difference between victors and martyrs.

Like any religion, i.e. the agreed cultural repository of the souls of a people, voudou was the most dangerous communicative ideology imported with the slaves. In Dahomey, Benin and other kingdoms, voudou was not only a religion, it was a centuries-old organizing principle of society. Royalty drew its authority from the orisha (or whatever the spirits were known as) and from the ancestors, and it was no mortal's place to challenge that. Priests as well as kings (who were also priests) were invested with politico-organizational authority; a theocracy as "natural" as democracy would later be argued to be by bourgeoisie Europeans. In the diaspora, priests often became the only leadership element with links to the cultural traditions; they were often implicated in shipboard rebellion, and continued their roles, under extreme duress, on the plantations.

Gayraud S. Wilmore (*Black Religion and Black Radicalism*, 1972), relying on the pioneering work of the anthropologist Melville J. Herskovits, who through studies in Dahomey and Haiti established the link of voudou from Africa to the New World, described a typical priest-leader scenario in the slave trade:

> One known source of such leaders was Dahomey, where dynastic quarrels produced persons who were then sold to white traders as slaves. Herskovits points out that the most intransigent among the people conquered by the Dahomeans were the local priests of the river cults. While compliant priests were retained in order not to incur the wrath of their gods, those who resisted, such as the priests of the river gods, were sold to the slavers and probably ended up in the New World.
>
> Herskovits comments on the implication of this for the incipient development of resistance among the slaves: "What indeed could have more adequately sanctioned resistance to slavery than the presence of priests who, able to assure supernatural support to leaders and followers alike, helped them fight by giving the conviction that the powers of their ancestors were aiding them in their struggle for freedom? (p. 8)

In the Caribbean basin, notably Haiti, the conditions of rural isolation, large unit cultivation and extreme oppression noted by Genovese, Hunt, Simpson and others allowed the priest-leaders to retain considerable influence—in their traditional social form. In the United States, closer socio-economic supervision and widespread Protestant evangelism led to a transformation of the priest that would have far-reaching consequences.

Wilmore and Sterling Stuckey (*Slave Culture: Nationalist Theory and the Foundations of Black America*, 1987) were among many scholars of African-American theology who, especially since the 1960s, have noted the link first publicly observed by DuBois: the priest became a preacher. "If the African religious leader was to operate in the open," observes Stuckey, "the safest cloak to hide behind was that of Christianity. . . . [T]his helps explain the authority of the black preacher through slavery and later" (p. 38). According to Wilmore, "the point that needs to be stressed is that the early spiritual leaders among the slaves in the West Indian and American colonies were the representatives of the traditional African religions . . . the prophets and preachers who evolved out of the class of African medicine men among the slaves . . . called the people to a sense of pride, solidarity and the first stirrings of resentment against slavery" (Wilmore, p. 25).

The paradox this development posed for the United States would have effects lasting past slavery or the Civil War. Two factors came into strange union. As the priests of African culture gave way to the preachers of the "invisible church," slave Christianity, the tools of knowledge of the Christianity of the masters were delivered into the minds of the slave preachers. Great evangelical movements in the eighteenth and nineteenth centuries put tremendous pressure on white churches to extend the Gospel to the pagan slaves. According to *DeBow's Review* (January 1859, p. 118) the South under slavery Christianized five times more blacks than all the missionaries in the world, combined. Total black membership in southern Protestant churches alone climbed from 348,000 in 1847 to 465,000 in 1859, according to the pro-slavery journal, which said those figures represented only about a third of those blacks who regularly attended services. At the end of the nineteenth century, church membership climbed to 2.7 million among a total black population that had grown to 8.3 million (Stuckey, citing Albert J. Raboteau, p. 367). That increase, which was both absolute and proportional, either indicates an earlier resistance to Christianity under slavery or a gradual succumbing to cultural domination, depending on how you want to see it.

The conversions, however viewed from a marketing standpoint, created a schizophrenic spiritual debate. What about slaves once they had been Christianized? Jesus says all saved souls should be free. Did he mean slaves, too? The role of the churches split—in the North towards abolition; in the South towards rationalization of slavery within a Christian context. Ultimately this debate laid the basis for a further split, that of the Negro Church (now the Black Church) as a separate American theological movement, beginning with Richard Allen's breakaway African Methodist Episcopal Church in Philadelphia in 1816 and evolving into the rise of Black Theology in the 1960s. It also led to the permanent segregation of Christianity in America— about ninety percent of African-American Christians worship, by choice, in separatist congregations (Simpson, p. 313).

The more immediate effect was to create a major source of sedition. The slave preachers shared a similar agenda—how to get free. There was the solution offered by the new religion, a place in heaven after a life of tribulation on earth, or there was armed struggle. The patchwork of laws restricting slave worship grew, not coincidentally, alongside that dilemma. But the brunt of the legal restrictions were aimed at limiting education and communication; difficult goals when you are also trying to teach people about the Bible. Sooner or later someone has to learn to read it. The preachers were those people, and they read the same subtext of liberation that Desmond Tutu and Bishop Romero and the Jesuits in Central America today have read. They also read the liberation polemics, such as *Walker's Appeal*, coming from the North. Here and there, the slave preachers decided to do something about it. In virtually every major revolt in the antebellum South, a black preacher, or the folk equivalent, was the organizational cadre.

It is easy to see the progression that led Du Bois to observe in 1939, through what Stuckey termed "a leap of intuition based mainly on concrete experiences," (Stuckey, p. 255) that as "the slave preacher replaced to some extent the African medicine man . . . gradually, after a century or more, the Negro Church arose as the center and almost the only social expression of Negro life in America" (W. E. Burghardt Du Bois, *Black Folk Then and Now: An Essay in the History and Sociology of the Negro Race*, 1939, p. 198). Ultimately, this would affect American political life in a massive way, in which the critical role of the black preacher in, for example, the civil rights struggle, was as remarkable as the strange denial of the African religion which pre-figured it. By 1963, old line theorists of the "Negro Church" were insisting, as did E. Franklin Frazier (*The Negro Church in America*, 1963), "It is impossible to establish any continuity between African religious practices and the Negro Church in the United States. In America the destruction of the clan and kinship organization . . . plunged Negroes into an alien civilization in which whatever remained of their religious myths and cults had no meaning whatever. . . . It is our position that it was not what remained of African culture or African religious experience but the Christian religion that would provide the new basis of social cohesion" (p. 13).

The overwhelming evidence, however, points to African culture—not European Christianity—as the most potent link among African slaves, and the extension of Christianity a purposeful fifth column designed to co-opt revolutionary ideology. "The inescapable conclusion [is] that the nationalism of the slave community was essentially African nationalism, consisting of values that bound slaves together and sustained them under brutal conditions of oppression," Stuckey argued in *Slave Culture* (p. ix). The point I offer beyond that is that "nationalism" was far less a factor than "values that bound slaves," which were values outside relatively modern concepts of nationhood. The values were those of a common religiosity, and it wasn't Christianity.

Why else the tremendous suppression? If Christian worship itself was restricted among slaves out of fear of its potential for providing the leadership and communication networks for insurrection, consider the "disappearing," to use another New World term of political repression, of voudou. Allowing African worship to be practiced among slaves—in any form—came to have only one meaning for white colonial and antebellum government and society: Bloodshed and apocalypse, exactly what came to pass in Haiti. On many plantations, voudou was banned outright. In Louisiana, to use but one example, "planters felt they had to be especially alert for 'voudous,' who used fetishes and special ceremonies to conjure evil and instill fear in other slaves" (Touchstone, pp. 52, 54). Christian slaves were potential trouble enough; slaves beholden to gods that could in no way be reconciled to the theological gymnastics of their masters were the very stuff of a planter's nightmares.

Not surprisingly, government, church and economic elites became allies in an unrelenting war—martial law, statute law, exorcisms, intellectual dismissal—against any overt form of voudou practice in the United States. It would be entirely missing the point, as many historians have, to see this pogrom as the by-product of oppression. It was the chief aim. "Religion was probably the greatest acculturalizing force which worked upon the plantation slave," observed Tulane historian Blake Touchstone. "The social control supposedly instilled by religious instruction was meant to be a deterrent to slave revolts and abolitionist inroads. . . . [Plantation owners] only thinly disguised the fact that they favored religion for the reason Karl Marx said capitalism should—as an opiate which would help black bondsmen to endure a most difficult and degrading experience" (pp. 52, 54).

Genovese observed, regarding the failed Muslim and voudou (Yoruba and Hausa)-led revolt in Bahia in 1835, a point closer to my own:

> Where religious movements could take such non-Christian forms the slaves were being called to arms by a deep commitment that, by its very nature, divided master from slaves and black from white. It had to be immeasurably more difficult to win slaves to a purely revolutionary cause, the ideological and emotional content of which actually linked them to their masters on some levels while separating them on others.
>
> In the hands of a skillful anti-Christian leader the religious cry could be made to separate the slaves totally from the white community and thus transform every rising into a holy war against the infidel. When master and slave appealed to the same God, the same book, the same teachings, the task of the Nat Turners became much more difficult. . . . The difference came not with the abstract character of the Christian tradition but with the reduction of revolutionary potential inherent in the deeper separation of religion from class and especially ethnicity. (p. 32)

Every law aimed at baptism, at forbidding dancing and singing and drumming (integral parts of voudou worship), at gatherings, and, by extension to even Christianized worship, and

Baptist preachers, was an overt attack, covertly coded, against the belief system and culture of the African slaves, i.e., voudou, and the insurrectionary potential therein contained. The very fact that the attack did not even dignify its target with the legitimacy even the Nazis afforded Judaism—at least acknowledging its theological existence—only attests to the scorched earth intensity of the strategy.

But it should never again be possible not to see the destruction of voudou as the lynchpin of African subjugation in the United States. As for the compensating role of Christianity—those for whom an alien religion became a substitute were not saved, and, if sociological data is correct, are yet to be liberated on this earth. What they were was brainwashed. Purposely, systematically, profitably, and under duress equal to that of concentration camp or gulag. They were converted all right. Literally and figuratively, into disposable machines of the productive process. That's what happened to voudou in America.

# GLOSSARY OF VOUDOU TERMS

[Note: accent marks and precise renderings of African words and voudou terminology into standard English or Spanish varies considerably among adherents and scholars. These renditions appear to be among the most commonly used.]

Aláfia—Yoruba greeting, a wish of peace, or good health.

Alagba—chief of the Egungun Society, the society of the ancestral dead.

Ashé—also aché; sacred power from the spirits. In santeria usage: ocha.

Apataki—a parable used in explaining readings in Ifa divination.

Awo—the mysteries, another way of referring to the spirits.

Babalawo—father (baba) of the mysteries (awo); highest form of priest in the Ifa system of divination.

Babalorisha—father of the spirits (orisha); a male priest below the rank of babalawo. Babalocha in santeria.

Babalu Aye—or Babaluaye, or Babaluaiye; the orisha associated with illnesses and terrible diseases. Also known as Shokpona or Sonponna. Syncretized with St. Lazarus and planet Saturn.

Bimbé—or bembe; ceremonial party.

Botanica—strictly speaking, a store selling herbs, but in practice a store which sells a variety of religious supplies and implements, including those for voudou or santeria.

Cowries—small seashells at one time used as monetary units in West Africa. Sixteen are used in a form of Ifa divination. Known as the caracoles in santeria, where the sixteen-shell method is called the dilogun.

Creole—originally, New World born; subsequently has been widely used to mean of mixed African and European race.

Dambada-Wedo—or Damballa-Hwedo, Damballah-Wedo; serpent god entwining the earth. Mate of Aida-Wedo.

Ebo—sacrifice.

Egun—spirits of the dead ancestors.

Egungun—costumed figure representing the egun; also the name of the festival for the ancestors.

Elegba—also Esu, Eshu; powerful orisha considered the guardian of the crossroads of the Yoruba spirit world. Syncretized with St. Michael, St. Peter or St. Martin de Porres, and with the planet Mercury. Baron Samedi or Papa Legba in Haiti. Elegua or Elleggua in santeria.

Eleke—beaded necklace, in various colors, worn by voudou initiates.

Florida water—generic name for an herbal, slightly perfumed clear liquid toilet water commonly sold in botanicas. Used by Catholics as well as voudous.

Gelede—costumed figures representing spiritual witches summoned by the deity Yemonja to deliver village gossip in annual gelede ritual. (GEL-eh-DAY, hard G sound.)

Gris-gris—popular term used in Louisiana and New Orleans for a small bag, usually of red cloth, filled with herbs or secret ingredients and used as a talisman for luck.

Hoodoo—old Southern term for folk hexing and spell-casting; sometimes used interchangeably with "voodoo," from which it probably derives, or from "ju-ju", a term for African magic.

Houngan—Haitian male vodoun priest.

Ibeji—twin orisha, male and female, representing concept of duality. Syncretized with St. Damian.

Ikin—palm nuts used for casting in the most authoritative form of Ifa divination ritual.

Ifa—or Orunmila, the orisha controlling fate; also the name of the Yoruba system of divination. Orula in santeria. Syncretized with Christ and with the sun.

Ire—Yoruba term for a positive sign to a reading.

Itá—ceremonial life reading given during santeria voudou initiation.

Italero—a santeria priest specializing in giving the itá.

Imale—an alternate Yoruba term for the orisha.

Iyalorisha—a female priest; mother (iya) of the spirit (orisha).

Loa—Haitian vodoun term for spirit. Also lwa.

Lukumí—or lucumí; Cuban usage, the Yoruba people. From the Yoruba word olukumí, meaning "friend."

M'ambo—Haitian female vodoun priest.

Mojo—term used in Southern hoodoo in a variety of ways: as negative magic, as power, as an alternative to gris-gris. In strictest usage, the bone of a black cat used in hexing.

Ndóke—Kongolese term for a burlap bag holding dangerous spirits.

Ngánga—a burlap bag used to hold the spirits of the dead, not necessarily dangerous, in the palo mayombe religion. In American practice the ngánga is frequently an iron kettle, called a prenda in santeria.

Oba—Yoruba term for king.

Obatala—orisha of the intellect and organization. Syncretized with Jesus Christ and planet Jupiter.

Obeah—form of voudou practiced in Jamaica; less syncretized than Haitian or Cuban forms.

Obi—coconut husks, originally kola nuts, used in a form of Ifa divination.

Ocha—santeria term for power; roughly equivalent to the Yoruba ashé.

Ochosi—orisha of hunting and the forest. Along with Ogun, one of the Warriors (Los Guerreros in santeria) necessary early in the initiation sequence. Syncretized with St. Norbert and the constellation Sagittarius. Especially popular in Brazil.

Odu—Yoruba term for any of the specific configurations obtained in an Ifa casting of cowries or the opele.

Ogboni Society—society of landowners, one of the most powerful in a voudou community.

Ogun—orisha of war and metal. Syncretized with St. Anthony or St. George and the planet Mars. Ogum or Oggun in santeria.

Olorun—also Olodumare, Orishnla. The supreme deity in the voudou pantheon. Not syncretized but equated with the Christian concept of God. Cannot be prayed to directly, but reached through the other orisha. Olofi in santeria.

Omo—Yoruba term for a new initiate. Short for omolorisha, or child of the spirits.

Opele—instrument used by babalawos in Ifa divination. Consists of a chain with eight palm nut halves affixed to swivels. Ekuele in santeria.

Oriaté—type of priest unique to santeria divination ceremonies; similar to babalawo but not generally considered of equal ranking. Uses caracoles for readings.

Orisha—the Yoruba word for spirit; see also vo-du.

Osanyin—hermit-like orisha of medicines. Considered close friend of Ochosi.

Oshun—orisha of beauty, love and sexuality. Syncretized with the Virgin of Charity, the patron saint of Cuba. Also equated with the planet Venus and the Egyptian goddess Isis. Erzulie or Freda in Haiti. Ochún in santeria.

Osobo—negative sign in a reading.

Oya—orisha of the wind, of cemeteries, of the passage to death. Syncretized with Our Lady of Candelaria, St. Catherine, St. Theresa, and with planet Pluto. Ghede in Haiti. Rival of Oshun.

Oyekun—orisha said to represent the African race.

Padrino/a—spiritual godfather/godmother in santeria. Term also sometimes used in orisha voudou in the United States.

Palero/a—person who has been initiated into palo mayombe. Sometimes called mayombero/a.

Palo mayombe—Kongolese religion emphasizing use of dead spirits.

Prenda—santeria term for the iron kettle, also called a palo pot, used in palo mayombe for keeping spirits of the dead. Roughly equivalent to the ngánga.

Root doctor—Southern term for a practioner of hoodoo or other folk magic. Also known as hoodoo man or hoodoo woman; sometimes as prophet or divine healer.

Santeria—Afro-Cuban religion based on a syncretization of voudou and elements of Catholicism, especially the santos, or saints. Also santería.

Santero/a—one who practices santeria.

Serviteur—Haitian term for vodoun worshiper, one who serves the loa.

Shakeree—or shekeré, or acheré, an Afro-Cuban musical instrument consisting of a largish hollow gourd draped in a netting of beads or shells. Sounds similar to a maraca.

Shango—passionate, cigar-smoking orisha associated with thunder and fire; often considered the "macho" deity. Also Songo, Xangô. Syncretized with St. Barbara and the planet Uranus. Changó in santeria. Especially popular among Cubans.

Spiritual Church—Independent charismatic denomination, with elements of Protestant, Catholic and African voudou ritual, found mostly in Louisiana and the South. Not part of the mostly white Spiritualist churches, although there are some past connections.

Supera—porcelain soup tureen used to hold, or "feed," the essences of a specific voudou spirit. Sometimes called an awo, or awo pot, meaning a pot holding the mysteries. Govi in Haitian usage.

Vêve—Haitian spirit drawings.

Vo-du—the word for spirit in the Fon language of Dahomey, now the country of Benin. Roughly interchangeable with orisha.

Voudou—pantheistic belief system developed in West Africa and transported to the Americas during the diaspora of the slave trade. Here, used as the generic term for a number of similar African religions which mutated in the Americas, including santeria, candomble, macumbe, obeah, Shango Baptist, etc. Also voodoo, vaudoux, vodou, etc.

Yaguó—santeria term for new initiate. From the Yoruba term, iyawo, mother (iya) of the mysteries (awo). In this usage, iya also assumes the inverse meaning of child, or sometimes bride.

Yemonja—orisha of fertility and the seas. Syncretized with Our Lady of Regla, and with the moon. Olokun is the male version. Agwe in Haiti. Yemayá in santeria.

Zombi—or zombie, a soulless body, originally from Haitian usage.

# BIBLIOGRAPHY

Abimbola, 'Wande. *Ifa: An Exposition of Ifa Literary Corpus.* 1976, Oxford University Press, Nigeria.

Adefunmi, Oba Oseijeman. *Olorisha, A Guidebook into Yoruba Religion.* 1982, Great Benin Books, Oyotunji, South Carolina.

Albanese, Catherine L., ed. *America: Religions and the Religious.* 1981, Wadsworth Publishing, Belmont, California.

Allman, T. D. "After Baby Doc." *Vanity Fair* (January 1989): 74–81 + .

Amelsvoort, V. Van. "Thanatomania in an ASMAT Community: A Report of Successful 'Western' Treatment." *Tropical and Geographical Medicine* 28 (1976): 244–48.

Barthes, Roland. *Mythologies.* 1957, reprinted 1988, Noonday Press, New York.

Bascom, William L. "The Focus of Cuban Santeria." *Southwestern Journal of Anthropology* 6 (1961): 64–68.

_____ . "Sociological Role of the Yoruba Cult Group." *American Anthropological Association* 1:2 (January 1944): 5–75.

_____ . *Ifa Divination: Gods and Men in West Africa.* 1969, Indiana University Press, Bloomington.

_____ . *Sixteen Cowries: Yoruba Divination, Africa to the New World.* 1980, Indiana University Press, Bloomington.

Baudrillard, Jean. *Simulations.* 1983, Semiotext(e), Columbia University, New York.

Blassingame, John W. *Black New Orleans, 1860–1880.* 1973, University of Chicago, Chicago.

_____ . *The Slave Community: Plantation Life in the Ante-Bellum South.* 1972, Oxford University Press, New York.

Blier, Suzanne Preston. *African Vodun: Art, Psychology, and Power.* 1995, University of Chicago Press, Chicago.

Brandon, George. *Santeria from Africa to the New World: The Dead Sell Memories.* 1993, paperback 1997, Indiana University Press, Bloomington.

Brown, Karen McCarthy. *Mama Lola: A Vodou Priestess in Brooklyn.* 1991, University of California, Berkeley.

Cable, George Washington. *The Grandissimes.* 1889, Charles Scribner's Sons, New York.

Cabrera, Lydia. *El Monte.* 1954, second edition, 1971, Rema Press, Miami.

_____ . *Reglas de Congo: Palo Mayombe.* 1979, Peninsular Printing, Miami.

Caldwell, Erskine & Margaret Bourke-White. *You Have Seen Their Faces.* 1937, Modern Age Books, New York.

Campbell, Joseph. *The Hero With a Thousand Faces.* 1949, reprinted 1973, Princeton University Press, New Jersey.

_____ . *The Masks of God, Vol. 3: Occidental Mythology.* 1964, reprinted 1976, Penguin, New York.

_____ . *Myths to Live By.* 1972, reprinted 1984, Bantam, New York.

Cannon, Walter B. "'Voodoo' Death." *American Anthropologist* 44:2 (April–June, 1942): 169–81.

Chesi, Gert. *Voodoo: Africa's Secret Power.* 2nd ed., 1980, Perlinger Verlag, Austria.

Comfort, Alex. "Sorcery and Sudden Death." *Journal of the Royal Society of Medicine* 74 (May 1981): 332.

Cortes, Enrique. *Secretos del Oriaté de la Religion Yoruba.* 1980,. Vilaragut Articulos Religiosos Corp., New York.

Curtin, Phillip D. *The Atlantic Slave Trade, a Census.* 1969, paper,1972, University of Wisconsin, Madison.

Davidson, Basil. *The African Genius.* 1969, Little, Brown, New York.

_____ . *The African Slave Trade.* 1961, rev. 1980, Little, Brown, New York.

Davis, David Brion. *The Problem of Slavery in Western Culture.* 1966, Cornell University Press, Ithaca, New York.

Davis, Rod. "Behind the Voodoo Mask." *America* (Spring 1986): 28–36.

_____ . "Children of Yoruba." *Southern* (Feb. 1987): 34–41 + .

Davis, Wade. *The Serpent and the Rainbow.* 1985, Simon and Schuster, New York.

_____ . *Passage of Darkness: The Ethnobiology of the Haitian Zombie.* 1988, University of North Carolina Press, Chapel Hill.

Deren, Maya. *Divine Horsemen: The Living Gods of Haiti,* 1953, reprinted 1970, McPherson & Co., New York.

Desmangles, Leslie G. *The Faces of the Gods: Vodou and Roman Catholicism in Haiti.* 1992, University of North Carolina Press, Chapel Hill.

Dorson, Richard M. *American Negro Folktales.* 1956, reprinted 1967, Fawcett, New York.

Draper, David Elliott. "The Mardi Gras Indians: The Ethnomusicology of Black Associations in New Orleans." 1973, unpublished Ph.D. dissertation, Tulane University.

Du Bois, W. E. B. *Black Folk Then and Now: An Essay in the History and Sociology of the African Race.* 1939, Henry Holt Press, New York.

_____, ed. *The Negro Church.* 1903, Atlanta University Press.

Edwards, Gary and John Mason. *Onje Fun Orisa* (Food for the Gods), 2nd edition, 1987, Yoruba Theological Archministry, Brooklyn, New York.

Ellwood, Robert S. *Religious and Spiritual Groups in America.* 1973, Prentice-Hall, New York.

Epega, Afolabi A. *Ifa: The Ancient Wisdom.* 1987, Imole Oluwa Institute, Bronx, New York.

Franklin, John Hope. *From Slavery to Freedom.* 1947, Knopf, New York.

Frazier, E. Franklin and C. Eric Lincoln. *The Negro Church in America: The Black Church Since Frazier.* 1974, Schocken Books, New York.

Frucht, Richard, ed. *Black Society in the New World.* 1971, Random House, New York.

Gayarré, Charles. *History of Louisiana, Vol. I.* 1882.

Genovese, Eugene D. *From Rebellion to Revolution: Afro-American Slave Revolts in the Making of the Modern World.* 1979, Louisiana State University Press, Baton Rouge.

_____ . *Roll, Jordan, Roll: The World the Slaves Made.* 1972, Pantheon, New York.

Gilroy, Paul. *The Black Atlantic: Modernity and Double Consciousness,* 1993, Harvard University Press, Cambridge.

Gleason, Judith. *Orisha: The Gods of Yorubaland.* 1971, Atheneum, New York.

Golden, Kenneth M. "Voodoo in Africa and the United States." *American Journal of Psychiatry* 134:12 (December 1977): 1425.

Gonzalez-Wippler, Migene. *Santeria: The Religion: A Legacy of Faith, Rites and Magic.* 1989, Harmony Books, New York.

_____ . *The Santeria Experience.* 1982, Prentice-Hall, Englewood Cliffs, New Jersey.

_____ . *Rituals and Spells of Santeria.* 1984, Original Publications, New York.

Goodell, William. *The American Slave Code*. 1853, New York.

Gover, Robert. *Voodoo Contra*. 1985, Samuel Weiser, Inc., York Beach, Maine.

Griffith, Ezra E. H. and George E. Mahy. "Psychological Benefits of Spiritual Baptist 'Mourning.'" *American Journal of Psychiatry* 141:6 (June 1984): 769–73.

Hamilton, Charles. *The Black Preacher in America*. 1972, William Morrow.

Haskins, Jim. *Voodoo and Hoodoo*, 1978, Stein and Day, New York.

Herskovits, Melville, J. *Cultural Anthropology*, 1955, Knopf, New York.

_____ . *Cultural Relativism*. 1972, Random House, New York.

_____ . *Dahomey: An Ancient African Kingdom*. Vol. 2, 1938, J. J. Augustin, New York.

_____ . *Life in a Haitian Valley*. 1937, Knopf, New York, reprinted 1964, Octagon Books, New York.

_____ . *Myth of the Negro Past*. 1941, Harper, New York.

Hunt, Alfred N. *Haiti's Influence on Antebellum America: Slumbering Volcano in the Caribbean*. 1988, Louisiana State University Press, Baton Rouge.

Hurston, Zora Neale. *Dust Tracks on a Road: An Autobiography*. 2nd ed., 1984, Harper & Row, New York.

_____ . *Mules and Men*. 1935, J. B. Lippincott, Philadelphia.

_____ . *Tell My Horse*. 1938, reprinted 1981, Turtle Island, Berkeley, California.

Huxley, Francis. *The Invisibles: Voodoo Gods in Haiti*. 1969, McGraw-Hill, New York.

Jacobs, Claude F. and Andrew J. Kaslow. *The Spiritual Churches of New Orleans*. 1991, University of Tennessee Press, Knoxville.

Johnson, Paul. *A History of the American People*, 1997, HarperCollins, New York.

Jones, Charles Colcock. "Suggestions on the Religious Instruction of Negroes in the Southern States." *The Biblical Reporter and Princeton Review* 20 (January 1848): 1–30.

Kaslow, Andrew J. and Claude Jacobs. "Prophecy, Power and Healing: The Afro-American Spiritual Churches of New Orleans." 1981, unpublished manuscript, National Park Service, Jean Lafitte National Historical Park, New Orleans.

Lampe, H. U. *Famous Voodoo Rituals and Spells.* 1982, Marlar Religious and Occult Series, Minneapolis, Minnesota.

Lawson, E. Thomas, *Religions of Africa.* 1984, Harper and Row, New York.

Levine, Lawrence W. *Black Culture and Black Consciousness: Afro-American Folk Thought from Slavery to Freedom.* 1977, Oxford Press, New York.

Lincoln, C. Eric, and Lawrence H. Mamiya. *The Black Church in the African American Experience.* 1990, Duke University Press, Durham, North Carolina.

Lyell, Charles. *Second Visit to the United States of North America.* Vol. II, 1849, New York.

Manning, Marable. *African and Caribbean Politics: From Kwame Nkrumah to Maurice Bishop.* 1987, New Left Books, New York.

_____ . *W. E. B. Du Bois: Black Radical Democrat.* 1986, G. K. Hall & Co., Boston.

Martinez, Raymond J. *Marie Laveau, Voodoo Queen, and Folk Tales Along the Mississippi.* 1956, Hope Publications, New Orleans.

Mason, John. *Black Gods—Orisa Studies in the New World,* 1985, Yoruba Theological Archministry, Brooklyn, New York.

_____ . *Four New World Yoruba Rituals.* 1985, Yoruba Theological Archministry, Brooklyn, New York.

McLaughlin, James. "The Black Code." *Mississippi Valley Historical Association Proceedings* 8 (1914–1917): 211–16.

Melton, J. Gordon. *The Encyclopedia of American Religions.* Vol. 2, 1978, McGrath Publishing Co., Wilmington, North Carolina.

Metraux, Alfred. *Voodoo in Haiti.* 1959, reprinted 1972, Schocken Books, New York.

Mintz, Sidney and Richard Price. *The Birth of African American Culture.* 1976, reprinted 1992, Beacon Press, Boston.

Mitchell, B. R., ed. *International Historical Statistics of the Americas and Australasia.* 1983, Gale Research Co.

Morrow, R.C. "On Obeah, Myalism and Magical Death in Jamaica." *West Indies Medical Journal* 32:4 (1983): 4–6.

Murphy, Joseph M. *Santeria: An African Religion in America.* 1988, Beacon Press, Boston.

_____ . *Working the Spirit: Ceremonies of the African Diaspora.* 1994, Beacon Press, Boston.

Myrdal, Gunnar. *An American Dilemma: The Negro Problem and Modern Democracy.* 1974, Harper & Row, New York.

Navard, Andrew Jackson. *Louisiana Voodoo.* Pamphlet available in Tulane Louisiana Collection.

Olmstead, Frederick Law. *Journey in the Seaboard Slave States.* 1856, New York.

_____ . *Journey in the Back Country.* 1860, New York.

Owen, Mary Alice. *Voodoo Tales, As Told Among the Negroes of the Southwest.* 1893, reprinted 1969, Negro University Press.

Parkinson, Wenda. *"This Gilded African": Toussaint L'Ouverture.* 1978, Quartet Books Ltd., London.

Plekhanov, George V. *Fundamental Problems of Marxism.* 1969, fourth printing, 1980, International Publishers, New York.

Porteous, Laura L., "The Gri-Gri Case." *Louisiana Historical Quarterly* 17 (January 1934): 48–63.

Puckett, Newbell Niles. *Folk Beliefs of the Southern Negro.* 1926, University of North Carolina Press/Oxford University Press.

Raboteau, Albert J. *Slave Religion: The "Invisible Institution" in the Antebellum South.* 1978. Oxford University Press, New York.

Ray, Benjamin C. *African Religions: Symbol, Ritual, and Community.* 1976, Prentice-Hall, New Jersey.

Reed, Ishmael. *Mumbo Jumbo.* 1972, Atheneum, New York.

"Religious Instruction of Slaves," *DeBow's Review* (26 Jan. 1859): 107–108.

Rhodes, John Storm. *Black Music of Two Worlds.* 1972, Original Music, Tivoli, New York.

Rigaud, Milo. *Secrets of Voodoo.* 1953, reprinted 1985, City Lights Books, San Francisco.

Riva, Anna. *Voodoo Handbook of Cult Secrets.* 1974, International Imports, Toluca Lake, California.

Sandoval, Mercedes Cros. "Santeria." *Journal of Florida Medical Association* Vol. 70, No. 8 (August, 1983): 628.

_____ . "Santeria: Afrocuban Concepts of Disease and Its Treatment in Miami." *Journal of Operational Psychiatry* 8:2 (1977): 52–63.

_____ . "Santeria as a Mental Health Care System: An Historic Overview." *Social Science and Medicine* 13B (1979): 137–51.

Schlesinger, Arthur M., Jr., ed. *The Almanac of American History.* 1983, Bison Books, Greenwich, Connecticut.

Seligman, Kurt. *The History of Magic and the Occult.* 1948, reprinted 1975, Harmony Books, New York.

Simpson, George Eaton. *Black Religions in the New World.* 1978, Columbia University Press, New York.

_____ with J. Milton Yinger. *Racial and Cultural Minorities: An Analysis of Prejudice and Discrimination.* 1985, Plenum Press, New York.

"Slavery and Conversion in the American Colonies." *American Historical Review* 21 (April 1916): 506–507.

Smith, Michael P. *Spirit World.* 1984, New Orleans Folklife Society.

Steber, Maggie. "Paradise Lost: Haiti Without Trees." *Alicia Patterson Foundation Reporter* 11:3 (Fall 1988): 14–23.

Stuckey, Sterling. *Slave Culture: Nationalist Theory and the Foundations of Black America.* 1987, Oxford University Press, New York.

Taylor, Joe Gray. *Negro Slavery in Louisiana.* 1963, Louisiana State University Press, Baton Rouge.

Tallant, Robert. *Voodoo in New Orleans.* 1946, reprinted 1983, Pelican, Publishing Co., Gretna, Louisiana.

Teish, Luisah. *Jambalaya: The Natural Woman's Book of Personal Charms and Practical Rituals.* 1985, Harper & Row, New York.

Terry, Sir Richard P. *Voodooism in Music.* 1934, Burns, Oates and Washbourne, Ltd., London.

Thomas, Hugh. *The Slave Trade: The Story of the Atlantic Slave Trade 1440–1870.* 1997, Simon & Schuster, New York.

Thompson, Robert Farris. "The Circle and the Branch: Renascent Kongo-American Art," in *Another Face of the Diamond: Pathways Through the Black Atlantic South.* 1988, INTAR Latin American Gallery, New York.

_____ . *Flash of the Spirit: African & Afro-American Art & Philosophy.* 1983, reprinted 1984, Vintage Books, New York.

Touchstone, Blake. "The Large Plantation and the Religious Instruction of Slaves," 1970, unpublished M.A. thesis, Tulane University.

_____ . "Voodoo in New Orleans." *Louisiana History.* 13:4 (Fall 1972): 371–86.

Ungar, Sanford J. *Africa: The People and Politics of an Emerging Continent.* 1989, 3rd edition, Touchstone/Simon & Schuster, New York.

Violette, E. M. "The Black Code in Missouri." *Mississippi Valley Historical Association* 6 (1912–14): 287–316.

Wade, Richard David. "Catholicism, Protestantism and Afro-Christian Cults in the New World." 1976, unpublished M.A. thesis, Tulane University.

Washington, Joseph R. Jr., *Black Sects and Cults.* 1973, Anchor Press, Garden City, New York.

Webb, Julie Yvonne. "Superstitious Influence—Voodoo in Particular—Affecting Health Practices in a Selected Population in Southern Louisiana." 1971, unpublished M.A. Thesis, Tulane University.

White, Timothy. "Luisah Teish, Daughter of Oshun." *Shaman's Drum* (Spring, 1986): 41–45.

Wilmore, Gayraud S. *Black Religion and Black Radicalism.* 1972, Doubleday, Garden City, New York.

Zuckerman, Edward. "The Natural Life of Zombies." *Outside* (May 1985): 41–44 + .

# INDEX

*Numbers in italics indicate a
photograph or illustration on that page.*